CICERO

CICERO

CICERO

A STUDY

BY

G. C. RICHARDS

GREENWOOD PRESS, PUBLISHERS
WESTPORT, CONNECTICUT

Originally published in 1935
by Chatto & Windus, London

First Greenwood Reprinting 1970

Library of Congress Catalogue Card Number 79-109830

SBN 8371-4321-7

Printed in the United States of America

TO MY FRIEND

WALTER BEATTIE ALLAN

OF SUNDERLAND

Caesar would have comprehended our lives and our interests without effort, and Catullus could have described us as we are, for one great civilisation is very like another when the same races are concerned.

F. MARION CRAWFORD

Preface

THE editors of the *Loeb Library* have kindly permitted me to use some of the translations in the text.
Anyone who is interested in the subject cannot do
better than consult their volumes that have appeared.
I have also to thank Messrs Macmillan for permit-
ting me to use two passages from Mr A. W. Pollard's
translation of Sallust's *Catiline* and Miss Olive
Purser for a similar permission to use Professor
Purser's exquisite translation of Plutarch's account
of Cicero's death. Mr R. Syme, Fellow of Trinity
College Oxford, has been good enough to check the
historical statements in the book: he is not responsible for my opinions.

G. C. RICHARDS

Contents

ix

PROLOGUE

THE events of our own time, the collapse of empires and kingdoms, the political unrest everywhere producing a crop of dictators or chiefs of state who assume exceptional powers, the temporary eclipse of democracy, lead our thoughts back to the Dictator Julius Caesar, the sole begetter of the imperial idea, and the initiator of a period which only definitely closed in 1918. Much as has been written about him, a satisfactory biography can never be achieved, because we know too little about the man from himself. But about his contemporary Cicero we know as much as can be known about any figure of the past, because in his Letters we have his thoughts, sometimes from day to day, over a number of years, as shared with an intimate friend. Self-revelation, if carried to such a point, might impair the reputation of any of the world's great men: in the case of Cicero it has led to an unfair depreciation of him as a man. Posterity must to a certain extent defend such a man against himself and point out what line he took in the end, however much he wavered beforehand.

Cicero has also suffered because he has been too exclusively judged as a politician. Like every other Roman of the upper and middle classes, he aimed at holding in succession those public offices to secure which was the laudable ambition of every man of ability. But it was only the accident of two great

emergencies, one during his consulship and one after
the murder of Caesar, which made him a leading
statesman.   Having once attained that position he
could not help himself: what he said and thought
was of importance to the future of Rome.   It has
been said of him that he began on the Left wing and
for selfish reasons went over to the Right.   As a
matter of fact he was all his life a Moderate, inclining
more and more to the Right as revolution seemed
to threaten the foundations of the Republic.   But
Cicero's political rôle was thrust on him rather than
sought.   He was no unreasoning conservative who
wished to preserve all the abuses of senatorial rule.
He only opposed the autocratic and foreign methods
by which Caesar sought to reform Rome, and, without having read the Gospels, he knew that they who
take the sword can only perish by the sword.   Had
he lived into the age of Augustus he would certainly
have been his powerful ally in reforming the state on
traditional Roman lines.

But Cicero was far more than a politician.   He
it was who first made his mother tongue into a
magnificent vehicle of speech whether in oratory
or writing, and he it was who preserved the best of
Greek thought to the following ages by translating
it into exquisite Latin.   Thus during the long centuries when Greek was practically unknown to the
western world, some tincture of Greek thought was
preserved to it in the writings of Cicero.

An orator speaks in order to persuade, and to those
who heard him Cicero was irresistible.   When Plutarch in his *Parallel Lives of Greek and Roman States-*
men had to find a pair for Demosthenes, Cicero was
his choice; and the author of the *Treatise on the*

Sublime similarly compares the two. When supreme command of rhythmical language is united with intense patriotic feeling, as it is in Cicero's Catilinarians and Philippics, the result is the greatest oratory. So Cicero takes his place by Mirabeau, Burke, Webster, as one of the Immortals.

Nor must his influence on the civilisation of the world be ignored. He introduced Greek culture, which was what he meant by the word philosophy, hitherto only the possession of a few, for the first time to the masses of his fellow countrymen. Without him the Latin language could not have permanently lived. When after a brief interval of experiment in the Silver Age the taste of cultivated Romans turned back to Cicero, his style once more prevailed. Soon the Christian Church also found in him an *anima naturaliter Christiana*, and he was a source of inspiration to Ambrose and Augustine. If Cicero himself set most store by the title 'Father of his Fatherland', his truest description is that he was 'Father of Humane Letters', the first parent of that international culture which strives to incorporate in one the best from every source, and which assuredly is the only hope for the future to-day.

Chapter 1

EARLY YEARS AT ARPINUM AND ROME
106-89 B.C.

Whenever it is possible for me to be out of town for several days, I come to this lovely and healthful spot.

CICERO, *De Legg.* ii. 1, 3

MARCUS TULLIUS CICERO, the third successive bearer of that name, was born at Arpinum in the Volscian hills on January 3rd, 106 B.C.:[1] on September 29th of the same year Gnaeus Pompeius Magnus was born. Thus both were six years older than Gaius Julius Caesar.* Cicero, Pompey, Caesar; round these three names the history of Rome was to revolve for many a year, and the life story of one inevitably entails a judgement of the other two.

Two other men also materially affect Cicero's career. His life-long friend Atticus was three years his senior; his only brother Quintus was four years his junior. With the former his attachment was uninterrupted; with the latter there was one serious estrangement, but the forgiving disposition of the elder brother brought about a reconciliation.

* The day of Caesar's birth was July 12th, but the year is uncertain. Mommsen said 102 B.C., but 100 is now generally accepted. Carcopino has recently argued plausibly for 101 (*Mélanges Bidez*, pp. 35-69). Caesar was then forty-one just before the consular elections of 60 B.C.

4

The Volscians to whom Cicero belonged were in early times very dangerous neighbours to Rome while the Romans were still a small agricultural community, centred around the Palatine Hill; but after the earlier stock of Rome had been reinforced by sturdy Sabine highlanders, the Volscians, like the Latins and Hernicans, threw in their lot with the rising Republic, and seem to have never repented of their decision. What historical truth there is in the legend of Coriolanus, and the wars described in Livy's first decade, who shall venture to say? The attachment of the Volscian hill towns to the constitution of the Roman state, their local patriotism and their voting strength are brought out fully in Cicero's speech for his friend Plancius in 54 B.C., in which he made a handsome return for the protection afforded him by Plancius at Thessalonica in the gloomy days of exile.

Just at the time of Cicero's birth, Arpinum was following with intense interest the fortunes of the greatest man the little town had ever produced. Gaius Marius, by sheer force of character, had broken into the ring of 'noble' families which then monopolised the high offices of state: he was therefore described as a 'new man'. Cicero, another new man, can adduce only two ancient and two modern parallels to Marius.[2] This shows how close a preserve had been the offices of state, and to how comparatively few patrician and plebeian families (*gentes*) they had been confined. Marius, a soldier of great ability, had wrung leave of absence from his commander-in-chief, a proud Metellus, and had held the consulship. Now, having superseded his noble chief, he was engaged in a fierce struggle in

Africa with one of Rome's most dangerous adversaries, Jugurtha, though the laurels of the victory were to be largely shared by a younger and noble lieutenant, destined to be his bitterest enemy, Lucius Cornelius Sulla.

During Cicero's infancy the most thrilling scenes of Roman history were enacted. Marius, who luckily had already reorganised the Roman army, saved Roman civilisation by annihilating in two great battles a mixed horde of Germanic invaders, the first of many similar waves of barbarians. During these campaigns, he held the consulship for five successive years; but at the end of this time his political supporters, the party opposed to the domination of the Senate, and called *populares* or champions of the people (*populus*), went too far; and their leaders met the usual fate of anti-senatorial politicians, assassination. The star of Marius then declined, while that of Sulla, the senatorial general, rose higher.

There followed the Social War, in which the rest of Italy, being denied civic rights, determined to break away and found a new federal capital Italica, a city representing Italy. But they were beaten in the field, and then granted the rights they had vainly attempted to gain, first through the *populares*, and then through the senatorial party, the so-called *optimates*, a term which meant to Cicero 'supporters of the best programme'. After his consulship Sulla went to the East, to fight Mithridates, king of Pontus, Rome's relentless enemy, and was away from Italy for more than three years. While he was absent, the popular leader, another Cornelius, Lucius Cinna, held sway, with the old Marius at

his back; but the expected return of Sulla with a
victorious army made inevitable the ultimate re-
establishment of the Senate's authority.   While consul for the eighth time, Marius died, having sullied
his fame by a horrible massacre of his opponents,
only just in time to escape destruction at the hands
of Sulla, his rival in popularity and military glory
for twenty-five years.   Among such stirring scenes
and in such anxious times the youth of Cicero was
spent.

The name 'Cicero' is supposed by Plutarch to have
been given to an ancestor who had an excrescence
on his nose like a vetch (*cicer*).   But the analogy of
Fabius (the bean-man) and Lentulus (the pulse-man)
suggests that Cicero means the vetch-man,[3] one perhaps who introduced its cultivation.   On beginning
to sue for public office the orator was advised to
drop the name, but refused, saying that he would
make it more glorious than those of the Scauri and
Catuli.   His grandfather was alive when he was
born.   He was a sturdy old yeoman who thought
that a knowledge of Greek was a certificate of rascality.[4]   Little did he dream that his infant grandson
was to be the interpreter of Greek literature to Rome,
and the real founder of Greco-Roman civilisation.

Of Cicero's mother Helvia we only know that she
was noble,* and from her son Quintus that she was
in the habit of sealing her wine-flasks, even when
they were empty, so that her slaves can have had
small opportunity of pilfering.[5]   But his father, who
had delicate health, was more than a mere gentleman-
farmer, being devoted to reading.   He enlarged the

---

* Virgil, *Aeneid,* xi. 340 (Drances). 'His mother's nobility gave him
a proud lineage: no one knew what was his father's origin' (p. 211).

family dwelling into something superior to a farm-house; and having two sons, determined to give them the advantage of a good education at Rome, so that they might vie with the Marian family.

There seem to have been connections between the Cicerones and the Marii: at any rate Cicero's grand-mother Gratidia had a nephew, who was adopted by a Marius and thus became Marcus Marius Gra-tidianus. He was twice praetor under Cinna,[6] de-livered harangues to the mob,[7] and was murdered in a revolting manner by Catiline.[8] An impostor too, who pretended to be Gaius Marius, grandson of the general, claimed relationship with Cicero in May 45 B.C.[9] The family of Cicero therefore had associations with the *populares*, but it does not in the least follow that they were of that political colour. Cicero's early poem on Marius shows that he regarded him as a national hero; but who was there who did not admire Marius, at least till he, a mere soldier, fell into the hands of astute politicians and sullied his fair fame by cruelty? The family belonged, as St Jerome tells us, to the 'knights', that middle or mercantile class, of great financial interests and political influ-ence, which stood between the nobles and the com-mons. Whence Jerome got his idea that Cicero was descended from the old Volscian kings, we know not: all we can say is that his was one of the few leading families of Arpinum which linked the self-governing country-town to the great world of Rome.

The knights, as they were called, stood for order and stability. Those of their number who were engaged in business were organised in joint-stock companies, and controlled the commerce of the day. They looked on the provinces, which one by one were being brought under the direct government of the Roman Republic, as their legitimate sphere of exploitation. This they were enabled to do, first by the fact that the nobles invested spare capital in the companies, and secondly because the companies' profits depended largely on the goodwill of the particular noble who governed the particular province. The knights were the party of material interests, and therefore it was generally their policy to keep on good terms with the majority of the Senate. But they maintained their independence; and were glad enough to put the screw on provincial governors by acting as members of the courts which tried charges of bribery at elections or of provincial extortion. Gaius Gracchus had won the support of the knights by composing Roman juries entirely of them; but that system lasted only from 123 to 80 B.C., when Sulla once more restored the juries to the Senate. After ten years Pompey divided the jury membership equally between senators, knights and a lower class called *tribuni aerarii*. These latter seem to have been even more venal than the others, and were abolished by Caesar; but Augustus had in effect to readmit them.

By his family connexions and upbringing Cicero belonged to this party of material interests. He became the natural leader of all the knights who came from the towns of Italy. Unfortunately for him the policy of the party was largely directed by the ablest financier of Rome, Marcus Licinius Crassus, who had acquired immense wealth in the proscriptions of Sulla by buying up property cheap, and to whom many of the leading men of Rome were in debt. Crassus was almost childishly jealous of Pompey: and in the vain hope of rivalling him as a soldier he met his end in the sands of Mesopotamia. Cicero never could abide him. 'What a rascal!' he exclaimed to Atticus, just after a formal reconciliation and the departure of Crassus to the Parthian campaign; and in his last work, a treatise on Ethics, he quoted with disgust Crassus' dictum that a man who aspired to be leader in the state could never be said to have money enough for the purpose unless with his income he could maintain an army.[10] Caesar found Crassus exceedingly useful at times: but Cicero, having some stubborn principles, could not put up with him, and posterity confirms his opinion.

When Cicero became consul, and thus reached the summit of his political ambition, he relied mainly on the support of the knights. His chief aim was to maintain a close alliance between them and the majority of the Senate: this he called 'harmony of classes' (*ordinum concordia*). It was essentially a conservative policy. At its best it secured the stability of the Roman Republic, and was a safeguard against anarchic .revolution, massacre and repudiation of debt; the suppression of the conspiracy of Catiline in the year of Cicero's consulship, 63 B.C., was the triumph of this policy. At its worst it meant the merciless exploitation of the provincials abroad and the comparative impotence of the lower classes at home. It was not a heroic or far-sighted policy, but it is no serious reproach to Cicero that he advocated it up to 56 B.C. From that time to the outbreak of the Civil War, he submitted under coercion to the domination of Pompey and Caesar: when it came to a choice between the two, he followed Pompey, because he believed him to be like-minded with himself in essential loyalty to the constitution.

Cicero may be described as feeble or short-sighted, but he cannot justly be called 'a political trimmer or weathercock', appellations applied to him by Mommsen, or a 'most eloquent and accomplished trimmer', which is the verdict of Macaulay. However, Macaulay had never made a special study of the life of Cicero. Had he done so, he might have come to think that one who believed that an Italian was as good as a Roman, that provincials were entitled to decent government, that freedom of speech was essential to freemen, and that nothing could compensate for the loss of liberty, was almost, if not quite, a Whig. Macaulay himself included Cicero in his noble description of the debt we owe to the great minds of former ages. 'These are the old friends who are never seen with new faces, who are the same in wealth and in poverty, in glory and in obscurity. With the dead there is no rivalry. In the dead there is no change. Plato is never sullen. Cervantes is never petulant. Demosthenes never comes unseasonably. Dante never stays too long. No difference of political opinion can alienate Cicero.'

For the education of his sons, the elder Cicero acquired a house in Rome, on the Carinae, a respectable but not fashionable quarter of the city, where he lived each year from October to June. It was subsequently occupied by Quintus, and in February 50 B.C. Marcus informs him that it has been let to 'respectable tenants' called Lamia; it was only later that a mythical genealogy was given to the Lamiae by Horace, while later still Juvenal takes them as types of the nobility who suffered under Domitian's reign of terror. The summer months were spent more cheaply at Arpinum; and so in 49 B.C., when Caesar

was marching on Rome, Cicero advises his wife to
economise by taking the town staff to the old home
in the country.

We know nothing about Cicero's schooldays. If
he had been a pupil of the great grammarian Lucius
Aelius Stilo, he would surely have told us so. His
early penchant for verse writing was probably derived from association with the Greek Archias of
Antioch, whose civic status he was later successfully
to defend (p. 226), though he failed to induce
Archias to write a poem on his consulship.[11] Among
Cicero's own poems we possess fifteen lines of a heroic
poem in honour of the great memory of Marius: of
this poem Quintus Scaevola prophesied that it would
be immortal.[12]   The earliest possible date for this
poem is 85 B.C., but some have thought it a supple-
ment to his 'Consulship', a poem of 60.   Some fragments of translation from the Iliad and Odyssey may
have been school exercises, and Plutarch speaks of a
'Pontius Glaucus' in tetrameters.   The rendering of
the astronomical poem *Phaenomena* by the Alexan-
drian Aratus was certainly an early production.   His
translation of Aratus' other poem 'Weather Portents'
is mentioned in a letter of 60 B.C., when he promises
to send it to Atticus with some 'poor speeches' for
publication: [13] it may have been only a revision of a
boyish work.

At that time he was celebrating his consulship in
verse, and for two lines in this poem he has been unmercifully ridiculed from Quintilian and Juvenal to
the present day.*   Cicero was not a poet.†   He ought

---

* The jingles they contain, 'cedant . . . concedat', 'fortunatam . . .
natam', may have pleased some ears at the time. Cp. *Phil.* ii. 20;
Quint. xi. 1, 24; *Juvenal,* x. 123.

† Professor Henry Nettleship said, 'Cicero was half a poet'.

to have known this, but he did not, and it is a part
of his vanity that he regarded these efforts with as
much complacency as the Philippics. But authors
are not always the best judges of their own works.
Miss Burney set as high store by her *Diary* as by
Evelina and *Cecilia*: and Scott insisted on *St Ronan's
Well* being as good as *Old Mortality*.

But in the history of the Latin hexameter Cicero's
effusions are not without importance. They are on
a technical level with Catullus' *Peleus and Thetis*, and
though lumbering as compared with the hexameters
of Virgil, it is interesting to compare them with the
rugged force of Lucretius.*

Greater importance attaches to his early prose
translations. He tells his son,† that he translated
the *Oeconomicus* of Xenophon, when he was much
about his age, namely nineteen or twenty: of this
enough remains to show that the ancient translator
aimed at giving the sense rather than the words of
the original. At the same time, probably in early
life, he also translated the *Protagoras* of Plato, and
the speeches of Demosthenes for, and of Aeschines
against, Ctesiphon.‡ These were simply relaxations
in the intervals of the serious business of rhetorical
training. They show Cicero's often repeated conviction that success in oratory is only to be obtained
on the basis of general culture and philosophy.

* It is necessary to express some opinion on the much discussed
reference to Lucretius in a letter to Quintus (also a tragedian and a poet
to boot) of 54 B.C. (*Q.F.* ii 11). The meaning seems to be: 'I agree with
you about the poem of Lucretius. It shows much of the genius of Ennius
and the older poets, but also touches of newer Alexandrine style' (Catullus).
The thought, being Epicurean, is beneath Cicero's notice.

† *De Off.* ii. 24, 87.

‡ We possess a short preface to these translations which mentions the
trial of Milo, and was therefore written not before 52 B.C.

Every young Roman of the upper or upper middle classes who hoped to play a part in public life—and who stood aloof? certainly not Cicero with the example of Marius before him—did his best to perfect himself as a speaker, and generally tried to make his name by appearing at an early age as prosecutor of some notorious offender. Caesar did this at the age of twenty-one, but Cicero preferred to wait till he was twenty-six, and then appeared for the defence.

His preparation for the courts, the Forum and the Senate House was unusually long and exacting. He assumed the white toga of manhood in 91 B.C., but it was ten years at least before he took a brief and appeared before the public in the trivial case *Pro Quinctio*, his first extant speech, though it must be admitted that during most of this time the political troubles made a public appearance impossible. As a stripling, he listened to the leaders of Roman oratory, Marcus Antonius, grandfather of the triumvir, and Lucius Crassus. Along with his friend Atticus, he also studied civil law under Scaevola the augur and jurist, and after his death under Scaevola the *pontifex maximus*: but Cicero had not a legal mind, and did not leave his mark in any way on Roman jurisprudence.* At the age of nineteen in 87 B.C. he had the good luck to hear the lectures of a famous teacher of rhetoric, Apollonius Molon of Rhodes, who was then in Rome: and nine years later he undertook the journey to Rhodes to complete his rhetorical training under the same man. As a teacher of the subject Molon had a high reputation. Of one

* He may have influenced the conception of the Law of Nature as the source of positive law. In some places he comes near to identifying the 'law of nations' with the 'Law of Nature'. See Bryce, *Studies in History and Jurisprudence*, vol. ii. pp. 135-8.

Favonius, who also went to study under him, Cicero, with his usual liking for a pun, said: 'He spoke so poorly, that you would imagine he spent his time at Rhodes working at the mill rather than under Mill (Molon)'. It seems curious, but it is the case, that it was the Rhodian who checked in Cicero his early tendency to the florid Asiatic style (p. 229), to which his rival Hortensius remained faithful.

In these early years at Rome he did not neglect philosophy, the other branch of Roman higher education, but attended the lectures of Philo of Larissa, the Academic, who, as he carried on the traditions of Plato and Aristotle, made a more profound impression on him than any other thinker; and even before he met Philo, Atticus had induced him to hear Phaedrus, head of the Epicurean school, 'when we were boys'. But into that school Cicero refused to follow his friend, and in 57 B.C., when writing to Memmius—whose only claim to distinction is that it was to him that Lucretius dedicated his poem—to ask a favour for a later head of the Epicurean school, he feels bound to say 'In philosophy I totally disagree with him'. Much greater influence on his early years was exercised by Diodotus the Stoic, who became an inmate of Cicero senior's house in 87 B.C., and seems never to have left the family. Diodotus died in Cicero's mansion on the Palatine in 59, and left him his fortune, but whether it was large or small it is impossible to say.* Not that Cicero became a Stoic either: he often controverts their dogmas, and the impracticable attitude and perversity of Marcus

---

* *Ad Att.* ii. 20, 6. £80,000 or £800. Are we to judge Cicero's feelings by telegraphic brevity in letters? No more surely than in the much discussed reference to his father's death *Ad Att.* i. 6.

Porcius Cato in politics made him still less inclined
to that school. Yet in the end of his life he largely
adopted their ethics and certainly appreciated the
strong points of the Porch.

Cato, who was born in 95 B.C., could not have been
an early associate of the Ciceros, but there is no
reason to doubt the statement made by Cicero in
56 B.C. that his brother and he were friendly with
Caesar in early life.[14] With Pompey he first came in
contact in the following way. When the Social War
(p. 6) broke out, his studies were interrupted for the
time being. He served a military apprenticeship
under Pompey's father, in the course of which he
and Pompey must have rubbed shoulders, probably
for the first time. But his soldiering did not last long.
It was really his only experience of actual warfare as
a combatant. Later in Cilicia, though of course he
got the credit, he was probably only a spectator of
the successful military operations conducted by his
brother Quintus and the equally able legate Pomptinus. 'Let arms give place to the gown', said he in
the much abused verse; and if in an eloquent passage
of one of his speeches he extols the life of the soldier
above that of the lawyer, at any rate he does not
express his real thoughts when he says 'Valour in
warfare is superior to all other excellencies'.[15]

Chapter 2

DEBUT AT THE BAR
98-77 B.C.

I spent my life in the popular eye: I haunted the Forum.
Pro Plancio, 27, 66

DURING the reign of terror under Marius and Cinna, and—after Cinna's death—Carbo, the Cicero family from Arpinum were of course quite safe. The knights as a body were opposed to the Senate's party, but it does not follow that they liked or approved of what happened: Cicero always hated bloodshed. Until Sulla's return from the East and the turn of the tide, we hear little of the brothers.

Marcus, probably often in the company of Quintus, was applying himself daily to rhetorical practice, 'declamation' as the Romans called it, not only in Latin, but also in Greek, in which language he became proficient, though he never had such entire mastery of it as of his native tongue. He could translate correctly from Greek authors, he used Greek phrases in his letters exactly as we use French,* he conversed with Greeks freely in their own language: but he would never have ventured to address

* The late Rev. G. E. Jeans, a most accomplished scholar, in his translation of Cicero's Letters, had no difficulty in always finding a French expression which fits Cicero's Greek like a glove.

a Greek audience in Greek, knowing too well how
some trifling slip or mispronunciation would have
offended their fastidious ears. As a provincial governor, he did not compromise the official dignity by
the use of the Greek language, but employed an
interpreter.[16] About this time his friend Atticus,
at the age of twenty-three, settled permanently at
Athens, which he found suitable as a centre of
culture, and a convenient business headquarters for
money-lending on a large scale: his Epicurean creed
made him determine not to mix himself up with
politics. He soon found that, being professedly no
politician, he received the secrets of all parties, and
as he was a safe man, continued to receive them all
his life. He did not return to Rome till 64 B.C., and
then only at Cicero's urgent request, that he would
help him by his presence to attain the ambition of
his life, the consulate.* Accordingly he then stayed
nearly three years in Rome.

Meanwhile Pompey, who had met Cicero on his
father's staff when they were only seventeen, had
begun his career in a phenomenal way. He had raised
a legion in Picenum, whence his family came, joined
Sulla, been saluted as *Imperator*, slain the consul
Carbo in Sicily, settled affairs in Africa, been saluted
as 'The Great' by Sulla, and celebrated a triumph,
when he was only a knight and had held no public
office. All this was before he was twenty-six.
Cicero on the other hand had, by close application
and a fresh dose of Molon's tuition, developed into a
first-rate speaker; and his first public appearance

* Would that he had not; for then we should have had letters from
Cicero to Atticus between 64 and the end of 62, for which three years
we have none. What descriptions we have thus lost.

(apart from the trivial civil case already mentioned), in a criminal case, which was in the latter half of 80 B.C., established his reputation.

Before this is described, it is necessary to give a brief sketch of Sulla's return from the East. At the end of 85 B.C. he wrote to the Senate complaining of what had happened in his absence, and announcing that he would return to wreak vengeance on his enemies. Cinna and Carbo secured their re-election as consuls for 84 and prepared to resist force by force. Cinna was at Ancona intending to cross over to Greece to meet Sulla, when he was murdered, and Carbo was left sole consul. The consuls for 83 were more moderate Marians. Sulla landed at Brundusium early in 83 with an army of 40,000 veterans, whom he was determined not to disband till he had led them to victory. Heavy fighting took place in various parts of Italy for a year and a half, until Sulla ended the war by a decisive victory outside the Colline Gate of Rome.

He was now master, and he used his power remorselessly. Both consuls had been killed, Carbo in Sicily, the younger Marius at Praeneste. Lucius Valerius Flaccus was nominated by the Senate as *interrex*, and by a startling innovation carried a bill in the Assembly of the People, by which Sulla was appointed dictator without time-limit, 'for drafting laws and *constituting* the Republic'. Cicero twice alludes to the Valerian Law in terms of strong condemnation. Once when opposing the agrarian law of the tribune Rullus in 63 B.C., he mentions it as 'the most unjust of all laws and most unlike a law, as ratifying beforehand all the acts of Sulla, and constituting a tyrant by law'. But odious as it is, he says, it may be excused on the ground of being a product of the times, not of its author: Rullus' proposal is in some ways more shameless. The second allusion is in Cicero's treatise *On the Laws*, where he quotes the law in the form 'that the dictator might with impunity put to death any citizen he wished without trial'.[17] That is, in effect, what the proscriptions meant. Proscription means public advertisement of the sale by auction of the confiscated property of one outlawed, whether only sentenced to death and liable to be slain at sight, or already executed.

For a year and a half lists of names were constantly appearing, and no one knew whether his name might not shortly be included in them. The phrase 'constituting' or 'giving a constitution to' the Republic is precisely that which Cicero used in pleading for Marcellus to Caesar in September 46 B.C., 'it is to constituting the Republic that you must now devote your efforts': and—to compare small things with great—that very year he says he has caused his son and an intimate friend to be elected aediles—there were three, but two if acting together would have full powers—at his native town of Arpinum 'with a view to constituting the municipality'.

Into the Cornelian Laws passed by Sulla it is unnecessary to enter: but the precedent he set for others to follow needs to be stated accurately. Without ceasing to be dictator, he allowed two partisans to be elected consuls for 81 B.C.: one Ofella, who presumed to offer himself as a candidate without Sulla's leave, was promptly put to death. For 80, Sulla was elected consul along with Metellus Pius, and at the end of the year, when the consulship expired, he laid down the dictatorship too, and retired to enjoy him-

self in Campania. There he died in 78, while his
enemy Lepidus as consul was trying to undo his
work. He had set the example of being simultaneously dictator and consul, but in the end he had
resigned. Recently M. Jérome Carcopino* has
maintained that he wanted to be tyrant for life, but
was prevented from being so by Metellus and
Pompey. This, if true, would be some slight justifi-
cation for Caesar's subsequent behaviour: but it is
very unlikely. It seems inconsistent with the fact
that Sulla retired to a life of luxurious ease without
any fear for his life. But the phrase 'the monarchy
of Sulla', which was correct in substance, if not in
name, was often in Cicero's mind in the anxious early
months of 49 B.C., when he had the gloomiest antici-
pations in the event of either Pompey or Caesar being
victorious. 'How often have I heard Pompey say',
he writes, 'Sulla was able; shall I not be able?' But
Caesar, in accepting a dictatorship for life, and insti-
gating his friends to procure for him the title of king,
went far beyond Sulla.

The proscriptions closed officially on June 1st,
80 B.C. One of Sulla's chief agents in them, and one
universally feared, was his favourite freedman Lucius
Cornelius Chrysogonus, whom Cicero calls, as he
calls himself, *adulescens*, and who therefore was under
thirty years of age. According to Cicero he had lent
himself to an act of private greed and animosity.
Sextus Roscius of Ameria, a man of exactly the same
position in an Umbrian town as Cicero's father at
Arpinum, was murdered one night at Rome. The

* *Sylla, ou la Monarchie manquée*, Paris 1931. Caesar, however,
said Sulla did not know his A B C when he laid down the dictatorship.
(Suet. *Julius*, 77.)

news was promptly sent off by a relative to Ameria, and at daybreak was communicated to another member of the family, equally hostile to the deceased. Thence it was hastily passed on to Chrysogonus in Sulla's camp at Volaterrae in Etruria. Though the proscriptions were over, Chrysogonus treated the property as if Roscius had been proscribed, and bought for £16 what was worth £48,000, handing over a part to the informer as his reward. Then to cover up the traces of the crime, he caused the son who had managed the land and now was evicted to be accused of parricide. The son took refuge with a noble lady at Rome, and the young Cicero was briefed for the defence.

The speech is equal in vigour and effectiveness to any he ever delivered in later life. He has little difficulty in fixing the crime on Titus Roscius who profited by it,[18] or in refuting the statement that the deceased had quarrelled with and made a working farmer of his son, the defendant, or in vindicating the honourable calling of the farmer; in so doing he reminds the jury of the great men of the past who were summoned from the plough to be supreme magistrates. His dexterous flattery of Sulla, who, no more than Jove himself, can he held responsible for everything that happens, or be omniscient, enables him to denounce with the greater vehemence the extravagance and greed of the hated freedman; a lacuna has deprived us of some of the invective, but what remains is sufficiently unsparing and telling. 'Who is happy enough'—Sulla bore the surname of Felix, 'the happy'—'not to have some rascal among his slaves or freedmen?'

The most interesting passage is that in which he

declares his own political attitude. 'I am not afraid of anyone thinking that I was opposed to the party and programme of the nobility. To the extent of my poor powers . . . I supported the victory of those who have been victorious. The preservation of the party meant the retention of dignity at home and authority abroad. I see clearly that this has been brought about by the will of the gods, the zeal of the Roman People, the sagacity, authority and good fortune of Lucius Sulla.' He goes on to say that, while he does not censure the punishment inflicted on the popular party, the struggle was not engaged in to give free scope to creatures like Chrysogonus to assail the lives and fortunes of innocent men. 'Did the nobility wake up, and recover the constitution by the power of the sword, merely that the freedmen and slaves of the nobles should, at their own sweet wills, harry the fortunes of you, gentlemen, and all of us? If this is what has come about, I was wrong in taking this line: I was mad to have advocated it.' If they drop Chrysogonus, he says, they will dignify their party and programme. The bold speaker would probably have had cause to rue his outspokenness, but for the support that Caecilia Metella, who was related to Sulla's wife, had given to the defendant. He ends with a spirited protest against cruelty at home, which blunts all the natural feelings of human nature. 'If the cruelty which has prevailed of late in the state, has—which assuredly is past belief—hardened and soured your minds, judges, all is over: better to dwell among wild beasts than to go on living among such inhuman men.' Could a representative of the knights have made a plainer protest against the excesses of the reaction, or stated more clearly the conditions under which alone they would continue to support the Senate?

There are other passages in the speech which are deservedly famous. Thus there is the rationalising explanation of the legendary Furies, that they are the stings of a guilty conscience: and there is the famous comparison of accusers to the geese and watch-dogs kept on the Capitol. 'Some of you are geese, who only cackle and can do no harm: others are dogs who can both bark and bite. We see that you are fed: but you ought to single out for attack those who deserve it. That is what the people like best. Then you may, if you like, bark, when it is probable that a man is guilty: under suspicious circumstances this may be conceded to you. But if you accuse a man of having killed his father, and cannot say why or how, and only bark when there are no grounds for suspicion, no one, it is true, will break your legs, but if I know the gentlemen of the jury, they will brand on your foreheads the letter K [for "false accuser']—that letter which you dislike so much, that the first of the month [Kalends, when interest was due] has become odious to you,—so that in future you can accuse nobody, but only inveigh against your own bad luck.'

Cicero was as independent in criticising Sulla's acts next year, when he defended the right of a lady of Arretium (Arezzo), which town had been disfranchised by Sulla, to sue and be sued. That this was in Sulla's lifetime, he asserts later, when, as Curule Aedile, he is defending Caecina of Volaterrae, another disfranchised town. In connection with the courage thus shown by Cicero at the very outset

of his public life, we must bear in mind that he was
constitutionally nervous and timid. It always, he
tells us,[19] cost him a great effort to begin to speak,
and he repeatedly describes his sensation of shrink-
ing. When we know what it meant to him physically to take a bold stand, we give him greater credit,
and are less inclined to accept the common verdict
of cowardice pronounced against him. It is possible
that the fear of Sulla's resentment may have contributed to his absenting himself from Rome for some
time. So Plutarch says; but in the *Brutus* Cicero
simply says he went abroad for the sake of his health.
He was very thin, and his neck was long and slender,
he had overstrained his voice, and the doctors feared
a decline. We may well accept this as the reason:
for Sulla, who had somewhat unwillingly allowed
Caesar, who had directly disobeyed him, to escape,
was in his retirement much too indolent to notice so
young a man as Cicero.

Accompanied by Quintus, and his cousin Lucius,
whose death eleven years later he felt deeply, Cicero
joined Atticus at Athens. There for six months he
attended the lectures on philosophy of Philo's successor, Antiochus of Ascalon, while he also took
instruction in rhetoric from Demetrius, called the
Syrian. During this stay, he was initiated in the
Eleusinian Mysteries, of which he speaks highly in
his treatise on *The Laws*: 'we have received from
them the secret of living happily and dying with a
better hope'. After a sojourn in Asia, he paid a
second visit to Rhodes, where Molon took pains to
prune the redundancies of his style, and to shape it
into something between the florid Asiatic and the
plain Attic styles. At Rhodes he also sat at the feet

of Posidonius, 'the greatest of the Stoics':[20] for in
early as in later life he always combined the study
of philosophy with that of rhetoric, thereby, as he
held, vastly improving the latter.

On his way back, he stopped at Delphi, though in
his work *On Divination* he speaks of the Oracle as
having fallen into contempt. Plutarch tells us that
the Pythia bade him follow nature, and not take the
opinion of the multitude for the guide of his life: it is
a pity he did not pay more heed to this advice, for,
in the words of Plutarch, 'his immoderate love of
praise and passion for glory always remained with
him and interrupted his best and wisest designs'.

He returned to Rome, not only better for his
studies, but physically a new man: his voice had
strengthened, and he was determined to use the bar
as a help to his political career. Sulla was now dead,
and there was more scope for talent and ambition.
To complete his preparation, he took lessons in
elocution from Roscius and Aesopus, who were respectively the leading comic and tragic actors of the
day.

It must have been soon after his return that he
married Terentia. It is clear that she considered herself superior in social standing to her husband. The
Terentian family had certainly held high office: one
was a tribune in 54 B.C.,[21] but a Terentius is also
spoken of as a tax-farmer, which implies equestrian
rank. Certainly Terentia had social ambitions and
pushed on her husband to make his name in public life.
Plutarch says she was an arrogant and domineering
woman, who later urged him to take a strong line
against the Catilinarians, and caused him to incur
Clodius' hatred by demolishing his alibi when he

was prosecuted for sacrilege. That she was a masterful woman is plain. With her 'the native hue of resolution' was never, as so often with her husband, 'sicklied o'er with the pale cast of thought'. Plutarch quotes Cicero as saying that 'she took a larger share with him in politics than she permitted him to take in domestic affairs', and we can well believe it. He says to her once that she has a spirit equal to that of any man. She was punctilious in the performance of her religious duties, which Cicero implies he left to her; and it must have been one of the proudest moments of her life when, on December 3rd, 63 B.C., as the consul's wife, she presided over the mysteries of the *Bona Dea*, performed by women only, and the dying fire on the altar shot up to the roof-tree, which the women all took for an omen of glory.

After the consulship her desire to rise in society must have prompted the crippling purchase of the mansion on the Palatine Hill, and her social ambitions were certainly gratified: for here she received a visit from Cornelia, a great lady, to ask a favour for her husband. She had brought Cicero a dowry of £3400, had property of her own[22] and a steward to manage it. Later on Cicero writes during his exile begging her not to sell her property. She got on well with Atticus, and in April 59 her husband shows her a letter from him with which she is delighted; he had helped her with advice in a business dispute. Something she did, without consulting her husband, in his absence seems to have annoyed him: for in October 57 after his return, when he says, 'My other anxieties are a dead secret: my brother and daughter are devoted to me', he plainly implies that his wife is not. During the provincial governorship she

hurried on the betrothal of Tullia to Dolabella, so
that the father had to accept the match as an accomplished fact and make the best of it. When the
marriage turned out unhappily, no doubt Terentia
bore the blame. Finally the defalcations of Philotimus, her man of business, in Cicero's second long
absence roused his ire: he repeatedly asks Atticus to
interfere with this 'cooker of accounts', whom he
charges with appropriating some of the property
bought for his master at Milo's sale.* He is particularly anxious that Philotimus should not touch a
legacy recently left to him. But Terentia and Philotimus fell out. In 47 Cicero writes: 'Terentia should
satisfy her creditors: Philotimus reports she is behaving dishonestly'. Finally he makes this specific
charge: 'You (Atticus) wrote to her to remit me by
bill of exchange £96, stating that that was the balance.
She sent me £80, and added that that was the whole
balance. If she appropriates such a trifle from a
small sum, you can see what she has been doing with
larger sums.' [23] His letters to her became shorter
and shorter till the last of October 1, 47, which, as
has been well said, is such as a gentleman would
hardly send to his housekeeper. 'I think I shall
arrive at my Tusculan villa either on the 7th or the
following day. See that everything is ready there:
for I shall have several visitors, and I think we shall
stay some time. If there is no hand-basin in the
bath-room, see that one is put. Also everything else
needful for living and health. Good-bye. Venusia
Oct. 1.' Nothing about the 'most faithful and best of
wives' or 'my sweetest and most longed-for wife', and
such expressions, of which his earlier letters are full.

* Milo's property was sold for a mere song (Asconius *In Mil.* 48).

Shortly afterwards he divorced her and left his friend Atticus to settle how the dowry was to be repaid, only insisting on the satisfaction of all her claims: * and this after a married life of thirty-one years. It made things no better when soon afterwards he married his young ward. His old friend Plancius, now in exile himself, wrote expressing the hope that 'his arrangements might turn out well and happily'. In January 45 he replies in a tone of bitterness about domestic difficulties, and says that 'finding no safety within the walls of his house' he found it necessary to secure himself 'by a new alliance against the treachery of the old'. But this is a quite isolated outburst. If it is true that Terentia subsequently married Sallust the historian, she had the almost unique experience of two literary husbands. With Sallust she got great wealth but no better blood: for he was of an obscure Sabine stock and never got beyond the praetorship.

It is difficult to judge Terentia. She cannot have been altogether an easy wife to live with, but was Cicero an easy husband? It is extremely probable that his haphazard ways about finance often drove her to the verge of desperation: and his annoyance with her, be it noticed, arose during his two absences from Rome, each of a year and a half, and the first under very trying circumstances when Terentia had taken refuge with her half-sister, a Vestal Virgin, and in spite of that had borne her share of persecution.† But Cicero had no romantic side and was essentially a man's man. In 46 B.C.[24] he describes how unex-

---

* That this was easier said than done appears from *Ad Att.* xvi. 15, 5.
† *Ad Fam.* xiv. 2. She had been obliged to go to the *Tabula Valeria*, possibly a bank, or a tribune's court, to make some affidavit about her husband's estates.

pectedly he met at a dinner party the gay lady
Cytheris, whom Antony had taken round Italy in an
open litter in 49; and he thinks it necessary to say
that he did not seek such society. 'I was never
affected by anything of that sort, when I was a young
man, much less now that I am old.' Good conversation and good company were what he liked, and that
he chiefly got from men.

The marriage had as its fruit a daughter, Tullia,
born probably in 76 B.C., and a son, Marcus, whose
birth he laconically announces in 64. Tullia was her
father's darling: she seems to have had more intellectual interests than her mother and may even have
been, for Roman society, a bit of a blue-stocking.
Her first marriage, arranged when she was very
young, left her a widow at twenty-two. Her second
husband apparently dissolved the marriage in 51: he
is mentioned as visiting Cicero at Formiae in March
49.[25] Her third was an aristocratic rascal, of whom
there will be much to say.

The son was dull and disappointing: he needed the
spur, as his cousin needed the curb, said Cicero, who
devoted much time and patience to their education.

An unfortunate marriage was also arranged by
Cicero and Atticus between Quintus Cicero and
Pomponia, Atticus' sister. The lady seems to have
been no less arrogant than Terentia, with whom she
got on very badly, and was perpetually complaining
of her husband. It took endless diplomacy on the
part of Cicero and Atticus to keep them together.
Very soon after the marriage Cicero writes to Atticus:
'Pomponia herself will tell you how much trouble I
have taken to make Quintus behave properly to her
. . . judging from his recent letters, I trust things are

as they should be and we should like them to be'. A
little later: 'My brother is, I think, getting on with
Pomponia as well as we can wish'. Still later: 'My
brother's affairs are, as I have always wished them to
be and tried to make them. Everything points that
way and not least the fact that your sister is *enceinte*.'

The young Quintus grew up to be a regular mis-
chief-maker, now siding with his father, and now with
his mother. Thus we find in a letter of 45 B.C.:
'What incredible hypocrisy to write to his father that
he would have to leave home because of his mother,
and to his mother a letter full of affection'. But the
uncle had been too indulgent with him, and listened,
when he should not have done so, to his amusing
gossip about 'our ladies'. The inevitable divorce
was staved off till 44 B.C., when Marcus could no
longer lecture Quintus about it, having taken the
same step himself.

There was then some talk of Quintus marrying
again, and his son loudly protested that he would not
stand having a particular lady for a stepmother; but
nothing came of it, and on April 26th of that year
Marcus writes: 'Quintus is so averse to marrying
again that he declares a bachelor's couch is the most
comfortable in the world'.

Chapter 3

EARLY POLITICAL LIFE
76-66 B.C.

*You know the race I have started to run, how I must not
only keep in with everybody, but make new friends.*
Ad Att. i. 1, 4

In the year 76 B.C. Cicero's political career began.
Sulla had raised the number of Quaestors to twenty,
fixed the minimum age at thirty,* and arranged that,
when their office was over, they became senators.
After the quaestorship came the offices of Curule
Aedile and Tribune of the Plebs; if a man preferred
the latter, he had to be a plebeian, or if he was a
patrician, had to be adopted into a plebeian family.
Most patricians therefore sought the office of curule
aedile, which however was very expensive.   Clodius,
of whom we shall presently hear, was exceptional in
holding both offices in succession.   The next stage,
the praetorship, was not attainable till a candidate
had reached the age of thirty-nine; and the crown of
all, the consulship, could not be held till a man was
forty-two.   Cicero climbed the ladder without any
defeat, and in each case 'in his year', at the exact time
when he became eligible.

In 76 he spoke for Roscius the actor in a pecuniary

* According to Carcopino 29 for candidature, 30 for holding the office.

32

dispute, had other important briefs, was elected quaestor, and in 75 was sent to Sicily, where he was finance officer of state for the western half of the island, with headquarters at Lilybaeum. His chief, Sextus Peducaeus, was a model governor, destined to be followed by the iniquitous Verres, who behaved so badly that his successor was obliged to revert to the arrangements of Peducaeus. It was the son of this Peducaeus whose advice Cicero found so valuable in later life. In 45 B.C. he says: 'All I felt for his father, I have given to him, and I love him for himself as much as I loved his father'.[26] When Cicero talks about the tie that should exist between a governor and the quaestor assigned to him by lot, that is by the will of Heaven, it is therefore no mere conventional phrasing, but a sentiment based on his own experience.

During his stay in Sicily he visited Syracuse, and discovered the neglected grave of the great scientist and practical mechanician Archimedes, who had by his ingenuity made the city hold out so long against the Roman besiegers in the year 212 B.C. In a period of scarcity, he contrived notwithstanding to send large cargoes of corn to Rome. On leaving the island in 74, he addressed the people of Lilybaeum, and told them he should be proud henceforward to add himself to their list of patrons; whenever they called on him, they could depend on his services as an advocate. Little did he think how soon he would be asked to be as good as his word.

On his return he landed at Puteoli, the chief commercial port on the west coast of Italy; in reference to this, he gives us an amusing story at his own expense. He was so full of his doings in Sicily that he naïvely thought they had made him the talk of

D

the city. The first man he met said to him: 'Oh, what day did you leave Rome, and is there any news?' 'No,' said he, 'I am returning from my province.' 'Oh yes, Africa, wasn't it?' 'No, Sicily.' Then a by-stander said: 'Why, don't you know he has been quaestor at Syracuse?' He had actually been at Lilybaeum. 'After this', says Cicero, 'I swallowed my vexation, and made myself one of the pleasure-seeking crowd. But it taught me the lesson that, while the ears of the Roman People are dull, their eyes are sharp, and I decided thenceforward to keep myself perpetually in the public eye.' It has often been pointed out that, if a man can tell a story against himself in this way, his conceit is of an amiable and harmless kind: Cicero's self-conceit was quite consistent with a realisation of his own failings. He knew he was ambitious and vain, and to his other self, his closest friend, he freely confesses these foibles.[27] But he would not have been human, if he had not been ambitious; and if he was vain, he had that in him of which he might well be proud.

During the next years he was extremely busy at the bar: his friends, the tax-farming companies, found him plenty of work, and his intimacy with them stood him in good stead, when his first great opportunity came. The resentment of the knights against the senatorial tribunals had been growing more and more acute. There was a particularly gross offender to be brought to book: for Verres had been governing Sicily for three years in an abominable manner. In addition to his other faults, he was boastful and incautious in his speech. He declared quite openly that his first year filled his purse, his second provided him with the best advocates, and the third and most profitable of all would be devoted to bribing his judges: even this took no account of the loot of every kind which he carried away, defrauding the revenue-collectors by arranging to be charged no customs-duties. This had become a notorious scandal, and there was much talk of a change in the constitution of the courts.

The senatorial leaders seem to have felt that the strength of a chain depends on its weakest link, and to have determined to get Verres acquitted. The powerful Metelli were on his side. The great orator Hortensius, whom he had secured to defend him, was elected consul for the year 69 b.c. along with Quintus Metellus. If the trial could have been post-poned to that year, Marcus Metellus would have been the praetor presiding in the court before which provincial governors were arraigned, while another brother, Lucius, was governing Sicily and could suppress evidence against Verres. But the blind optimates did not realise the strength of public feel-ing that had been aroused, nor did they understand how energetic and determined Cicero could be in a righteous cause. They opposed him in his candi-dature for the curule aedileship, but were unable to prevent him from being elected.

At this moment the Sicilians placed their cause in Cicero's hands. He saw that he must strain every nerve to get the case tried before the year 70 came to an end. His first task was to assert his right to be prosecutor against a man of straw set up by the other side. This was one Quintus Caecilius, who had been quaestor to Verres and was therefore implicated in the charges against his official superior in connec-tion with the corn-supply, if not with other charges.

But he alleged that he had quarrelled with Verres, and complained of wrongs done to himself. The process by which the court selected the prosecutor was called 'divination', and the speech which Cicero delivered is called 'Divination against Quintus Caecilius'.

He has an easy task in dwelling on the close relationship that should exist between a provincial governor and his finance officer: it was bad form, if not positively irreligious, for a quaestor to disregard this solemn tie. He quotes as many as three recent instances, in which an outsider was preferred to a quaestor, and selected to lead a similar prosecution: in one case the representative of the Sardinians was preferred on the specific ground that he was the man of their choice. Nor can, Cicero says, a quaestor decently prosecute on charges in which he himself is implicated. Cicero is treading more delicate ground when he contrasts the entire inexperience of Caecilius in public speaking with his own training and experience of the courts, especially in cases affecting the tax-farmers.[28] On the whole he succeeds in avoiding the appearance of boastfulness while saying everything he wants to say: Cicero was a past master in the art of contriving to say things while professing not to say them. Except for some rather cheap jokes at Caecilius' 'book of the words', compiled for him by some hack out of other people's speeches, the banter is not in bad taste and quite amusing. 'Hortensius', he says, 'will have an easy task in making Caecilius ridiculous: I know and can guard against all his wiles.' On the other hand Caecilius' juniors will have to moderate their efforts so as not to surpass their leader, just as on the Greek stage the deuteragonist and tritagonist must be careful not to outshine the leading actor. That he himself had studied Greek literature at Athens and Latin at Rome, is implied rather than expressed, when he says Caecilius had learnt his Greek at Lilybaeum—Sicilian Greek was like the French of Stratford-atte-Bowe, not so much incorrect as totally different—and his Latin in Sicily.* After all, the telling point was that the Sicilians repudiated Caecilius, and demanded himself.

Cicero was then granted a hundred and ten days to collect his evidence. He obtained all he required in fifty, and returned in time for the trial to begin on August 5th. He spoke very briefly: the first Pleading, as we have it, may be substantially what he said. He describes the bribery and intimidation that had been employed. He states that Hortensius, when elected consul, had met Verres and publicly informed him that the result of the elections had assured his acquittal, and he complains that every effort had been made, but in vain, to defeat himself in his candidature for the curule aedileship. The Sicilians had been browbeaten both at Rome and by Lucius Metellus, the new governor of Sicily. He then produced his long series of damning evidence, and in nine days all was over: Verres had gone into voluntary exile.

Whether the Sicilians received compensation—they had through Cicero demanded £400,000—is doubtful, but at least a notorious offender had been disgraced, and his career as a Roman was over. Subsequently Cicero published the series of speeches,

---

* Plutarch says Caecilius was a Jew. This is very improbable, but Caecilius of Calacte in Sicily, a literary critic of the age of Augustus, may have been, and this might account for the mistake.

of which only the *Divinatio* and the first Pleading
were actually delivered. The second Pleading was
divided into five sections. In the first Cicero deals
with Verres' earlier life and his conduct as city-
praetor. Here he no doubt lays on the colour too
thick, but if we deduct half from all Cicero's charges,
enough remains to show how scandalously a Roman
magistrate could behave. There is one pretty touch
in this first section. He is describing the outrageous
interference with the will of one Annius, who wished
to bequeath his property to his only daughter. 'I
doubt not, gentlemen, that as to me, who love my
daughter dearly, so to you who have a like feeling of
affection for your daughters, these proceedings will
seem scandalous and outrageous.' [29] After beginning the second Pleading with a panegyric on Sicily,
the storehouse and treasury of the Roman Republic,
which in the late war 'with its supply of hides,
clothing and corn, dressed, fed and armed our
forces', he proceeds to detail the injuries done to
individuals; notably and at the greatest length he
relates the treatment of Sthenius, who had prevented
Verres from robbing the temples of his native town,
and had been obliged to flee to Rome and denounce
the governor there. He describes how every privi-
lege and office in the island had to be paid for to the
freedman Timarchides, how Verres had ingeniously
contrived to raise the number of taxing-officers to
a hundred and thirty, how he had appropriated three
million sesterces, nominally for the erection of
statues to himself, and how most of those which
were erected were thrown down after his departure,
in spite of all Metellus' efforts to prevent this happening. Finally Cicero describes how he had detected

Verres' frauds on the customs, how the account-books of the tax-farmers had been tampered with, the name of Verres being changed into an imaginary Verrucius, whom he challenges Verres to produce. As the customs-duties thus evaded at the port of Syracuse alone amounted to £480 on goods valued at £9600, he leaves to the imagination of his hearers how many articles had been smuggled out of the numerous other ports of Sicily, especially Messana, the inhabitants of which town were in collusion with Verres and sharers in his profits.

Into the detailed description of the frauds in connection with the supply of grain to the capital, and for the governor's use, it would be tedious to enter: they are set forth at length in the third Pleading. The fourth Pleading, *On Statues*, reads almost like a bit of the *Arabian Nights*. One might have supposed that only in the East could a governor sleep no night in anybody's house without begging, borrowing or stealing—as the case might require—any object of art that caught his fancy. Yet that is what Verres seems to have habitually done. One would like to know what became of the bronze Diana from Segesta, the Mercury from Tyndaris, the Apollo by Myron from Agrigentum (the Hercules was saved from a night attack led by Timarchides which was beaten off!), the whole contents of the temple of Juno in Malta, the Sappho by Silanion from Syracuse—the inscription on the bases of which he left behind to denounce him, 'not knowing a letter of Greek': probably most of them went into the melting-pot. The following passage will give a good idea of the behaviour of this art-connoisseur and the style of the orator:

'Those of you who have visited Henna have seen
a marble statue of Ceres, and in another temple one
of Libera: they are very large but not so very old.
There was one of bronze, of moderate size and unusual workmanship, carrying torches, very old, far
the oldest object in the temple. That he carried off,
but it did not satisfy his appetite. In an open space
in front of the temple of Ceres, there are two statues,
big and fine, one of Ceres, the other of Triptolemus.
Their beauty was their peril, their size their salvation:
for to pull them down and take them away seemed
very difficult. On the right hand of Ceres rested a
fine Victory: this he ordered to be wrenched off and
removed. What can be his feelings now at this re-
hearsal of his crimes, when in mentioning them I am
not only moved in spirit but thrill with horror? I remember the temple, its position, its sanctity: everything is present to my mind's eye. The day when I
arrived at Henna, the priests of Ceres met me decked
with chaplets and vervain. There was a public
meeting of the citizens, at which, when I addressed
them, such weeping and wailing arose, that you would
have thought the whole city was in mourning for one
dead. It was not of the exaction of tithes, nor the
plundering of their goods, nor the unjust sentences,
nor the outrageous lusts of Verres, not of the violence
and insults with which they had been overwhelmed,
that they complained. It was the deity of Ceres,
their ancient religion, the sanctity of the temple,
whose violation they desired to be expiated by the
punishment of this audacious wretch. The indignation was so great, that you would have thought Verres
a second Pluto, come to Henna to carry off not only
Proserpine but her mother as well. For that city is

not a mere city, but a shrine of Ceres: the people of
Henna believe that Ceres actually dwells among them:
I regard them not as citizens of the state, but all alike
are priests, neighbours and pontiffs of Ceres. Was
it from Henna that you had the impudence to carry
away a statue of Ceres? Was it from Henna that
you tried to tear Victory from the hands of Ceres and
rob a goddess of a goddess? Why, those who (in the
Servile War) occupied Henna, slaves, runaways, barbarians, enemies, never did anything so bad. They
were not so enslaved to their masters, as you to your
lusts: they were not such runaways from their masters,
as you from justice and law, nor so barbarian in speech
and nationality as you in disposition and character,
nor such enemies to men as you are to the immortal
gods.' For effectiveness it would be difficult to find
an invective in any language to surpass this passage.

In the last Pleading, on the capital punishments
inflicted by Verres, it may be felt that Cicero piled
on the agony, or even repeated false statements
made to him. When, however, we are inclined to
doubt whether Verres flogged a Roman citizen at
Messana, we may read a letter from Asinius Pollio,
addressed to Cicero from Corduba (Cordova) on June
8th, 43 B.C. In this he relates how his quaestor
Balbus has absconded to Africa with all the ready
money he could lay his hands on, and in the description of Balbus' enormities occurs the following:[30]
'At the gladiatorial shows there was a certain Fadius,
a soldier of Pompey; he had been pressed into the
gladiatorial school, and having twice defeated his ad-
versary without being paid for it, he objected to bind-
ing himself over to be a gladiator, and had sought
refuge with the people; so Balbus first let loose some

Gallic horsemen among the crowd (for stones were thrown at him, when Fadius was being dragged away) and then carried off Fadius, buried him up to the waist in the gladiators' school, and burnt him alive, while he himself, having lunched, strolled about barefooted and with his tunic ungirdled and his hands behind his back, and when the poor wretch shrieked out "I am a Roman citizen born", he answered "Off with you at once, implore the protection of the people".   It is a fact that he has thrown Roman citizens to the wild beasts, among them a certain itinerant pedlar who frequented sales, a very well-known character in Hispalis (Seville) on account of his deformity.   This is the kind of monster I have had to deal with.'

Such was the behaviour of a quaestor, but in the middle of the Civil War, when the animosity of parties had gone to great lengths: Verres was possessed of absolute power in Sicily in a time of profound peace.

Nor are Verres' shameful dealings with the pirates at all incredible.   They had become so outrageous in their insolence that in three years' time Pompey had to be given a special commission to round them up out of the whole Mediterranean area.

The pleadings against Verres remind us forcibly of the attacks of Burke and Sheridan on Warren Hastings, which roused the same kind of excitement in the fashionable audience at Westminster Hall that Cicero's plain speaking roused in his hearers: historians have successfully rehabilitated Hastings, but no one has yet attempted to whitewash Verres.   His amazing impudence in his treatment of Roman citizens surprises us most.   We see from the life of

St Paul how great an improvement in this respect
the Empire secured.

During the trial the Aurelian Law on the constitution of juries, which reduced the representation of
the Senate to one third, and added two other panels,
of knights and the so-called *tribuni aerarii*, possessed
of a somewhat lower amount of property, was formally promulgated. Cicero cannot therefore be given
the credit of abolishing the senatorial courts; what
he did was to express the popular indignation against
them, and prove to all future ages why they were
and had to be abolished. He rarely afterwards, apart
from occasional invectives, undertook the part of
prosecutor (see p. 160, note). He devoted himself for
a great part of his life to securing the acquittal of
persons, most of whom were notoriously guilty: but
there was no etiquette of the Roman Bar to prevent
his undertaking such briefs. In the case of Cluentius
four years later he boasted that he had thrown dust
in the eyes of the jury, and so successfully did he
defend his client, that to this very day we cannot tell
what was the truth in that extraordinary tissue of
crimes, which incidentally reflected more discredit on
the senatorial tribunals.

The next office which Cicero held was that of
curule aedile. For a comparatively poor man it was
difficult to hold this office without heavy borrowing.
Cicero had to give three sets of public shows: yet
in later life he tells his son that his expenses were
trifling. Plutarch says that the grateful Sicilians
helped him to defray the cost. In the same year he
defended, it is thought successfully, one Fonteius,
who, like Verres, was accused of misgoverning Provence, the 'province' of Gallia Narbonensis. Certainly

the charges against Fonteius were much less serious, that he had burdened the province with debt, made profit out of the building of roads, and instituted customs-duties on wine. In his speech Cicero under-rates the trustworthiness of Gaulish evidence, as he does at other times that of Greeks and Orientals. It was always a sure way of pleasing a Roman jury to disparage other nationalities. In this sort of thing Cicero is merely playing to the gallery.

In the year 68 Cicero with his wife's money acquired the suburban residence at Tusculum, which —though he put it up for sale unsuccessfully in 57— he occupied to his death. As on November 28th of this year his father died, he became possessed of the house in Rome (subsequently handed over to Quintus) and the family house and estate at Arpinum. He was now in easy circumstances and able to order Greek statuary to embellish his villa at Tusculum. To this he added five villas, and as many more humble lodgings in various parts of southern Italy, to facilitate travelling in days when there were no hotels. The expense of the upkeep of such a country-house today is not great, as it is always easy to find an Italian caretaker who will be only too glad to live rent-free. Those who have read modern novels the scene of which is laid in Italy will understand how little things have changed in centuries.

How Cicero avoided bankruptcy is a question less easy to answer. Probably it was Atticus who kept him solvent. Though advocates charged no fees at Rome, grateful clients like P. Sulla and C. Antonius found means of rewarding him, and he tells Antony that he received in all from legacies over £160,000. But unlike most upper-class Romans, he eschewed usury and provincial plunder.

In 67 B.C. Cicero was elected praetor. His duty was now to preside in the same court from which he had secured a conviction of Verres. In this capacity he condemned the historian Gaius Licinius Macer, though Macer had the powerful backing of Crassus. A sentence in his letter to Atticus on the subject [31] has been mistranslated. He says in effect: 'The verdict is popular. I had been inclined to favour him, but the popularity I have gained by his condemnation is more valuable to me (in view of my impending canvass for the consulship) than his support would have been, had he been acquitted.' Cicero had no doubt of Macer's guilt.

The most important event in Cicero's year of office was the proposal to confer a new and more important command on Pompey. By the Law of Gabinius, Pompey had been given considerable forces and authority to clear the Mediterranean of pirates: he had performed this task with great efficiency and speed, and he had prevented the recurrence of this evil; for instead of cruel executions he had planted out the ex-pirates as peaceful citizens. It has often been thought that Virgil's 'Corycian old man', who had a model garden at Tarentum, was one of these settlers.[32] Now the tribune Manilius proposed to supersede Lucullus, the senatorial general, and send Pompey to crush Mithridates and settle the East. Lucullus had been waging war with considerable success,—Macaulay even compares him with Trajan,—but he had never been able to bring the war to a successful conclusion: the wily king had evaded Lucullus and was still at large. On this occasion the knights united with the anti-senatorial party to carry the law. They were pleased with

Pompey whose consulship had restored to them
nearly, if not quite, their old ascendancy in the
courts, they admired his efficiency; and the taxes of
Asia were still in danger from Mithridates. Cicero
therefore, their usual spokesman, came forward and
delivered his first harangue to the people, in support
of this exceptional command for Pompey. It may
be remarked incidentally that Pompey justified all
the confidence reposed in him, and made settlements
in the East which were above criticism, during an
absence of four and a half years from Rome.

The praise of Pompey in Cicero's speech is very
emphatic, and there is no reason for thinking it
either insincere or undeserved. Pompey was clean-
handed, just and efficient. Lucullus was under the
same suspicion as other senatorial governors. This
is the way in which Cicero covertly attacks him:
'Who can be regarded as a general, in whose army
the post of centurion is or has been sold? What
great plan of campaign can we expect of a man,
who, when he has received an allowance from the
Treasury for carrying on the war, either distributes
it to magistrates because of his desire of a province, or is so avaricious that he banks it at Rome?
Your groans, fellow-citizens, make me think that you
recognise who have been guilty of such practices.
'I name no names; therefore no one can be angry
with me, except one who finds the cap fit.' In this
Cicero is, indirectly but unmistakeably, accusing
Lucullus of appropriating for his own purposes his
official allowance (*vasarium*), a charge which he expressly made, probably with more truth, against
Lucius Piso, when he went to Macedonia in 57 B.C.

Cicero was already under the spell of Pompey: he

clung to him pathetically down to the outbreak of
the Civil War, and even afterwards, when it would
have suited his interest far better to have thrown
in his lot with Caesar. It is certainly difficult to
criticise Pompey as a general or an administrator.
That he lacked some of the qualities of a statesman
and was hopeless as a political leader, was not as
plain at this time as it became later. Neither Cicero
nor anybody else foresaw this. Cicero's advocacy
of the Law of Manilius was dictated partly by the
interests of the knights, partly by his belief in
Pompey, but certainly also by his desire to be
Pompey's candidate for the consulship. He ab-
horred senatorial misgovernment in the provinces,
and he looked to Pompey as the strong man who
would make a just and lasting settlement in the East:
nor was he wrong. It is mere humbug, when he
says in his peroration that he has no design of
securing Pompey's good-will. He certainly hoped
for that, and he also felt sure the measure was in the
best interests of the Republic. Nor was he mistaken: for when Pompey returned it was not in the
manner of Sulla. He loyally disbanded his troops,
and hoped in vain that the gratitude of his fellow-
citizens would give them their due reward. In his
advocacy of the Law of Manilius, Cicero was acting
with the popular and anti-senatorial party and to
that extent ingratiating himself with them. But he
was not thereby identifying himself with their programme. He was supporting Pompey, not only
because it was the policy of the knights to send
Pompey to the East, but because he believed him to
be the man for the task.

Chapter 4

THE CONSULSHIP
65-63 B.C.

That consulship, which he, not unjustifiably but incessantly, praised.   SENECA, *De Brevitate Vitae*, 5

THE popular party had recovered much lost ground, since the reaction under Sulla had put them definitely under the heel of the Senate, or rather the conservative majority in the Senate; for there were always senators of popular sympathies, and now one who was an ideal political leader had come to the fore.

Gaius Julius Caesar was thirty-five, and a past master in the arts of electioneering and political wire-pulling. He was of the bluest blood of Rome, but the Julian family, like the Claudian, had long had democratic sympathies. His aunt was the wife of Marius, and he married the daughter of Cinna, whom he refused to put away at Sulla's order. When he avoided obedience by voluntary exile, Sulla said of him: 'In that young man lies many a Marius'. He then saw service in Asia, and won the civic crown,[33] at the siege of Mitylene. The story of his capture by pirates, and his exact fulfilment, after his release, of a jesting promise that if ever he caught them he would crucify them, illustrates the ruthless side of his nature. Like Cicero, he studied under Molon at Rhodes, and won fame at the age of twenty-one by his prosecution of Dolabella, one of Sulla's creatures, against the leaders of the Roman Bar, Cotta and Hortensius: from that time he was only second to Cicero as a public speaker. He had boldly revived old memories by displaying at the funeral of his wife Cornelia the wax likeness (*imago*) of Marius, and still more, when as curule aedile in 65 B.C. he restored the trophies and statues of Marius, which had been removed by Sulla. It was now his object to secure a democratic counterpoise to the power of Pompey.

The democrats had voted Pompey his Eastern command, but did not trust him, since he had begun his career as a supporter of Sulla. For a time Caesar hoped through the agency of Crassus, the wealthy financier (p. 9), to be sent to Egypt, which would have been a good way of restoring his financial solvency: it is probable that Cicero delivered the speech, which has not been preserved, on the 'King of Alexandria' in 65 B.C. in opposition to this scheme. The democrats had got the censorship restored; and Crassus as censor, though somewhat thwarted by his optimate colleague Catulus, was weaving one scheme after another for the defeat of Pompey.

That Crassus and Caesar were in each other's confidence at this time is highly probable. It is less easy to say whether they were cognisant of the desperate schemes of the daring and bankrupt aristocrat, Lucius Sergius Catilina, who is vividly portrayed to us not only in the orations of Cicero, but in the calm and judicial monograph of Sallust. The same picture of Catiline is drawn by both, and

E

many think Sallust chose the subject chiefly to defend Caesar against the charge of having been privy to Catiline's plans. But what were Catiline's plans?

That depends on the view we take of the so-called 'first conspiracy of Catiline', related by Sallust, which came to nothing. Catiline is supposed to have arranged with Autronius and Sulla, who had been elected consuls but unseated for bribery, to murder their substitutes Cotta and Torquatus on January 1st, 65 B.C., and to reinstate themselves. Thereupon, Suetonius tells us, one of them was to nominate Crassus as dictator: Caesar would then be appointed Crassus' 'master of the horse' [34] (see p. 142). A certain Piso was to be sent to Spain, but what exactly he was to do is far from clear.

Nothing happened of all this except that Piso did go to Spain and was murdered there. That Crassus would have liked to be dictator is obvious: but that either of them were foolish enough to enter into compromising relations with Catiline is exceedingly unlikely. Caesar had carefully avoided compromising himself with Lepidus' premature and abortive attempt to upset the Sullan constitution in 78: was it likely that he would have entered into direct relations with the bankrupt Catiline, who had been associated with the worst excesses of the Sullan reaction? Probably the democrats encouraged Piso in his schemes, whatever they were, and very possibly there was an assassination plot, prompted by private disappointment and animosity, which failed: for Cicero does say in his first Speech against Catiline (November 8th, 63 B.C.) that on December 31st, 66, Catiline had plotted to murder the consuls and the leading men of the state.[34a] Catiline may have often contemplated

murder; but any regular plot was certainly unknown
to Cicero, when he delivered his candidate's speech,
or to Quintus, when he wrote for his brother an
'Electioneering Manual': they would both have been
only too glad to make capital out of anything of the
kind. Therefore the 'first conspiracy of Catiline' is
a misnomer: nor can we believe that in 63 Caesar,
who had planned a series of constitutional moves on
behalf of the democratic party, gave any support to
an anarchist plot.*

Catiline then went to Africa and misgoverned the
province. On his return he was prosecuted by
Publius Clodius, and we are not particularly surprised
to learn that Cicero might, if he pleased, have defended him. That he did not do so is proved by
Asconius. Catiline was acquitted: the mixed juries
were as venal as the unmixed senatorial juries had
been. But it delayed his candidature for the consulship from 65 to 64, and so he was a formidable rival
to Cicero: for having begun as a violent reactionary,
he had gone round to the extreme left, and could
count on the democratic vote.

Early in 65 B.C. Cicero writes to beg Atticus for
a time to leave Athens, where he had lived for over
twenty years, and come to Rome to support his
candidature. Catiline, he says, if the verdict of the
courts is that the sun does not shine at midday, that
is if he is acquitted when notoriously guilty, will be
a dangerous competitor. But more dangerous still
is the prospect that some one will come from the East
and secure election as Pompey's nominee: therefore

* Suetonius (*Julius*, 9, 3.) quotes Cicero as saying in a letter to Axius
(lost to us), that Caesar as consul (59 B.C.) established the despotism which
he planned as aedile (65 B.C.). But see p. 58.

Atticus must try to secure the help of Pompey's supporters. Then he makes a little joke, which must
not be taken seriously: 'Tell Pompey, our friend, that
I will forgive him if he does not come in person to
support me'. Cicero certainly hoped that his useful
advocacy of the Manilian Law would be remembered
in his favour: and we may suppose it was, for Pompey
did not run a candidate. But neither did he indicate
that he was in favour of Cicero's election.

One phrase in the letter to Atticus is too vague to
be interpreted with certainty. 'I want you back as
soon as possible: for there is a widespread belief that
friends of yours in the upper classes will oppose my
election.' It has been interpreted as referring to
Crassus and Caesar: but Atticus was not in any close
relations with either. More probably it refers to
the senatorial leaders. They were perhaps annoyed
with Cicero for his advocacy of the ex-tribune
Cornelius in 65 B.C.

Cornelius, who had been Pompey's quaestor, as
tribune in 67 took a strong anti-senatorial line.
When Cicero was praetor in 66, Cornelius was accused before him of high treason, but the accusers
failed to appear and were supposed to have been
bribed to abscond. When he was prosecuted again
in 65, it may be inferred that Cicero accepted his
brief, partly because he had been Pompey's man, and
partly because the very tribune was now supporting
him, whose veto Cornelius was said to have ignored.

For some time past Cicero had been accepting
briefs without any regard to party politics, and thus
had been liable to offend the senatorial majority.
Yet it was certainly the votes they commanded which
brought Cicero to the head of the poll in 64. He

was an upstart, but at least he could be relied on to oppose the danger of constitutional change (Caesar) or downright anarchy (Catiline), though how soon the latter's designs became known is uncertain: Sallust at least definitely states that they became public property before the consular elections held in 63. Cicero's colleague was Gaius Antonius, uncle of the triumvir, an impecunious and shifty aristocrat, who was strongly suspected of revolutionary leanings: Catiline was defeated by a few votes. Cicero lost no time in securing the inaction, if not the support, of Antonius, by announcing his intention of not taking a province himself at the end of his year of office, and in addition managing to secure for his colleague the rich province of Macedonia.* The bait was greedily swallowed, and to all intents and purposes Antonius was as much a cipher in 63 as Bibulus was in 59 when Caesar was consul. Quintus, who often had a pretty wit of his own, hit the nail on the head, when, speaking of the joint candidature of Antonius and Catiline, he said: 'Catiline fears neither god nor man: Antonius is afraid of his own shadow'.

The democratic forward move began with the opening of the year. A tribune, Rullus, had advertised an agrarian law,† to provide land for needy citizens and discharged soldiers. A board of ten persons was to be appointed to hold office for five years: it was obviously impossible for Pompey to be one of them. They were to have full power to draw on the resources of the state, and all revenues acquired by conquest since 88 B.C., in order to purchase land

---

* To avoid the temptations of ambition ' commands should sometimes be refused'. *De Off.* i. 20, 68.

† E. G. Hardy, *Some Problems in Roman History*, p. 68 ff.

in Italy generally, and in particular to evict with compensation the tenants of the valuable state land formerly belonging to Capua, the so-called *Ager Campanus*, the holders of which through long tenure had come to regard their title as secure, provided they paid their rent. The measure was opposed to Cicero's convictions: for he associated agrarian laws with attempts at tyranny or revolution. He therefore spoke against it with great adroitness, and secured its rejection. It was a proposal, he said, to crown ten kings in Rome; who was Rullus that he should describe the inhabitants of the capital as a cesspool to be drawn off? It is amusing that Cicero used the same expression himself in discussing another agrarian law, which, to please Pompey, in 60 B.C. he wished to be carried with modifications suggested by himself: it probably stuck in his memory. Equally ingenious is his argument that the measure is an attempt to put money in the pockets of those who own either land confiscated by Sulla, or land which is worthless for agricultural purposes. Finally he attempts to prejudice the Romans by suggesting that it would revive the pride and arrogance of Capua, which once had been a rival of Rome itself. His words were convincing for the moment: but he could not conceal the fact that the law was an attempt to relieve the poor, and he had thrown it out. From this time dates Cicero's great unpopularity with the lower classes in the city.

Foiled in one article of his programme, and not yet ready to take up another, the enfranchisement of Italians north of the Po, Caesar determined to make a demonstration against the execution of any citizen by order of the magistrate without trial under cover

of the Senate's authority. The ancient Valerian Law
on appeal to the popular assembly dated back to
509 B.C.: the protection of the tribunes was an additional safeguard against official violence. The Senate,
however, held that it could arm the magistrate and
dispense him from the laws by passing the so-called
'ultimate decree': 'Let the consuls see that the
Republic takes no harm'. To protest against this
doctrine, the tribune Labienus, of course at the instigation of Caesar, prosecuted an old senator called
Rabirius for the murder of the democratic leader,
Saturninus, thirty-seven years before. It was notorious that Rabirius had not done the deed, but a slave
called Scaeva, who had been rewarded by freedom
and citizenship: but doubtless Rabirius had drawn
the sword and used it on the same day. So Caesar
and his uncle condemned the poor old man, who
could only appeal to the assembly of the people,
organised in centuries, which represented the army
of the Republic. In spite of the eloquence of Cicero,
he would certainly have been condemned to death,
had not the praetor dissolved the assembly by lower-
ing the flag on the Janiculum, the hill on the right
bank of the Tiber, which in old times used to mean:
'Romans, to arms: the Etruscans are on us'. After
this masquerade of outworn forms, the victim was
allowed to escape. But Cicero had his warning. It
is all credit to him that in a desperate emergency a
few months later he did not falter.

In the summer there was another demonstration
of popular feeling on the reintroduction of popular
election for the post of *Pontifex Maximus*, the official
head of the Roman religion. Caesar staked his last
farthing on success: he told his mother when he left

the house not to expect to see him back, unless he was elected. But though a free-thinker, who dismissed the idea of a future life as folly later in the year, he was triumphantly elected, and soon afterwards made praetor. At the end of his year of office he could look forward to restoring his finances in Spain.

For the year 62 Catiline was again a candidate for the consulship, but by this time he was organising a widespread conspiracy. Cicero describes six classes of those he had drawn into his net. 'The first consists of those who are heavily in debt, but unwilling to part with any of their lands to pay their creditors; the second of the indebted and ambitious (is this a covert reference to Caesar?); the third of the Sullan colonists, who though brave men and good citizens are so badly off that they wish for a return of the Sullan proscriptions; the fourth of all needy and turbulent adventurers; the fifth the criminal classes; and the last, Catiline's dissolute young associates, with their glossy hair, with their faces either smooth (because they were too young for hair to grow) or adorned with a small beard, with long sleeved tunics reaching to the ankles, and veils rather than *togas*, who keep their nightly revels. These striplings, so charming and effeminate, have learned not only to love and be loved, but also to brandish daggers and broadcast poisons. If they are not driven out, then even in the event of Catiline's death there will be a seed-plot of Catilines in Rome. How will they endure the Apennines with their frost and snows?'

Sallust lays on the colour even more unsparingly. 'Every debauchee, adulterer, and glutton who by the gratification of his passions had impaired his patrimony, everyone whose debts had been swollen to buy indemnity for some crime, all cut-throats from every quarter, all who had committed sacrilege, who had been tried and condemned, or whose deeds made them fear a trial, or who gained their living by polluting their tongues with perjury or their hands with their countrymen's blood, in fine, all who were driven on by crime, by need or the stings of conscience— these were Catiline's intimate associates. It was especially the intimacy of young men that Catiline affected: and their pliable and unformed minds fell an easy prey to his wiles. Complying with the several forms of youthful passion, he helped some to mistresses, bought hounds and horses for others, and in fine spared neither his purse nor his honour to make them his faithful creatures. I am aware that some believed that the young men who made Catiline's house their resort behaved with too little regard for decency, but the report obtained credence rather from other considerations than from any direct testimony.' He goes on to credit Catiline with intrigues with a high-born maiden, and with a Vestal virgin, and has no doubt that he killed a stepson in order to overcome Orestilla's objection to marrying him.

Nothing would by this time satisfy Catiline and the desperadoes with whom he was in touch all over Italy, but total abolition of debt, and a fresh proscription: in fact they were anarchists. It will be said perhaps that Cicero is prone to exaggeration and we have chiefly his authority to follow. Cicero certainly did not minimise the danger: but that plans were laid for firing the city and a general massacre, we can call Crassus to witness. In February 61

Crassus said in the Senate, to Cicero's immense surprise and gratification, that he owed his seat in the
House, his privileges as a citizen, his freedom and
his very life to Cicero. He worked up with great
effect 'that purple-patch, with which I so often adorn
the speeches of which you, Atticus, are so severe a
critic—about fire and sword—you know how thick
I lay on the colour'.[35] Crassus at least could not
have wished for anarchists to win the day nor Caesar
either. In none of his public utterances did Cicero,
in spite of great pressure, accuse Caesar of complicity
in the plot. He probably suspected that he knew
all about it, but felt it more politic to assume that he
did not. Later on he may have changed his mind.
At least the context of a passage in a letter of May
2nd, 49, shows that he is referring to Caesar, when
he says: 'I must obey men against whom the Senate
armed me with power to see that the Republic took
no harm'. It is clear from Plutarch [36] that in his
Greek memoir On the Consulship Cicero acknowledged help from Crassus in warning him of the conspiracy. But Plutarch says that, in a work only published after the deaths of Crassus and Caesar, he
accused them both of complicity: and it is argued
from Asconius 83, 21 and Charisius i. 146 that this
was called De Consiliis suis. In April 59 [37] Cicero
threatens to vent his feelings of disgust in a private
memorandum (anecdota). If he ever wrote this, it
was more likely to be an attack on Pompey. There
is no reason to connect this with the liber anecdotus
written but not yet revised in May 44 B.C.[38] The
context suggests it was an attack on Antony rather
than on Caesar. Anyhow a posthumous work of
Cicero does not refute the conclusion adopted above,

that Crassus and Caesar were much too wily politicians to have in any way patronised Catiline in the year 63 B.C. No impartial person will either accuse them, or deny that Cicero played the part of chief magistrate in a serious crisis with energy and efficiency and at great peril of his life.

By the meeting of the Senate on October 20th he had collected sufficient information of the armed rising planned for a week ahead at Faesulae (Fiesole above Florence), and accused Catiline of treason. The Senate passed the ultimate decree and postponed the consular elections to the 28th; and at these two reliable men, Silanus and Murena, were chosen and Catiline again rejected. The rebellion at Fiesole under one Manlius broke out, and still Catiline made no sign. At Rome Atticus organised a strong bodyguard of reliable knights to defend the consul's person. On the evening of November 6th a meeting of the conspirators was held, attended by Catiline, who was supposed to be in private custody at his own request but apparently was allowed a latch-key, and by an ex-consul, who having been expelled from the Senate had actually been elected and was acting as praetor at the moment: several others of those who met were members of the Senate. The mistress of a conspirator warned Cicero that two of the desperadoes would go next morning to murder him at his house, and the consul naturally was 'Not at home'.

He then convened the Senate at the temple of Jupiter, and as Catiline had the effrontery to attend the meeting, though no one would speak to or sit near him, Cicero denounced him in the First Catilinarian Oration (November 7th or 8th). Cicero perhaps expected he would be there: in any case his

presence gave him the opportunity to deliver the finest
piece of invective he or perhaps any orator ever delivered: it may have been slightly polished for publication, but it seems to be substantially what he said.
There were shorthand reporters at all these meetings
of the Senate.

'How long, pray, will you abuse our patience,
Catiline?' The opening words strike the schoolboy
who is spelling out the unfamiliar Latin, and equally
they stir the blood of those who have passed their
prime: they have won for themselves immortality. It
was a memorable scene. There sat the conspirator
all alone to be assailed by this torrent of telling and
truthful eloquence.

Cicero began by ranging himself uncompromis-
ingly on the side of the Senate on the constitutional
question. Ahala was right to kill Maelius, Scipio
Nasica to slay Tiberius Gracchus. The Senate armed
Opimius to put to death Gaius Gracchus and Fulvius.
The same decree armed the consuls Marius and
Valerius to slay Saturninus. (He does not add that
Marius did notwithstanding everything in his power
to save his friend.) 'That decree like a sword in its
sheath has been waiting for nineteen days. But while
I employ only words not weapons, there should at
least be walls between us.' The object of the speech
is to show Catiline that his game is up in Rome, his
movements are known, and to drive him out of the
city into the position of a public enemy. In spite of
his audacity Cicero tells us[39] that Catiline was struck
dumb. Sallust says that uttering violent threats he
left the house, assumed the state of a general of the
Republic, and hurried to place himself at the head
of the open insurrection in Etruria.

Cicero did not dare do anything but let him go:
for the situation in the capital was too difficult. Next
day, obviously with some anxiety as to the reception
he would get, he addressed the people, warned them
of the danger and strove to avert from himself any
unpopularity for having driven Catiline out, some
said to exile: for the existence of the rising was not
generally believed.

His speech begins effectively with the four untranslatable words for 'He is gone', *Abiit, excessit,
evasit, erupit*; but it is far less forcible than the first;
for it is overloaded with rhetoric. There are fourteen
descriptions of Catiline's associates, and fourteen contrasts of the qualities displayed on the opposing sides
in the coming struggle. But it probably served its
purpose; and the alarm was such that the Senate was
able without any public protest on November 19th
to declare Catiline and his lieutenant Manlius public
enemies: they could thenceforward be slain by anyone without fear of consequences. But the danger
was still acute. The insurrection was liable to break
out simultaneously in various parts of Italy. Worst
of all, there were the conspirators in Rome, including
actual senators, who refused to budge. Lentulus,
the praetor, was a vain and foolish fellow, who had
been led to believe that he was the third Cornelius—
first Cinna, then Sulla, then himself—destined to
bear rule in Rome. But Autronius, the unseated
consul for 65, Cethegus and Gabinius were fully the
equals of Catiline in audacity and forcefulness. If
Cicero is to be believed—and his backstairs information seems to have been very accurate—the City had
been mapped out in districts each to be fired by
a separate incendiary. Luckily the conspirators

decided to postpone the rising in Rome to the Satur-
nalia (December 19th), when amidst general merry-
making, at a time when masters usually gave their
houses over to the slaves, it was thought that the
plot was more likely to succeed.

Then by a stroke of great good fortune Cicero
secured damning evidence against the principal conspirators. There were present in Rome some ambassadors of the Allobrogian Gauls, from the country we
call Savoy. Lentulus had the folly and wickedness to
tamper with them. They informed their patron, a
Fabius, who passed on the information to Cicero.
At his request they obtained autograph letters from
the conspirators, and accompanied by one of the
latter, Volturcius, were arrested at the Mulvian
Bridge and the evidence was all seized, whereupon
Volturcius turned informer.

Even then Cicero only proceeded with the greatest
circumspection. He summoned the leading senators
to his house, and produced the prisoners and the
sealed letters for their inspection; but would not open
the letters till the Senate had met in the Temple of
Concord. There confronted with the Allobroges and
denounced by Volturcius the boldest among them
were unable to deny their guilt. Four of the nine
implicated managed to escape; but five were arrested
and given in charge, each to a different senator,
who was responsible for his safe-keeping. Cicero
was duly complimented and a public thanksgiving
ordered. After this Cicero addressed the people,
related the facts, described the conspirators as public
enemies (*hostes*) and bade them thank Heaven for
deliverance from a calamity which would have been
worse than any that had befallen the Republic in the

civil troubles of the past. But there is no boastfulness in the speech. He is content, he says, to suffer
unpopularity, if only he is allowed to do his duty. It
is for the citizens to save him from any injurious consequences. One would have expected the Senate to
show their gratitude to Cicero by safeguarding him,
but there was little gratitude for a 'new man'.

On December 5th they met to decide the fate of
the prisoners. Why they did not declare them public
enemies and order a military execution is not clear:
or a summary trial for high treason might easily have
been arranged: but they preferred to lay the onus on
Cicero. Silanus, consul-elect, proposed the extreme
penalty and others followed in the same sense.
Caesar, when it came to his turn, naturally could not
agree to this after the affair of Rabirius. He moved
an amendment that they should be imprisoned for
life in different Italian towns, with civil degradation
and confiscation of property, dire penalties being
threatened to any one who permitted or assisted them
to escape. This was, he observed, a severer punishment, as there could be no certainty of a future existence: thus spake the supreme pontiff of the Roman
religion. The speech—of course not verbally that
which Sallust puts in his mouth—made a great impression, and Silanus declared that perpetual im-
prisonment was a more 'extreme penalty' than death.
But if the Senate could not put them to death, how
could it imprison them for life? Was not the one
punishment as illegal as the other?

Cicero, with studied courtesy to Caesar, argued
against the proposal, but undertook to carry out
either sentence, if passed by the Senate. He did not,
however, point out that the sentences stood on a

similar legal footing, nor did he much emphasise the danger of the criminals escaping or being released by those who had fled, nor did he argue that the punishment suggested by Caesar was quite without precedent. Cato then spoke strongly in favour of the death penalty. This decided the waverers, and it was voted.

Cicero immediately hurried the prisoners off to the dungeon, where the brave African Jugurtha had met his end—which by a curious coincidence was called the *Tullianum*—and caused them to be strangled one by one. Then he came out and announced to the assembled crowd in one word that they were dead. He was escorted home by jubilant supporters, and Rome was illuminated for the occasion by all friends of the Government. But in the back streets of the capital there must have been curses loud and deep and vows of vengeance.

Cicero had incurred the responsibility of putting men to death without trial, and before long he had to suffer for it, being basely deserted by those who had ordered him to carry out their decree. He wondered sometimes what history would say of him after six hundred years: there are still those who after nearly two thousand years think that he saved the fatherland which he loved.

After the executions the insurrection did not spread, though Catiline was already at the head of ten thousand men. Luckily the unreliable consul Antonius left the crushing of Catiline and Manlius to able lieutenants. Being rounded up and prevented from escaping northwards, the rebels were annihilated at Pistoria on January 5th, 62 B.C. In his *De Officiis*, written in 44, after remarking what desperate efforts Catiline had made to bring about a general repudiation of debt, Cicero observes that, when all hope of defrauding their creditors had been removed from debtors, debts were immediately repaid.[40]

During these exciting days Cicero had to plead for Murena, consul-elect, who was tried on a charge of bribery; in addition to his other labours he took the brief, as under the circumstances it was highly dangerous for the Republic to lack one of its consuls on the coming New Year's Day. Sulpicius, a jurist of high repute, who had been an unsuccessful candidate, and Cato, who put principle before expediency,* were the prosecutors. After a sleepless night, Cicero delivered the wittiest and brightest of the speeches that have come down to us, and secured the offender's acquittal. With complete courtesy but irresistible effect he compares the lawyer's popularity with that of the soldier, and ridicules the unpractical maxims of the Stoics. This year was certainly not only the culmination of Cicero's ambition, but marked his zenith as an orator.

* But Cato did not object to the bribery which made his son-in-law Bibulus consul in 59 B.C. (Suetonius, *Julius*, 19, 1.)

Chapter 5

THE FIRST TRIUMVIRATE
62-59 B.C.

*Assert yourself in politics only so far as you can carry your
fellow citizens with you: it is as wrong to use violence to
your country as to a parent.*
PLATO, *Crito*, 51 C; *Ad Fam.* i. 9, 18

W HAT did Pompey think of all this? An ominous
sign of his displeasure was given by Quintus Metellus
Nepos, who had arrived post-haste from his camp
just in time to be elected tribune of the commons.
These plebeian magistrates came into office on
December 10th and had three weeks clear in which
to annoy the outgoing magistrates, show their hands
and intimidate those who were to come in on January
the 1st. When Cicero came forward to deliver his
carefully prepared valedictory speech, the tribune
interposed his veto. Cicero was simply allowed to
swear that he had served the state, and the people,
he says, confirmed his words by their applause: but
it was a grievous disappointment.

The fact was that Pompey was intensely chagrined
that events had moved too fast: there had been no
time to summon home the Indispensable One to set
all to rights. Again we have a clear indication that
Catiline's conspiracy, though secretly brewing for a

long time, did not take definite shape till his second
rejection at the consular elections. Nepos must have
started, before the news of that had reached Asia,
with general instructions to stage-manage the recall
of Pompey, but he was quite aware what line he
should take under all circumstances.

When Pompey had taken over the command in
Asia, Lucullus could not refrain from the taunt, that
what Pompey had done in the past to Catulus,
Metellus and Crassus, he was repeating once more,
stealing the laurels due to another. There was
enough truth in this for the sting to go home.
Notoriously, Crassus had been given less than his due
for the suppression of the rebellion of Spartacus. It
was therefore to be expected that Pompey would wish
to come back and behave as he had done before,
posing as the saviour of the state. Now, both in the
third and fourth speeches against Catiline, Cicero had
without any apparent relevance made highly complimentary allusions to Pompey. Unfortunately he
had been so tactless as to talk of his own achievements (*res gestae*), and thus to set the deeds of a
civilian by the side of the military glories of the
Great Man. This mistake he had repeated by sending an elaborate account of the suppression of the
conspiracy to Pompey. We possess neither this nor
Pompey's chilly reply. That Cicero was laughed at
for being snubbed is certain. When he was defending Plancius, the prosecutor had remarked that he
himself had sent home no dispatch about his provincial administration, because a letter sent by Cicero
to a certain person had done him harm. Cicero, as
usual when he is cornered, takes the bull by the
horns: 'I am not aware that it did any harm: I can see

that it might have done good to the state'. We have
a letter from Cicero to Pompey of (perhaps) June
62 B.C. In it he says Pompey's public dispatch has
profoundly upset his 'old enemies and recent friends',
that is Caesar's party, and that the private letter he
had received, 'though it contained but a scanty expression of your feelings towards me,' nevertheless
pleased him; for he was quite ready to do more for
Pompey than Pompey did for him. Had he stopped
there it would have been a dignified protest. But he
could not help showing his disappointment at receiving no acknowledgement of his services to the state,
and ended by proposing to play the part of Laelius
to Pompey's Africanus, a proposal which, however
complimentary, Pompey was in no mind to accept,
till he found out for himself whether Cicero was hope-
lessly discredited or still a force to be reckoned with.
It was impossible for him from a distance to keep in
touch with the shiftings of politics at Rome, at any
rate from Asia. In nothing do we see the vast intellectual superiority of Caesar to Pompey so much as in
the way in which he managed throughout his ten years
in Gaul to keep in touch with the politics of the City
and be felt all the time in his absence: even Cicero,
when later on he was in Cilicia, knew pretty much
what was happening in Rome.

In the offer of political alliance and mutual confidence which Cicero was formally making he did not
indeed realise that Pompey would only issue orders
to inferiors and could not unbosom himself to a friend:
but he did express a conviction that the state needed
a *princeps*, a wise leader who would control public
policy, like the great Africanus or Pericles in Athens.
He felt that Pompey had it in him to play this part.

But now he was snubbed, and he vented his feelings to Atticus in the letters of 61 B.C., notably on January 25th: 'He is totally lacking in courtesy, candour and distinction in politics, as well as in honour, resolution and generosity'. Yet the moment Pompey held out a finger, Cicero grasped it with his whole hand. The two men had totally different dispositions, Cicero ardent, sanguine, impulsive, almost insincere because of his rapid changes of feeling, Pompey cold, reticent, proud and very slow in gauging other men's thoughts. Because of this, Pompey has never received much appreciation, except from Mr Masefield in his *Pompey the Great*. The portrait there is essentially true.

Pompey was a humane man, who never soiled his record by unnecessary cruelty. In a very immoral age he was a model of domestic behaviour. He had five wives in succession, and to the last two of them we know that he was devotedly attached. He was a great soldier and military commander. Above all, he was a patriot and loyal to the Republic, a merit which outweighs many defects. But he was cold and slow in making or keeping friends. Thus he ought never to have allowed Caesar to win over the invaluable services of Balbus the Spaniard. Instead he seems to have relied too much on another agent, one Theophanes, though it is a gross exaggeration to say with Mommsen that the Greek had 'complete ascendancy over his weak master, and probably contributed more than anyone else to the outbreak of the war between him and Caesar'. It is probable enough that Theophanes hated Caesar, but Pompey was not weak except in intercourse with Caesar, who had learned how to dominate Pompey's shy, reserved and proud nature. Pompey knew his own mind quite well, but he was very chary of showing it to others: he had no great power of words, and he therefore found silence his best weapon. He got the reputation of being oracular often when he was only puzzled.* Probably often after listening to Cicero, he would go to Julia or Cornelia, and make the same remark as Queen Victoria made about Gladstone, 'He talks to me, my dear, as if I were a public meeting'.

The campaign of Nepos against Cicero went on vigorously in the early months of 62. He harangued the people in an invective: Cicero replied in unsparing terms, but the *Metelline Oration* has not come down to us. Nepos wanted by hook or by crook to summon Pompey back, but it was too late, and the Senate would not hear of it. Caesar, now praetor, threw himself with zest into the game of baiting the Senate. But the consul Murena was a resolute man and ready for strong measures. The Senate proclaimed a suspension of public business, suspended both Nepos and Caesar, and was quite prepared to pass the ultimate decree. Then Caesar, who knew when *reculer pour mieux sauter*, submitted and soon afterwards, apparently before the end of the year, went to Spain, where he found it an easy matter to get enough money in a year to pay his debts without even risking a prosecution; he was reserving himself for the consulship. Nepos in a dudgeon went off to Pompey, and would not resume the official duties from which he had been suspended. Pompey, unlike Caesar in January 49 B.C., refused to take any

---

* The disrespectful Caelius said: 'As a rule he thinks one thing and says another, and yet is not quite clever enough to conceal his wishes'.— *Ad Fam.* viii. 1, 3.

notice of the incident. The Republic did not need him: very well, he could afford to wait till the Republic came to him on bended knees imploring his aid. It did, but by that time Pompey was older and had lost nerve.

There was an amusing correspondence over the relations between Nepos and Cicero. Nepos' brother Celer, who owed to Cicero's kindness the province of Cisalpine Gaul and had been very useful in the suppression of the Catilinarian rising, wrote a curt and arrogant letter to Cicero, in not quite impeccable Latin, complaining of the way in which his brother and he had been treated. It seems that Cicero had actually raised a laugh against Celer in the Senate. He cannot deny the fact, but represents that the Senate laughed at himself rather than Celer. He is on surer ground when he says that he has not attacked Nepos, but only defended himself against a gross and unprovoked assault. He has appealed to 'your wife Claudia' (Clodia!) 'and to your sister Mucia' (wife of Pompey) to restrain Nepos, but in vain. He excuses Celer's threatening tone on the ground of brotherly affection, and adds that no just resentment against Nepos will prevent him from entertaining the friendliest feeling to Celer or, he is sure, make Celer disloyal to the state. The letter illustrates the contempt of a Metellus for a 'new man' however distinguished, and also the extent to which family pride overrode party ties. Celer was bound to disapprove of Nepos' conduct, but was the first to protest against his being publicly disgraced.

There can be little doubt that Cicero wearied and almost disgusted people by over-praising his own achievements. We must not, however, forget that it

was his only means of self-defence.   In 63 B.C., as
we have seen, he foresaw the danger to himself and
yet he did not flinch.   Now he could only avert the
consequences, if everyone agreed that he had saved
the capital and the Republic from a great disaster.
The triumphs of a soldier leap to the eye, not necessarily so the precautions of a statesman.   This was
the motive of Cicero's self-praise: it must be admitted
that he overdid it.*

Late in the year Pompey landed in Italy and to
everyone's surprise disbanded his army, trusting to
the Senate to provide for his veterans and to confirm
his Eastern arrangements.   A writer in the *Cambridge Ancient History*, following Mommsen, actually
says that by doing so Pompey made 'the great
refusal'.   So persistently do people allow their
knowledge of after-events to colour their judge-
ments of men who lived under the Republic before
the days of the Empire.   It should rather be
called a grand renunciation of the bad traditions of
Marius and Sulla; yet even Cicero does not mention
it.†   One can imagine Caesar hearing of it in Spain
and saying 'What a fool!   If I had had a chance like
that—but never mind, I shall, one day.'   It was in
the end to Caesar that Pompey had to have recourse
to get bare justice done to him.

According to Cicero, when Pompey got back to
Rome, he disappointed everybody by his first harangue. . . . 'The poor got no comfort from it, the revolutionary thought it meaningless, the rich were not

* Quintilian (*Inst. Orat.* XI. i. 17) says: 'His frequent mention of
what he did in his consulship may be put down to self-defence rather
than boastfulness.'

† Velleius Paterculus, who wrote his outline of Roman History in
A.D. 30, does justice to Pompey (*R.H.* ii. 40).

pleased with it, the conservatives thought it lacking in dignity: so it fell flat.' That was because Pompey had no intention of showing his hand: he would wait and see. When Cicero tried to corner him with questions about the suppression of Catiline, he took refuge in vague expressions of following the Senate's lead, and said to Cicero, as he sat down, 'That covers your case'.[41] But on this occasion Crassus pronounced an unexpected eulogy of Cicero (see p. 58), and at some later meeting of the Senate Pompey must have followed suit; for we read in the De Officiis that he said 'in the hearing of many, that he would have won a third triumph to no purpose, if the Republic had not had, thanks to Cicero, a place in which to celebrate the triumph'.*

When Pompey arrived, all Rome was talking about the latest scandal. At the December festival of the Bona Dea (see p. 27) Publius Clodius was discovered in Caesar's house disguised as a woman. As this reflected on Caesar's honour, he divorced Pompeia (though he refused to hold her as guilty) because 'Caesar's wife must be above suspicion'. The matter was taken up in the Senate, foolishly as Cicero thought, and referred to the authorities on religion, who, of course, reported it as a case of sacrilege. Whereupon a bill was proposed by which the jurors were to be chosen by the judge, lest Clodius if tried should escape. As this was against the first principles of Roman Criminal Law, it was naturally objected to by the democrats. An ordinary

* De Off. i. 20, 68. Cp. also Cicero's Speech to the Senate on his return (61, 29). 'Can I ever seem sufficiently grateful to Pompey, who not only to you (the Senate) who were all of the same mind, but to the whole people, said that the safety of the Roman People had been preserved by me and was inseparable from mine.'

jury was empanelled, and by a narrow majority owing to gross bribery, of which Cicero accuses Crassus, Clodius was acquitted. Unfortunately Cicero, who at first had held aloof from the sordid affair, at his wife's instigation it is said, gave evidence to overthrow Clodius' *alibi*. Had he foreseen the consequences, he might have been more prudent. Clodius vowed vengeance on him and kept his word. For the next ten years he caused him constant anxiety, and Cicero only breathed freely when Clodius was dead.

Publius Claudius Pulcher, to show his democratic sympathies, wrote his name in the way in which the vulgar pronounced it, Clodius. He had begun public life by prosecuting Catiline in a half-hearted way, but afterwards he had certainly belonged to the Catilinarian gang. He had however behind him all the prestige of an ancient family: he was related to most of the noble families by blood or affinity, and whatever pranks he played, it was certain that someone in high position would try to shield him. When Caesar took him up, his fortune was made, and Pompey, without Caesar, found him quite unmanageable. He became a power in the capital; for he was one of the first to organise *operae*, or hired armed bands of political supporters. They were simply the unemployed hooligans of Rome, who were glad to take anybody's pay and do his dirty work. Then, as now, a Southerner was ever ready to use his knife. Some countries seem to be full of *operae* to-day, and if we do not take precautions, we shall have the ugly phenomenon in this country. Perhaps without fresh provocation Clodius would have forgiven the ex-consul for his testimony, particularly as it was not credited. But Cicero could not

refrain from denouncing him: he was always unable
to resist making a witticism, and his words stung.
Clodius tried a fall with him in that odd sort of
sparring match (*altercatio*) which sometimes interrupted the flow of speech in the Senate or elsewhere.
'You bought a mansion,' said Clodius: it was recently
that Cicero had borrowed £28,000 to buy a house
on the Palatine. 'That is better than buying a
jury.' 'The jury did not credit you on your oath.'
'Twenty-five jurymen credited me: the other thirty-
one gave you no credit, but took care to get their
money in advance.' Later on Cicero remarked how
seldom Clodius' promises to pay were implemented.
But for the time Clodius went to Sicily, as quaestor,
following in Cicero's footsteps, and seemed to have
forgotten his animosity.

Equally notorious at the moment in Rome was
his sister Clodia, who was not happy unless she
had one of the gilded youth in attendance upon
her. She was an expert at dancing, which of itself
was enough to stamp her in the opinion of old-
fashioned Romans: Sallust similarly draws a portrait
of a 'new woman' in Sempronia, the mother of
Decimus Brutus and friend of Catiline. 'She was well
read in Greek and Latin literature, could sing, play
and dance more gracefully than an honest woman
need, and had many of the other accomplishments of
a riotous life. There was nothing she held less dear
than purity and honour; indeed, it would have been
hard to determine if she were more careless of her
wealth or her repute; so destitute was she of all
modesty that, more often than not, she was the first
to begin an intrigue. Often ere this she had broken
her engagements, forsworn her trust, and been an

accomplice in murder; an extravagance which outran her resources had hurried her downwards. Her talents, however, were by no means despicable; she could write verses, bandy jests, and talk modestly, voluptuously, or pertly at will; in short, she was a woman of much pleasantry and wit.'

That Clodia was beautiful is certain: she was probably nicknamed Juno because of her large lustrous eyes: [42] she had other more opprobrious nicknames. That she could inspire intense passion is shown by the thrilling verses of Catullus, who was supplanted in her favour by the young friend of Cicero, Caelius, who seems to have been a better dancer than the poet. She was the wife of Celer (see p. 71), to whom Cicero writes of her as Claudia. Almost the only other reference to her in the letters to Atticus is an indecent jest, a very unusual thing for Cicero—so unusual, that he promptly apologises for repeating it. 'Not quite a witticism for an ex-consul to make, you will say: but I hate her, so unfit to be a consul's wife. She is a revolutionary, she is at warfare with her husband': then follows a corrupt passage, which seems to refer to her zeal for Publius' interests. Publius in fact was accused of being one of her lovers: but that is obviously mere scandal.

What then is to be said of Plutarch's story, that she set her passionate eyes on Cicero and was quite ready to marry him, but Terentia got wind of it and took measures to prevent the scheme? If true, it would explain Terentia's dislike of the brother and sister. Terentia may well have been anxious: for there was shocking laxness at the time in Roman upper society. If a man divorced his wife, it was invariably supposed that he wanted to marry some

one else with whom he had already had illicit
relations: at any rate he generally did marry another
woman. Women freely divorced their husbands,
and usually had some one else in view. In 50 B.C.
Valeria Paulla divorced her husband on the very
day he returned from his province and immediately
married Decimus Brutus. In 44 B.C. Marcus tells
Atticus that their nephew Quintus has had a proposal made to him by a married lady, who is anxious
to divorce her husband. Naturally, Quintus senior
wants to know something about the lady's reputation. Can Atticus, who knows everybody's secrets
and always keeps on good terms with everybody,
find out? Only the uncle is not sure that this is not
one of Quintus' flights of imagination!

The most amazing instance of the strange way in
which the best Romans of the day looked upon the
marriage tie is the story Plutarch tells of Hortensius
the orator. He admired Cato so much, that he set
his heart on a matrimonial alliance with him. First
of all he requested that Porcia, Cato's daughter and
wife of Bibulus, should be lent to him, and if Bibulus
did not wish to part with her permanently, returned
to him. This amazing proposal having been turned
down, he then requested the loan of Cato's wife
Marcia. At first Cato refused, but finding Hortensius still importunate, he consulted Marcia's father,
who was agreeable to the transfer, though apparently
he objected to the loan. Marcia then became Hortensius' wife: and when she was a rich widow, Cato
took her back again.

The whole story is under suspicion of being an
invention to illustrate Cato's high reputation in
Rome; but even if invented it showed that such

things were possible in the state of society at the time.
It may therefore have been 'the fury of a woman
scorned' which made Clodia egg on her brother to
pursue Cicero with his hatred. Her husband Celer
was consul for 60 B.C., and when soon afterwards
he died, it was whispered that she had poisoned him.
We hear more particulars of this 'Medea of the
Palatine' when Cicero defended his young friend
Caelius in 56 B.C., *inter alia* against a charge of
attempting to poison her, which certainly Cicero
easily makes out to be a cock and bull story. Caelius
had thrown her over and had to pay the penalty of
standing this prosecution. In the speech Cicero
speaks of her cruelty to his family during his exile.
Decidedly she was as awkward a person to quarrel
with as her brother. But by 56 they had both shot
all their bolts and their vindictiveness was no longer
so much to be feared.

After serving as praetor in 62, Quintus went to
Asia as governor and remained three years, not
returning till the end of 59, so that Marcus lacked
his assistance just when he most needed it. It is
satisfactory to learn that Quintus did not unduly
enrich himself. His faults were chiefly due to his
irritability and bad temper: the fact was that his
wife led him such a life at home, that he took it out
of other people when he was away from her.

There was a very unsatisfactory state of things in
Rome in 61 and 60. The knights were annoyed,
because the Senate refused to release them from their
contract for farming the taxes of Asia, over which
they had lost heavily. Cicero would have let them
off, but Cato blocked the way. Pompey was
annoyed, because the attempt to get an Agrarian

Law passed for his veterans failed, in spite of Cicero's support. Cicero was annoyed, because the good understanding between the Senate and the knights, which he had established in his consulship, was completely at an end.

In this state of things Caesar arrived from Spain just in time to be a candidate for the consulship for 59, and threw up his chance of a triumph sooner than imperil his election. The Senatorial party could not defeat him at the polls, but provided him with a stupid die-hard colleague in Marcus Calpurnius Bibulus, Cato's son-in-law, more unpractical than Cato and far less able. Caesar at once grasped the situation and formed what has been called by modern historians the 'First Triumvirate'. But there was nothing official or even publicly known about this secret combination of three men to rule Rome according to their wishes. Pompey should have known better than to be joined to his old and undying foe Crassus by a cleverer man than either of them. But it was too tempting an opportunity of securing what he wanted. When Caesar cemented the partnership by giving him his daughter Julia in marriage, he found also a wife to his mind, and was a most affectionate husband to her till her death in 54. Had Julia lived longer, the Civil War might never have happened: at least the breach between Pompey and Caesar would not have become a chasm which could not be bridged.

We learn from Cicero's letters that he was definitely invited to join this secret combination, which, if he had accepted, would have been a Quattuorvirate. Cicero had toyed with the idea of making Caesar a more patriotic statesman, as 'he is now

sailing gaily before the breeze' (June 60), and
apparently he did not definitely refuse the offer until
Balbus, Caesar's confidential agent, came to him for
his final answer in December.[43] The fact was that
much as he admired Pompey, he felt that the new combination would be entirely hostile to the Senate and
he would be led into sanctioning all manner of things
against his conscience. As a man of principle, Cicero
acted rightly: had he been simply selfish, he would
have considered his own interest and never had to
go into exile. But the Senatorial party never showed
greater folly than in the last six months of 60 B.C.
They had irritated and alienated Pompey; Crassus
had his grudge against them; they had shown their
hostility to Caesar by assigning insignificant provinces to the consuls for 59,* a decision which Caesar
countered by getting a law passed providing him
with the opportunity he wanted.

As the year went on, they more and more realised
their impotence in the face of this strong secret
combination. The elders sulked, the younger men
raged. Cicero had become quite disgusted with them
for some time. The leading optimates, such as Lucullus, he nicknames the 'fish-fanciers', and says
bitterly of them that they are in the seventh heaven
if they can get bearded mullet to eat out of their
hands. Cato on the other hand is an unpractical
visionary, who fancies he is living in the Republic
of Plato, not in 'the dregs of Romulus'.

The first thing necessary was to get an Agrarian
Law passed, which Pompey had failed to secure.

* That these were not 'woodlands' and 'drift-ways', as Suetonius
states (*Julius*, 19, 2), is proved by Prof. J. C. Rolfe, in *American Journal
of Philology*, xxxvi. 3, 5. Which they were, we do not know.

This time Caesar took the line of going to the People
and disregarding the obstruction of Cato and Bibulus
or the vetoes of the tribunes. After rough usage in
the Forum, Bibulus shut himself up in his house and
issued foolish edicts, or watched the heavens for unfavourable omens. When Caesar had passed his first
law, he caused all the senators to swear not to resist
it: the opposition simply collapsed.* To the supple-
mentary law, which re-allotted the public estates in
Campania, Cicero had a much stronger objection:
when it passed, all senators but one, who made a
voluntary martyr of himself and went into exile, took
the oath. Cicero, who had retired to Antium on
the coast not far from Rome, watching events with
great anxiety and constantly unbosoming himself to
Atticus, made one great mistake. He prophesied
that the Campanian land would not support more
than five thousand people: on the other hand
Suetonius tells us that Caesar settled in Campania
twenty thousand citizens, who each had three or more
children. The twenty land commissioners went
rapidly to work, and by the end of the year Pompey's
veterans were provided for and a great many others
besides.

Caesar having done this job himself, the rest of
his legislation devolved on the tribune Vatinius. This
vulgar, good-humoured and impudent fellow proved
an excellent tool. Through his agency, Pompey's
Eastern settlement was ratified, the tax-farmers got
a remission of the third of their purchase price, and,
most important of all, by the Vatinian Law as to
Caesar's province, Caesar was given Cisalpine Gaul
and Illyricum for five years ending February 28th

* Hitler seems to have adopted this plan, only on a bigger scale.

G

54 B.C. Presently Transalpine Gaul fell vacant by the death of Celer, and on the motion of Pompey was conferred by the Senate on Caesar in addition. Caesar found time also to pass an act to curb extortion in the province, and introduced the publication of an Official Gazette (*acta*). He was now to be away from Rome for a long time; so he was determined to leave no one there capable of bringing about a reaction.

What was he to do with Cicero? First he tried offers. Would he be a land-commissioner? When that was declined with thanks, would he go on a special mission to Egypt? Perhaps that offer was not actually made, for Ptolemy Auletes arranged just then to pay the Triumvirs the enormous sum of six thousand talents for his restoration. Cato, however, when he was offered the task of annexing Cyprus, accepted and was thus removed from Rome for three years. 'If they could not soil Cato's honour', says Cicero, 'they could assert that they had plucked out his tongue.' [44]

Next intimidation was tried. About April Cicero was defending his former colleague Gaius Antonius in the courts and made some independent observations on politics. These were reported to Caesar after midday, and by three o'clock in the afternoon Clodius had been adopted by a plebeian younger than himself, thereby making it certain that he would succeed Vatinius as Caesar's tribune on December 10th. [45] The danger became therefore more menacing to Cicero. The offers began again. Would he be Caesar's legate? He need not leave Rome unless he liked. Or would he accept an unfettered commission, such as any senator might be granted, in the form of a permission to travel with official status? Still believing that Pompey would protect him, Cicero declined everything and stayed in Rome or near, relieving his feelings to Atticus or to young Curio, who was the boldest opponent of the Triumvirs: Cicero had introduced him to public life. At times hostile demonstrations in the theatre or public places gave Cicero some satisfaction. He tells how Diphilus the actor brought down the house by reciting with emphasis the line

Through our misery thou art Great (*Magnus*).

For it was part of Caesar's uncanny adroitness that all or nearly all the unpopularity fell on Pompey: it was Pompey, everyone thought, who was responsible for all this tyranny. Cicero coins one nickname after another for him, this 'Eastern Bashaw', 'this Jerusalemite who transfers people to the plebs': opposition is often all the more vocal when it is impotent.

In October there was a great sensation. One Vettius, who had been useful to Cicero as a spy in 63 B.C., divulged a plot against Pompey's life, which he alleged had been hatched by Curio and various young nobles. That he was a liar is obvious: but two points interest us. The first day he denounced young Marcus Brutus, then twenty years old, as an accomplice: the next day he withdrew his name. Cicero ascribes this without hesitation to the nocturnal intercession of Brutus' mother Servilia, whom Rome believed to have had an intrigue with Caesar and who certainly preserved her influence with him down to his death.[46] The other was an indirect denunciation of Cicero himself. 'An eloquent

ex-consul, who lived near Caesar, said it was high time
for a Servilius Ahala or a Brutus to arise.' Certainly
si non è vero, è ben trovato.

Cicero's own view is as likely as not correct, that
Caesar himself concocted the affair in retaliation on
the young nobles for their waspish opposition: others
have thought Vatinius was the instigator of Vettius,
which is much the same thing. One often wonders
how Cicero, who was so acute in seeing through other
people, was so unwary in his own behaviour.

On December 10th Clodius came into office and
showed his hand. He gave notice of a series of
measures, most of them very far-reaching, which
with the active help of the new consuls for 58 B.C.,
Lucius Piso, Caesar's father-in-law, and Aulus
Gabinius, a nominee of Pompey, he proceeded to
carry into law. First he conciliated the poor of Rome
by making the distributions of grain free: Caesar had
afterwards to reverse this. He then increased the
number of the days on which popular assemblies
could be held, and abolished the right of magistrates
to delay business by announcing unfavourable omens:
this was shortly afterwards repealed. He then legalised guilds or *collegia* in the capital, so that henceforward anyone might hire a gang of roughs without
fear of the law; and he limited the power of censors
to degrade offenders. Having then paid the consuls
for their support by awarding to Piso the province of
Macedonia and to Gabinius that of Syria, apparently
in both cases to stay as long as they chose, he directly
attacked Cicero by proposing 'that anyone who had
put to death Roman citizens uncondemned should
be outlawed'. Clodius held a public meeting outside
the walls, so that Caesar, who was waiting with his

army till Clodius had carried out his commissions, might speak. When called on, Caesar said that the execution of the Catilinarians was illegal, but *pro forma* deprecated retrospective action. Pompey was appealed to, but said he could do nothing against Caesar's will: he even, it is said, was mean enough to leave his house by a back door when Cicero came to call on him. The friends of Cicero put on mourning, but nothing was now of any avail.

On the very day on which Cicero left Rome, another bill was proposed and carried, this time naming Cicero and stating that he had been outlawed. The only mitigation of the penalty his friends could secure was a clause giving him permission to live at any place not less than five hundred miles from Italy. This prevented him from taking refuge in Sicily, where he had desired to be, and where not only the population of the island but the governor might have been expected to befriend him. He crossed over to Epirus, and then went to Thessalonica (Salonica) to stay with his friend Plancius, quaestor in Macedonia, prepared to go further East to Cyzicus if necessary. Meantime his enemies in Rome pulled down his house and the adjacent house of his brother on the Palatine Hill, and Clodius consecrated the site to Liberty. His villas at Tusculum and Formiae were also looted and destroyed. To a man of Cicero's acute sensibility the calamity that befell him was doubly painful. The ingratitude of his friends was hardly less galling than the cruelty of his enemies. Life away from Rome was to him worse than death.

Chapter 6

EXILE AND RETURN
59-51 B.C.

I am tired of surgery, and beginning a cure by treatment.
Ad Att. iv. 3, 3

IT was a cruel fate and quite undeserved. Cicero
with his mercurial Southern temperament utterly collapsed. At first he contemplated suicide, but luckily
thought better of it: for the world would then have
lost all his philosophical works and most of his higher
flights of oratory. Then he began to make queru-
lous and unjust complaints against his friends.
Hortensius, who had advised him to retire from
Rome, was a false friend: Atticus had not taken the
trouble that he should have done to defend him.
'Why did I not stay and fight it out?' he keeps on
saying. Even then he could not realise that to do
so would have been certain death.

Having disposed of Cicero for the time being,
Caesar hurried off—we wonder he could have waited
so long—to annihilate the Helvetii, and to drive the
arrogant German Ariovistus back over the Rhine.
When one considers that he had previously only conducted guerilla warfare in Spain and was over forty,
the military genius he suddenly exhibited seems to
have no parallel in history. All the while he was

in Gaul, he kept in the closest touch with Rome.   A
stream of Gallic gold flowed into the purse of all who
would take his pay—and accept his conditions: and
he did not fail to conciliate with presents the high-
born ladies whose husbands were not amenable.

The moment he was gone, Pompey was helpless.
He could not control Clodius: it required a Caesar to
do that.   We are therefore not surprised to learn that
by September, regretting that he had thrown Cicero to
the dogs, Pompey had written to ask Caesar's consent
to Cicero's recall.   The magistrates elected for 57
B.C. were mostly favourable to Cicero.   One consul,
Lentulus Spinther, was his warm supporter: the
other, his former opponent, Metellus Nepos, let it
be known that he would do nothing to hinder
Cicero's return.   Accordingly Cicero wrote to thank
him.   Nepos kept his word, and, though afterwards
he helped Clodius, his first cousin, to become curule
aedile, he must in the process have quarrelled with
him—it was not difficult—before he went to his
Spanish province: for he writes to Cicero from Spain
expressing contempt for the insults of 'an uncon-
scionable fellow', who can only be Clodius, and proposing to regard Cicero himself as a cousin in his
stead.   Decidedly the 'new man' was at last admitted into the inner circle of the nobles, when a
Metellus could thus condescend.   By this time
presumably the magnates were beginning to be
a little ashamed of themselves for their treatment
of Cicero.

Clodius did not give in without a struggle.   On
January 25th, 57 B.C., he filled the Forum with
bloodshed, when a bill for Cicero's recall was being
brought forward.   The mover was attacked and

driven away: the same thing happened to a tribune, and Quintus Cicero had to fly for his life. 'The Tiber was filled with corpses, the sewers were blocked up, and the Forum had to be sponged to clean it of blood.' [47] But the tribunes Milo and Sestius organised counter-bands, and the streets of Rome in consequence became very unsafe for the next five years, at the end of which time Clodius was killed. There were various signs of a revulsion of feeling in Cicero's favour, such as the applause given to Aesopus the actor, when in the *Andromache* of Ennius he contrived a reference to the subject (cp. p. 83). Finally by August crowds of country voters flocked into Rome, and the measure for Cicero's recall was passed on August 4th. Cicero had been for some months at Dyrrachium (Durazzo), the arrival of the proconsul Piso having terminated his stay at Thessalonica, and had anticipated things by crossing over to Brindisi, where on the 5th Tullia met him on her birthday, which was also the anniversary of the founding of Brundusium and the Temple of Safety near Atticus' house in Rome: the Latin word for safety has a special application to the civic status.

A curious dream is related by Cicero in his treatise *On Divination*. On his way to exile he dreamed that while roaming in solitude and dejection he encountered Marius attended by lictors with laurel-wreathed rods (*fasces*), who asked him why he was sad, and when he explained the reason, said to a lictor: 'Take him to my monument: there he will find safety'. Cicero's host at the time said this was a splendid omen, but Cicero had forgotten it, till he heard that the decree for his recall was passed in the Temple of Honour and Virtue erected by Marius.

After receiving the news on the 8th he made a circuit of the country towns, being everywhere received with joy—he was essentially the representative of the Italian towns—and at Rome his reception was equally flattering. Yet in a few days Clodius succeeded in stirring up trouble because of the price of bread: he said Cicero's friends had eaten it all up. Here was a fresh opportunity for Pompey: who so fit to reorganise the corn-supply as the man who had cleared the Mediterranean of pirates in three months (see p. 45)? Cicero at once spoke in favour of this appointment. A tribune proposed in effect to initiate the Empire, by giving Pompey supreme command on sea and land with authority overriding that of all provincial governors, putting him in the position which, by many years of patient and sagacious labour, Augustus ultimately attained. The consular proposal supported by Cicero was less far-reaching. As usual, it was impossible to read the mind of Pompey. 'He says he prefers the latter: his friends say he prefers the former.'[48] Marcus wanted no appointment for himself: his reward was that Quintus was placed on Pompey's staff and presently sent to Sardinia.

For the moment Cicero's chief concern was to obtain adequate compensation and rebuild his house and villas. But as the site of his house had been consecrated, he had to appeal to the College of Pontiffs to annul the consecration of Clodius, which they obligingly did. He then received £18,000, which was fairly adequate for the rebuilding of the town house for which he had paid such a fancy price: but he was very dissatisfied with £4400 for his Tusculanum and half as much for the villa at Formiae.

For some time he was busy with architects, which always, to the very end of his life, gave him great pleasure: he had much taste and experience in arranging the details of a domestic interior.[49] In his embarrassments he even put up his beloved villa at Tusculum for sale in October:[50] 'I can easily do without a suburban house'. But finding no purchaser [51] he changed his mind, and kept it to the end of his life.

Clodius however was still on the war-path. On November 3rd the workmen were dislodged by an armed attack, the adjacent portico of Catulus which was also being rebuilt was knocked down, and Quintus' house was smashed and fired. On November 11th Cicero, luckily not alone, was waylaid in the Sacred Way and had to take refuge in the first house which offered a door to enter. He remarks: 'Clodius himself might have been killed: but I am tired of surgery and beginning a cure by treatment'. On November 12th there was an attempt to storm and burn Milo's house. Milo was endeavouring to bring into court a prosecution for breach of the peace against Clodius: Clodius was attempting to evade this by being elected curule aedile, which was unusual for one who had already held the office of tribune; of course by this time he was a patrician again. Thus Milo was persistently delaying the election by the familiar trick, now once more legal, of *obnuntiatio* or reporting unfavourable omens. In these dodges Cicero took an intense and almost boyish interest. Here is a picture he draws of one of the night hours during the time.[52]

'It is now three o'clock in the morning of the 23rd, as I am writing. Milo has already occupied the

Election Ground. Marcellus, the candidate, next door is snoring loud enough for me to hear him. It is reported to me that Clodius' front hall is entirely empty, except for a few tatterdemalions with a canvas lantern. His side are complaining that I am directing all the operations: they little know the courage and wisdom of that hero. His valour is marvellous. I can't relate some new strokes of genius. But this is the matter in a nutshell. I believe the elections will not be held: and Milo will bring Publius into court, if he does not kill him first. If he gives him a chance in a riot, I can see Milo will kill him with his own hands. He has no scruples, he avows his intention, utterly undeterred by my own downfall. *He* has never followed the advice of a jealous and treacherous friend nor trusted in a weak noble.' It is to be hoped that Atticus did not apply the last words to himself! Cicero was however wrong in his prophecies. It was more than four years before Milo killed Clodius; the elections were held and Clodius was elected. Then instead of being prosecuted himself, he prosecuted Milo on the same charge. Rome in these days must have been exceedingly like Chicago, when Al Capone was on the war-path against the rival-gangsters.

Why did Pompey not restore order? The answer is that he had only moral authority within the walls. Caesar had utilised Pompey's veterans for purposes of intimidation in 59 B.C., but Pompey was not the man to do anything of the sort, unless he had lawful authority. This he did not receive till 52.

In February 56, when he appeared to support Milo at the trial, he was interrupted by shouting and abuse from the Clodian gangs, but went on undismayed, till he had finished all he wanted to say. 'When Clodius got up, our side gave him tit for tat and kept up a volley of abuse for two hours up to two o'clock, including even filthy verses against Clodius and his sister. Maddened and white with rage, he asked his partisans above the din, who the man was who was starving the people to death. The rowdies shouted: "Pompey". "Who was bent on going to Alexandria?" They replied "Pompey". "Whom did they want to go?" They answered "Crassus". Crassus was there at the time with no friendly feelings for Milo. About three o'clock the Clodians, as if at a given signal, began to spit upon our men. Then there was pandemonium. They began to hustle and try to dislodge us. Our side charged: and the roughs took to their heels. Clodius was ejected from the Rostra:* and I too ran away, for fear of anything happening in the meleé.' [53]

Decidedly the Triumvirate was not working well in the absence of its mainspring. The reference to Alexandria meant the restoration of Ptolemy, derisively called the Piper, whom for a vast bribe it had been decided to replace on the throne of Egypt to the great disgust of the Egyptians. Lentulus Spinther, Cicero's friend, now governing Cilicia, had good reason to expect the lucrative task; for it had been assigned to him in 57 B.C.[54] In the early months of 56 the matter took up most of the Senate's time. Cicero reports the discussions to his friend, whose interest he attempted to the best of his power to serve: he even directly appealed to Pompey on the

---

* The Rostra was a platform for speakers to the people in the Forum, the centre of the public life of Rome.

subject. Pompey of course had nothing but fair
words: but meanwhile his friends were working to
secure the commission for him.* To make mischief,
Clodius was working in the interests of Crassus. A
few days later, if Cicero may be believed, Pompey
implied in the Senate that Crassus had plotted against
his life, declaring that he was not going to suffer the
fate which Africanus had suffered from Carbo: it was
not certain but generally believed that in the year
131 B.C. Africanus had died by foul play, and that
Carbo was the author of his death. It was little
wonder that Cicero felt that the Triumvirate had
broken up, as it would have but for Caesar's energetic action.

Again on March 11th Cicero was greatly encouraged by the unanimous acquittal of Sestius, whom he
defended on a charge of breach of the peace in promoting his recall in the previous year. Thinking
therefore that this was a good opportunity of detach-
ing Pompey entirely from Caesar, as Pompey had
already detached himself from Crassus, on April 5th†
he gave notice in the Senate that on May 15th he
would move a motion to reconsider the Campanian
land settlement, that being the part of Caesar's
agrarian legislation which he had most disliked.
Never in all his life did Cicero make such a foolish
blunder. It offended Pompey: it utterly failed as a
rallying cry for the nobles. In his blindness he
boasted that it was an attack on the enemies' citadel:
it was a desperate and forlorn hope.

Pompey deliberately misled him. He showed no

* 'When I hear Pompey himself, I acquit him of all greed: but when
I look round his friends it is different' (Cicero to Lentulus *Ad Fam.* i. 2, 3).

† *Ad Quint. Fratr.* ii. 5, 1: 'There was a heated debate on the Campanian
land, when the Senate was nearly as noisy as a public meeting'.

sign of the annoyance he must have felt: for it was his veterans whose title Cicero proposed to question. A few days before Pompey left Rome professedly on corn-supply business, Cicero took the opportunity of seeing him and asking for his brother's return to Rome. Not a word did Pompey breathe on the political situation. Then he left Rome for Sardinia, as it was given out. As a matter of fact, he went straight to Luca (Lucca), the nearest town to Rome in Caesar's province.

Caesar had not been idle. Hearing of the breach between his two colleagues and Cicero's rashness, he had summoned Crassus to Ravenna, and satisfied him. Next he had to satisfy Pompey, which proved equally easy at Lucca. Nor was Pompey his only visitor at Lucca: it is said that a hundred and twenty senators, with two hundred attendant lictors, found themselves in that obscure and unattractive town, of course by accident. Gallic gold, and the prospect of employment in a country of the size of France, with the possible El Dorado of Britain to follow, were already working wonders with the needy aristocracy of Rome. Nor could Pompey ever resist the seductive personality of Caesar, when it came to an interview: and doubtless all Julia's influence was exercised over her fond husband. She was no more, when in 49 B.C. it came to the final breach: even then if the two could have met, a composition would doubtless have been arranged. Now it was easy for Caesar to give his colleagues what they wanted, provided that he could get what he himself wanted.

Pompey and Crassus were to be consuls for 55, and if any other candidates offered themselves, so much the worse for them: had not Sulla in 82 murdered Ofella for daring to oppose his nominees (p. 20)? After his consulship Crassus was to hold Syria and fight the Parthians, the only field left where military glory was to be sought. Pompey was to hold the two Spanish provinces, and to do the work by deputy, while remaining himself at the head of affairs in Rome. Meanwhile Caesar was to have an extension of his tenure of Gaul, which is frequently described as a second period of five years (*quinquennium*).* The restoration of Ptolemy was to be paid for in hard cash, and to be brought about by the trusty Gabinius then in Syria, Lentulus Spinther being left in the lurch. Such seem to have been the main points decided at Lucca: how much flattery, gold and intimidation were employed in dealing with individual senators, we can only conjecture.

We only know what happened to Cicero. That Pompey wrote politely requesting him to drop his motion is certain: for Cicero tells his brother that the motion announced for May 15th will not be made. 'In this business my waters are dammed. But I have said more than I had intended: so more when we meet.' But to Quintus in Sardinia Pompey was much more blunt and summary: 'You are just the man I wanted to see: nothing could be more opportune. If you don't make serious representations to your brother, you will have to pay up what you guaranteed on his behalf.' There is no question of money here: the meaning is, 'when I appointed you, it was on the distinct understanding that Marcus would be subservient. If he is recalcitrant, you will

* *E.g.* Velleius, *R.H.*, ii. 44 *in quinquennium,* 51 *prorogatae in idem spatium temporis provinciae.*

have to suffer.' Pompey doubtless wished to hint
that they would accompany each other into exile this
time, but the vagueness of the threat made it more
unmistakeably alarming. The threat or something
similar was conveyed direct to Cicero by one
Vibullius.

On receipt of this message he could do nothing but
submit. It was indeed swallowing a bitter pill, as
he puts it in writing to Atticus, and he felt submission to be a little discreditable. But he comforted
himself by the thought that he had really been betrayed by the treacherous and jealous optimates, who
had refused to follow his lead. He can only feel that
he had been a 'regular mule' in obstinately adhering
to those who had no power, and henceforth he must
win the affection of the powerful Three. He then
wrote a formal letter probably to Pompey, possibly
to Caesar, which we do not possess—for he would
not even show it to Atticus—which he calls his
Palinode (recantation). He yielded to *force majeure*
—nobody could have done anything else—and from
May 56 b.c. to the outbreak of the Civil War he had
to be at the beck and call of the Triumvirs. His
services were at once requisitioned and late in June [55]
he delivered his Speech *On the Consular Provinces.*
In this he eulogises Caesar for his achievements in
Gaul, which were so remarkable that any patriotic
Roman was bound to be proud of them. It was he
who had proposed in the Senate that a thanksgiving
of the unprecedented length of fifteen days should be
held in honour of unprecedented victories: Caesar in
his *Commentaries* remarks that no Roman general had
ever before had such an honour. Cicero would have
been unpatriotic, had he underrated Caesar's services

to the state: he acknowledged them handsomely.
Nor are his praises at all insincere in the speech. But
with extraordinary ingenuity he argues that Piso and
Gabinius ought to be recalled from their provinces,
and that this would provide for the consuls of 55,
without disturbing Caesar. His language about
these enemies is very violent, and we must not take it
to the foot of the letter. Piso was superseded by
Ancharius, and when he returned in 55 B.C. was
foolish enough to protest in the Senate against
Cicero's — certainly unjustifiable — attacks. This
caused Cicero literally to empty all the vials of his
wrath upon him in the invective which we possess.

Strong things were said in the English language
in the seventeenth century. Thus Coke said of
Raleigh, 'Thou hast a Spanish heart, and thyself art
a spider of hell. I will now make it appear to the
world that there never lived a viler viper on the face
of the earth than thou.' Scroggs at the trial of the
Five Jesuits in 1679, and Wyld at the trial of Green,
Berry and Hill for the murder of Sir Edmund Bury
Godfrey, used very violent language. Still stronger
things have been said in religious controversy, of
which this is a choice specimen.[56] 'I shall not suffer
my pen to rake into the filthy ulcers of this feeble
Lazar, but be content with pointing at them as we
pass along, that you may take notice of the infection
to avoid it.' But Cicero's Latin is worse than anything one can find in the English language with its
offensive personalities. The beginning of the speech
is lost: what we have starts thus, 'Now do you see,
beast, now do you perceive what people complain of
in your brazen face?' It is the one speech by Cicero
of which we feel ashamed. It only illustrates what a

H

Southerner is capable of saying when he gives way to temper and has a great command of vituperative language. The speech against Vatinius is vulgar, but is not so ungentlemanly as the attack on Piso.* What military reverses Piso had in Macedonia, whether he pillaged Byzantium and Achaia in the manner of Verres, whether he concealed a vicious life under the cover of philosophy, passes our knowledge: but it is at least incredible that, as Cicero avers, maidens of high rank threw themselves into wells to escape from his persecution.

Caesar does not seem to have resented these attacks on his father-in-law: perhaps he thought Piso was quite able to take care of himself, and his own achievements were handsomely acknowledged in the speech (§§ 81-82). But he subsequently compelled Cicero to defend Vatinius. This later on stood Cicero in good stead: for the good-natured vulgarian showed his gratitude by being very obliging to him, when he needed it most. It was an equally bitter pill to have to defend Gabinius for extortion in the courts, just after Gabinius had returned and insulted Cicero in the Senate by calling him an exile. Cicero must have performed his task very badly on purpose: for Gabinius was condemned, while Vatinius got off, and we have no *Oratio Pro Gabinio*.†

But it was not often that Cicero had to do what he considered dirty work. On the contrary Pompey gave him much of his society. Thus he writes to Atticus, on May 22nd, 55 B.C., to say how much he is enjoying the library of Faustus Sulla, but alas,

---

* Of this, alas, Cicero was proud. He tells his brother that schoolboys read his *In Pisonem* as a school exercise (*Q.F.* iii. 1, 11).

† Josephus (*Ant.* xiv. 104) speaks with high praise of Gabinius as a general, and does not censure his settlement of Jewish affairs.

Pompey has arrived and he will have to take pro-
menades with him. On the 26th he writes again to
say that the Great Man actually paid him a visit but
was in bad humour, expressing contempt for all provincial governments. Obviously to escape from him,
Cicero left on the 25th for Pompeii, where he also
had a villa.[57]

For the most part he found refreshment in literary
pursuits. By November 55 B.C. he had finished and
dedicated to his brother a treatise in three books
On the Orator, an imaginary dialogue between
Crassus and Antonius, the leaders of the Roman Bar
in his early days. He then set to work at a treatise
on the model of Plato, *On the Republic*, only fragments
of which are preserved to us. He then began, still
following Plato, to write *On the Laws*, but did not
then complete the treatise.

Caesar, who could always make himself agreeable
to those who were not opposing him, gladly welcomed
the submission and adhesion of this distinguished
orator and man of letters. He was himself enough
of both to appreciate Cicero's genius: and no doubt
would have been highly delighted if he could have
carried Cicero off with him in the spring of 58. As
he could not get the elder brother, he took the
younger. Since he had written to Cicero to say
'Recommend anyone you please to me', Cicero could
suggest this, as Quintus was out of employment.
The letter of recommendation, when it reached
Caesar, was illegible, having been soaked in transit;
but Caesar says he hopes he is right in guessing its
purport, which is more than he had ventured to hope.
Quintus justified the appointment: are not his heroic
defence of the winter quarters among the Nervii,

and his failure to obey orders next year, written in the *Commentaries* of Julius Caesar on the Gallic War?

In his correspondence with his brother, Marcus shows some curiosity about our island. Caesar posts a letter in Britain, and Cicero receives it at Rome after only twenty-seven days in transit. To Trebatius, a legal friend, whom he had recommended to Caesar, he alludes jocosely to Britain. He says 'The Lawyer in Britain' would be a fine stage character, and Trebatius must see that he is not captured or taken in by the drivers of war-chariots. But Trebatius would not go to Britain, and Cicero writes: 'As we hear there is no gold or silver in Britain, I counsel you to capture a war-chariot and make haste home to me'.*

In a speech of 54 for Rabirius Postumus Cicero inserts a eulogy of Caesar's private generosity to individuals, and says it is as admirable as his public services. This illustrates the fascination that Caesar then exercised upon him: for a little later he would certainly have described the relations between Caesar and Rabirius in a very different way.

The death of Julia this year was an equal blow to her father and to her husband; it removed a very strong link between the two men. When in June 53 Crassus fell fighting the Parthians on the fatal field of Carrhae, not only was a great disgrace inflicted on the Roman army, but it became clear that Pompey and Caesar could not long be friends. The death of young Publius Crassus caused a vacancy

---

* But on hearing that Trebatius has not gone to Britain, he says: 'I am glad, because you are spared the fatigue, and I your descriptions!' (*Ad Fam.* vii. 17, 3).

in the augural college.   Cicero had not concealed his
ambition to be elected an augur: but of course he is
not serious when in 59 B.C. he says that it is the only
bait by which the triumvirs could catch him: [58] for
he adds jestingly, 'See how unprincipled I am!' Now
on the nomination of Pompey and Hortensius he was
elected to the vacant place, to the chagrin of Antony,
as Antony himself later admits,[59] and seems to have
regularly attended the augural dinners, except during
the period of mourning for his daughter.   In the
Thirteenth *Philippic* he proposed to nominate Sextus
Pompey for the place occupied by his father.[60]   The
augural college was a sort of select club for prominent Romans, and was to Rome what the Athen-
aeum is to London.

Things went from bad to worse in Rome: the
whole constitutional machine seemed to have got out
of order.   The consuls for 53 were only elected in
July of that year.   Bribery was scandalously rife, and
a disgraceful bargain between the late consuls and
the two candidates was divulged, and this ruined at
any rate one who had been a party to it.

The year 52 B.C. opened without any consuls.   On
January 18th Milo, who was still hoping to be consul
with Cicero's active support—he had written to Curio
in Milo's favour—met Clodius at Bovillae and killed
him.   This led to riots in the course of which the
Senate house was burned.   In despair the Senate
turned to Pompey, who had been waiting calmly for
this to happen.   On the proposal of Bibulus, supported by Cato, Pompey was elected sole consul:
misery makes strange bedfellows.   Later in the year
he married Cornelia, the daughter of an optimate of
the optimates, Metellus Scipio, and associated his

father-in-law with himself as consul for the last
months of the year. At last, being fully authorised
thereto, he showed that he could restore order as
perfectly as Caesar, if he was given the authority.
The rowdies of both parties were dealt with sum-
marily. Milo was condemned and had to go into
exile at Massilia (Marseilles). This was the only
fiasco of Cicero as a pleader. He was intimidated, as
were others, by the display of military force: he knew
that whatever he said was useless. Subsequently he
published the very elaborate and sophistical speech
which we possess.[60a]

Pompey, all his life, was an exception to all rules
(see p. 18). In this year he was sole consul, a contradiction in terms, and he held the consulship again
after an interval of two years, when the law proscribed
ten: this point was soon to be important. He then
proceeded to carry a law insisting on a personal canvass, explaining that he did not thereby mean to
cancel the leave to sue for the office in absence already
granted to Caesar by a law. His law, however, also
prescribed an interval of five years between office in
Rome and the tenure of a province. What he gave
Caesar with one hand, he thus took away with the
other. For it would be possible to provide Caesar
with two successors to his two provinces, Cisalpine
and Transalpine Gaul on March 1st, 49 B.C., whereas,
under the previous system, no one would have been
available before January 1st, 48 B.C., when everybody
had assumed that Caesar would enter on his second
consulship, without the necessity of previously re-
signing his provincial command, leaving the protection of his army and exposing himself to the certainty
of prosecution and condemnation in Rome. Under

this new law, very unwillingly* Cicero had to undertake the government for at least a year of the province
of Cilicia.

* Mr. Froude says: 'Cicero had preferred characteristically to be out
of the way at the moment when he expected the storm to break and had
accepted the government of Cilicia and Cyprus'. He also says that Cicero
held his government for two years. Did he ever read Cicero's Letters?

Chapter 7

THE PROCONSUL
5 1 - 5 0 B.C.

*I cannot express how terribly I miss life in Rome and how
intolerable to me is the boredom of life here.*
                                            Ad Att. v. 11, 1

QUINTUS,˙who had not long before arrived from
Gaul, was able to accompany his elder brother to
Cilicia: it was fortunate that so competent a soldier
was available as staff-officer (*legatus*) in view of the
excursions and alarms that were to follow.

The brothers met at Arpinum, their birthplace.
As Atticus had recently begged Marcus to make
things as easy as possible for his sister Pomponia,
Marcus instantly broached the delicate subject to
Quintus, and as a result of the talk, informed Atticus
that if there had been any disagreement on money
matters between husband and wife, Quintus was at
present quite amiably disposed to Pomponia. He
then gives an amusing description of a lunch at
a country-house belonging to Quintus on the day
following the conversation.[61] 'When we arrived,
Quintus with the utmost politeness said, "Pomponia, please welcome the ladies, I will see to the
men". Nothing, as far as I could see, could have
been more gentle than his words or intention or

looks. But in the hearing of us all she said, "I'm only a stranger here", because, I suppose, Statius* had been sent on ahead to get lunch ready for us. "There you are", says Quintus to me, "that's what I have to put up with every day." You may say there was not much in that. Indeed, there was a good deal: she quite upset *me*; for she answered with such uncommon asperity of word and look. I concealed my annoyance, and we all sat down to lunch without her: Quintus sent her something from the table, which she refused. In a word, I thought my brother as good-tempered and her as cross as could be, and I omit a good deal which annoyed me more than Quintus himself. I went on to Aquinum, and Quintus stayed behind. When he joined me next morning, he told me that she refused to sleep with him, and when he was leaving, she was as cross as when I saw her. You can tell her if you like, that in my opinion she showed very bad manners that day. Now it is *your* turn to give *her* a little good advice.' One wonders whether Atticus did, and suspects that he lacked the courage.

The province of Cilicia at that time was from the administrative point of view as awkward as possible. To begin with, it included the island of Cyprus, which had been recently taken over into the Roman system by Cato's mission (p. 82), and in addition to Cilicia Proper a number of administrative districts (dioceses) north and west of the great Taurus range, some of them such as would more naturally have formed part of the province of Asia. Cicero did not

* Statius was Quintus' freedman and confidant. For fear of gossip Marcus objected to Statius' manumission, which took place while Quintus was governor of Asia (*Ad Att.* ii. 18, 3; ii. 19, 1). Quintus promptly sent Statius to Rome (*Q.F.* i. 2, 1) to clear himself.

go to Cyprus, though, as we shall see, he did something for the Cypriots. He made haste to reach the easternmost part of his province. There, after his campaign, he left Quintus, recrossing the Taurus before the pass was blocked with snow: this, we learn, lasted till June. The first half of 50 b.c. he spent by holding courts at Laodicea for various districts. When this was over, he paid a flying visit to Tarsus, the capital of Cilicia Proper, and counted himself fortunate to be able to leave his province in July exactly when his year of office had come to an end. After this brief outline, the details of his administration may be sketched.

The journey to Cilicia was long and awkward. It was delayed by the failure of Pomptinus to turn up. He was a very able staff-officer, who had seen service against the Allobrogian Gauls and actually aspired to a triumph. Even when he arrived, he did not stay the whole year: Cicero hints there was a lady, on whose account he was anxious to get back to Rome. But his military experience was to prove extremely valuable.

We are exceptionally well informed about the year of office, because we have not only numerous letters to Atticus, but the lively and even slangy correspondence of Caelius, the clever young man whom Cicero had introduced to public life and had subsequently saved from the vengeance of Clodia (see pp. 76, 78). Besides we have a whole book of letters to the outgoing governor.

This was Appius Claudius Pulcher, brother of Cicero's enemy, consul in 54. Since then he had been governing Cilicia for two years and a half with rapacity and cruelty. He was annoyed at being

robbed of six months in office by the law of Pompey
which provided him with an unwanted and unexpected successor in the month of July 51 B.C., when
under the previous state of things he would not have
been superseded before 50 B.C.   His patrician arrogance, commented on even by Vatinius, who did not
lack plebeian cheek, the long feud of Cicero with his
deceased brother and his present chagrin made it certain he would give trouble.   Cicero was obliged to
be civil to him, as his three daughters were married
respectively to Pompey's eldest son, to Brutus, and
to his benefactor Lentulus Spinther, to whom he
largely owed his restoration from exile: and indeed
Pompey had made a special point of reconciling
Cicero to Appius.   Lentulus in writing to ask
Cicero the reason for his changed political attitude
expressly says he has no objection to his reconciliation with Appius.[62]   We possess a polite letter of
Cicero to Appius written in the year 52 B.C., which
expresses satisfaction at the renewal of friendly relations, and offers kindly offices—always desirable for
a provincial governor—which he promises will not
be against the grain.   Here he uses the Latin phrase
'not against Minerva's will': and adds, 'If I get (a
statue of) her from your collection, I shall call it not
Pallas Athene (Minerva) but Pallas Appias'.[63]   This
is almost certainly an allusion to the statue of Minerva
dedicated by Cicero in the Capitol, before he went
into exile.   No doubt it had been confiscated by
Publius Clodius, and now very probably was in the
hands of Appius.*   This is the only allusion in the

* In March 43 Cicero writes to Cornificius that he pleaded his cause
in the Senate 'with the goodwill of Minerva': for that very day it was
decided to re-erect this statue in the Capitol.

letter — if it be an allusion — to Publius Clodius'
vagaries, and is ingeniously turned into a compliment.

In spite of all that had preceded, Appius behaved
with great rudeness.   At Brindisi Cicero met one of
his dependants and enquired at which part of the
province Appius would like him to land.   At this
man's suggestion he agreed to enter the province at
Sida in Pamphylia, though he disliked the idea of
coming in as it were by a back door.   But at Corcyra
he found another dependant, one Lucius Clodius,
who asked him to go straight to Laodicea, the first
city of importance in the western part of the province.*

He then wrote to Appius, who certainly received
the letter, to acquaint him with the change of plan.
What was his surprise on landing at Ephesus, to
learn that Appius had gone off to hold a court at
Tarsus, when he had been already superseded, and
apparently had taken the available military force,
three cohorts, with him.   No wonder Cicero resents
an action as illegal as it was discourteous.   He says
to Atticus: 'On seeing that I was near at hand, our
friend Appius left Laodicea and went all the way to
Tarsus.   He is holding a court there while I am in
the province.   I am not (publicly) resenting the
slight he has put upon me: for I have enough to do
in healing the wounds he has inflicted on the province,
and I am trying to do this with as little reflection on
him as possible.   But please tell your friend Brutus,
that it was not gentlemanly behaviour of his father-in-
law to go away as far as possible on my arrival': and
he might have added, from the very place he had
appointed as a rendezvous.

* Laodicea is one of the Seven Churches of the Apocalypse.

Nor was this the worst. In order to avoid meeting Cicero, he sneaked past his camp by an alternative road, and Lepta, Cicero's chief engineer (who had previously served with Caesar in Gaul), when sent to meet him, reported that he had already gone too far to be overtaken.*

After this it was consummate impudence of Appius to write and complain that Cicero would not go to meet him, as he had gone to meet his predecessor Lentulus. Cicero's reply is dignified. 'No Appiism or Lentulism weighs more with me than the distinction conferred by virtue. Great names in themselves are nothing: the men who bequeathed them to you were great. This is the opinion of Pompey, than whom no better man ever lived, and of Lentulus, whom I consider a better man than myself.'

A little later Cicero was placed in an awkward position. In his absence in Cilicia, Tullia, his beloved daughter, became engaged to Dolabella, a wild young nobleman, only eighteen years old, who just then proposed to make his début in public life by prosecuting Appius for high treason; and Cicero says: 'I am doing all I can for Appius here consistently with my honour'. Appius was acquitted. Since 53 B.C. Cicero had had to meet him as his colleague in the College of Augurs; indeed he had already received from Appius the dedication of a book on augural lore.[64] But he retained his bad opinion of him, and at the beginning of the Civil War called him the 'prince of trimmers'.

* Mr. L. W. Hunter (*Journal of Roman Studies,* iii. 73-97) thinks that Cicero did meet Appius near Iconium on September 3rd. *Ad Fam.* iii. 7, 4 certainly makes this very unlikely.

Now after he had been a week in his province, from the evidence of his own eyes and from daily complaints, he was finding out how Appius had misused his position. The poll-tax had been ruthlessly enforced and those unable to pay had had to sell out their investments in order to do so: Appius had behaved so inhumanly that Cicero vents his indignation to Atticus, by calling him a savage wild beast. After this we read with some disgust what he says to Caelius, who had begged him to support Appius by his authority as governor: 'My own measures and policy differ to some extent from his ideas of provincial administration, with the result that certain people have suspected that my disagreement with him is due to the clash of incompatible temperaments, and not to a mere difference of opinion. Now I have never either done or said a single thing with the intention of disparaging his reputation. Indeed, since this trouble caused by our friend Dolabella's indiscretion, I am putting myself forward as his intercessor in the day of his need.' What Cicero wrote to Atticus was certainly never divulged: but we cannot believe that he had not said the same in other quarters. Anyhow Appius cringed when he needed Cicero's help, and Cicero at once responded in a friendly way. 'At last I have read a letter worthy of Appius Claudius, a letter full of kindly feeling, courtesy and consideration. Evidently the urban aspect has restored to you your pristine urbanity.' We hope Cicero did nothing very bad to save Appius from disgrace. At least he tried to limit the expense of embassies to Rome to what was permitted by the Cornelian Law.

Nor is Cicero's letter to Appius to congratulate

him on his acquittal any more pleasant reading: it was an awkward one to write, as some reference had to be made to Tullia's marriage. If Cicero may be believed, Appius had expressed the hope that it might turn out happily: very probably he felt sure it would not, as it did not.

What was Cicero then to do for the poor provincials? He was determined to do what he could. In the first place he caused them as little expense as possible for himself and his staff. With one exception, he proudly says, his staff took their cue from him. He would accept nothing but bare lodging, not even what was allowed by the law of Caesar, and preferred to sleep under canvas. So everywhere he was welcomed. Secondly, he allowed no billeting. He makes the almost incredible statement that the people of Cyprus paid £40,000 per annum to avoid having soldiers billeted on them, and that other rich states did the same; he would not take a farthing himself. Thirdly, he compelled fraudulent magistrates to refund their peculations. Thus, he says, the provincials were able to pay the arrears of their taxes, and he is in high favour in consequence with the tax-farmers. Fourthly, his justice cost nothing: there was no 'backstairs jobbery'. He was accessible and held receptions every morning before daybreak, as he used to do in old days when a candidate for office at Rome. In all respects he was a great contrast to nine-tenths of the greedy nobles who usually governed provinces.

Notwithstanding, those who love Cicero as a man can only wish that he had done better in resisting the pressure put upon him from Rome. His experience shows how difficult it was for the most upright of men to resist the demands of their friends, and even of their acquaintances, let alone of people of the type of Appius Claudius. The test case is the affair of the citizens of Salamis in Cyprus.

A deputation from that town met Cicero on his landing at Ephesus and told him a tale of woe. One Scaptius, a business man, had received a troop of cavalry from Appius with which to bully the Salaminians. They had shut up the town council in their town-hall, so that five of them were starved to death. Cicero instantly ordered the cavalry to leave the island. When he reached Tarsus, Scaptius and the Salaminians appeared at his judgement seat. At this time he knew no more than that Scaptius had been recommended to his favour by young Marcus Brutus. Subsequently he found out why. Young Brutus had, to use Professor Tyrrell's neat phrase, 'invested in Cappadocians and Cilicians', but, as Pompey had first claim on Cappadocians, was all the more anxious to wring all he could out of Cilicians. He was now twenty-eight years of age, and according to Cicero, even when he asked a favour, 'wrote in an arrogant, impudent and tactless way'. Matius told Cicero later that Caesar said about Brutus, 'Whatever he wants he wants badly'.[65] Shakespeare makes him at the age of thirty-six say:

> By heaven, I had rather coin my heart
> And drop my blood for ducats than to wring
> From the hard hands of peasants their vile trash,

but, having been misled by Plutarch, he did not know that Brutus thought that peasants only existed to fill the pockets of such as himself!

P119 — flue moved more sitters for my corner

The debt incurred by Salamis was of long standing. Brutus must have been very young when he lent the money. The debt was running at 48 per cent. This Cicero refused to recognise: in his edict issued to the province he had stated he would not recognise at law any higher rate than 12 per cent. Then Scaptius flung at his head two decrees of the Roman Senate five years old, ordering the governor of Cilicia to recognise the loan as valid, in spite of the Gabinian Law forbidding loans to provincials; another instance of the way in which the Senate granted exemption from the laws. Cicero agreed to 12 per cent compound interest, but would not hear of 48 per cent. The Salaminians promptly offered to pay the sum which Cicero recognised; and failing that, asked to be allowed to deposit the money in a temple, so that interest would cease to run. Scaptius demurred, and though Cicero thought him a shameless rascal, he did not insist on the settlement of the debt as he could easily have done. It was weak of him to be anxious not to offend Brutus (though he did not at the time know Brutus was the actual creditor) and to leave the Salaminians to the tender mercies of his successor Sestius. As Brutus subsequently hurried to Cilicia, being only summoned from there by his uncle Cato to Pompey's camp in Macedonia, it is to be feared that Cicero's weakness cost the Salaminians dear. This is the only blot on Cicero's administration of Cilicia. But what other Roman would have done as much as he did? Would even Cato have refused to oblige his nephew?

In another matter Cicero was less weak-kneed. Curule aediles who had to give shows vied with each other in importing wild beasts from the provinces,

I

of course at the expense of the provincials. Two of these officials thus worried Cicero to supply panthers from Cibyra. One he refused outright: the other, Caelius, his intimate friend and correspondent, he put off with jokes. 'There are very few panthers just now, and the few there are complain that in my province no snares are set for any living creatures but themselves, and so they have decided to emigrate *en masse* to Caria.' To Caelius' other calm request for a contribution from the province for the expenses of his shows he gave a flat refusal: 'you who accuse other people should live more cautiously yourself'.

One good act Cicero claims to have done to the neighbouring vassal state of Cappadocia. The young king Ariobarzanes came to him with the news that his mother had plotted with the high priest of Comana to dethrone him in favour of his brother Ariarathes, who had generously informed him of this conspiracy. Cicero settled him firmly on his throne, which he retained for many years: and in return squeezed money out of him for Brutus! Incidentally he tells us that Cappadocia was so deeply in debt to Pompey that every month £8000 worth of taxes went to the Great Man. One begins to understand how Pompey paid for his great Theatre, his temple of Venus Victrix and the unprecedented Games of 55 B.C.

Cicero's first anxiety on entering his province was as to its military defence: for a Parthian invasion, which might fall on Cilicia or Syria or both, was expected. On reaching his camp at Cybistra in Cappadocia he had news of their crossing the Euphrates. He summoned Deiotarus of Galatia to join him, thus doubling his forces, and raised levies from all the Roman citizens in the province.

Meanwhile the Parthians had invaded Syria, and Cassius, the future conspirator against Caesar, who had escaped from the fatal field of Carrhae, repulsed them from Antioch. Meanwhile Cicero crossed the Taurus and proceeded to attack the hostile mountaineers of the Amanus range, took some mountain fortresses, and—strange experience for a civilian proconsul—was saluted as *Imperator* by his soldiers on Alexander's battlefield of Issus. Was there ever a more humorous coincidence? No doubt in Quintus and Pomptinus he had able legates, and Lepta was a first-rate chief engineer. It is quite possible that these operations, as he put it, gave heart to Cassius and inspired fear in the Parthians. After their retreat, he besieged and took the mountain town of Pindenissus. He imagines Atticus exclaiming, 'Who the deuce are the Pindenissitae? I never heard the name,' and remarks, 'That is not my fault. Could I turn Cilicia into Aetolia or Macedonia?' The soldiers received all the spoil but the horses, and the sale of the captives realised £100,000.

Naturally after this Cicero expected a triumph: Pomptinus had had one for some small operations in Savoy. We possess an interesting letter from Cicero to Cato (January 50 B.C.) asking his support in the Senate, though avoiding the word 'triumph'. He describes his provincial administration, his interference in Cappadocia and his military successes, and asks for Cato's vote 'in the name of philosophy which we have both introduced into public life'. A thanksgiving was voted in honour of Cicero's successes, but against the opposition of Cato. In April 50, Cato, whose Latin style was as stiff as his mind, conventionally praises Cicero in reply, but bluntly says, 'I thought a vote of thanks more complimentary to you than a thanksgiving and so supported that. If you prefer "chance" to get the credit rather than yourself, I am glad you have what you prefer. But don't think that a triumph necessarily follows a thanksgiving. I have written at greater length than is my wont.'

In August 50 B.C. Cicero replies, beginning with a quotation which has the parallel in English 'Commendation from Sir Hubert Stanley is praise indeed' (he had once said to Atticus, 'Cato to me is as good as a hundred thousand'). He then warns Cato he has heard about his speech in the Senate, of which his friends sent him a verbatim copy, and ends, 'I mean to try for a triumph; and if I get it, I hope you will be equally ready to rejoice that I got what I preferred'. Privately he remarks: 'Cato was discreditably malevolent in his behaviour to me'. Seeing that Cato supported the ridiculous application of Bibulus, his son-in-law, for a thanksgiving for having shut himself up in Antioch, we shall be inclined to agree with Cicero in this judgement.

The two Cicero boys went with their parents to Cilicia. When they reached the camp at Cybistra they were sent on a visit to Deiotarus of Galatia and ultimately went to pursue their studies at Rhodes. The young Quintus was already shifty and deceitful, and his uncle had much difficulty in controlling him. The young Marcus was more slothful and obviously led by his cousin. Dionysius, their Greek tutor, was perpetually at warfare with them. The boys complained of his violent temper, but they obviously needed a strong hand. When the time came for Cicero to return to Rome, he picked them up at Rhodes.

There was no obstacle to Cicero's leaving his province when the year was up, as the Parthian invasion was over. The only question he had to decide was whom to leave in charge. After long hesitation he passed over Quintus, probably to the latter's dissatisfaction: but he confides to Atticus that he was afraid Quintus might give way to his violent temper and do regrettable things: so he chose the new quaestor, who though young and inexperienced was the official allotted to him.

Seeing that Cicero was quite a scrupulous governor, the fact that he banked a sum of £17,600 at Ephesus, before he left, shows what the illicit profits of Republican governors must have been. In January 49 B.C. he tells his quaestor Mescinius, who was dissatisfied with his share, that he had placed this sum at Pompey's disposal for the expenses of the Civil War.[66] Yet in January 48 in a letter to Atticus he speaks of the sum as available.[67] Was he lying to Mescinius? We prefer to think that Pompey, though authorised to do so, had not actually then taken any or all of the sum. But in March 47 he says to Atticus: 'All the money I had I handed over to Pompey at a time when it seemed advisable to do so'.[68] So it would seem probable that Cicero never reaped any pecuniary benefit at all from his provincial governorship.

On October 1st he finally sailed from Ephesus, having heard 'awful news' about Caesar, that he would refuse to disband his army, and that Pompey was inclined to retire to Spain. So to a perplexed Italy returned a perplexed proconsul, accompanied by lictors bearing laurel-wreathed bundles of rods and hoping against hope for a triumph. These wretched lictors accompanied him everywhere till at least December 48: for he then writes that Sestius, his successor in Cilicia, had also been allowed to retain his lictors.[69]

Chapter 8

CIVIL WAR AND SUBMISSION TO CAESAR

49-47 B.C.

The bogey-man is dreadfully alert, rapid and energetic.
Ad Att. viii. 9, 4

DURING Cicero's absence of nearly a year and a half from Rome, he had received the political gossip from the obliging Caelius. That able but unprincipled young man* was rapidly falling out with the leading nobles, and, though still nominally on the Senatorial side and elected curule aedile by their votes, enjoyed very much the defeat of Domitius, brother-in-law of Cato, when Antony was elected augur in the place of Hortensius, who had recently died. This was really a trial of strength between the Caesarians and the Senatorial party; but the latter rallied and secured both the consuls for 49 B.C. Caelius at first had written, begging Cicero to support his predecessor in the matter of his prosecution by Dolabella. 'If you don't do it, it will be supposed that you were insincere in your reconciliation with him, and it will be doubly awkward, because he is being accused by your son-in-law, though you can't help it, being away from Rome.'

---

* Velleius (*R.H.* ii. 48 and 68) describes him and the younger Curio (p. 83) as 'artists in rascality' (*ingeniosissime nequam*).

Yet the same Caelius a few months later, having been refused a temporary accommodation by Appius, then censor, violently quarrelled with him, and prosecuted the official guardian of public morals for unnatural vice, thus making him very ridiculous. Both Cicero and Caelius enjoy the success of Caelius in securing the post of curule aedile, when he defeats Hirrus, a politician of some note and a partisan of Pompey. Cicero facetiously calls Hirrus *ille* (*that man*), because being afflicted with inability to say the letter '*r*' he pronounced his name Hillus.

Cicero could seldom refrain from a joke; yet in his serious moments he viewed with great alarm the widening breach between the two parties, and deprecated all violent action on his own side. Thus when the consul Marcus Marcellus found at Rome and scourged a native of Como (founded by Caesar as a Roman *colonia* under the name of Novum Comum), in order to question the validity of the Vatinian Law and to show that in his eyes he was only a provincial, Cicero strongly condemns his action.[70] It was a colony with Latin rights anyhow, and Latins were never scourged: if, however, the man *was* an ex-magistrate he was certainly a Roman citizen. It was very shortsighted of the Senate obstinately to refuse the citizenship to the Transpadanes. Had Cisalpine Gaul been incorporated earlier, Caesar, as a provincial governor, would have had no authority in North Italy, and, to invade Italy, would have had to cross the Alps instead of the Rubicon!

Events were now moving fast, and rumour exaggerated them. At Athens, Cicero was told that Caesar was going to send four of his eleven legions to Placentia on October 15th, within striking distance

of the frontier.   Even in August, Caelius had said
that there would be war within a year, unless either
Pompey or Caesar would go to fight the Parthians.
On the excuse of an imminent Parthian war the
Senate had ordered them to supply a legion each.
Pompey demanded back the legion he had lent to
Caesar, and Caesar surrendered one of his own.
These two legions were now encamped in Italy very
much against their will, and from Pompey's point
of view were anything but reliable.   With his in-
veterate levity Caelius says to Cicero: 'If it could
happen without personal risk to yourself, a grand and
magnificent spectacle is being staged for you by
Fortune'.

As the danger came nearer, an overwhelming
majority of the Senate actually voted that both
Caesar and Pompey should lay down their commands.   Pompey, who had a good deal of obstinacy
in his character, would go no further in concession
than to allow Caesar to stay in his province till November 13th, 49 B.C.   But even this was a futile
suggestion: for it left Caesar defenceless for six
weeks, before he entered on his second consulship on
January 1st, 48, and Cato had publicly announced
that he would prosecute him on the day he returned
to Rome.   The fact was, as Caelius saw and said, that
Pompey, though he had himself been thrice consul
(the last time after only a two years' interval), dreaded
nothing so much as a second consulship for Caesar.
Every one assumed as a matter of course that if
Caesar was admitted as a candidate, he would be
elected.   If Pompey had repeated his magnanimity
of 62 B.C. and gone to fight the Parthians, history
would have had no complaint against him.   As it

was, he contributed to the outbreak of the civil war
by his obstinacy.   He felt himself constitutionally in
the right, but by his legislation to Caesar's detriment
he had created the impasse.

How was it that he did not realise the irresistible
strength of Caesar as compared with his own?   No
doubt, he had been greatly encouraged by the
universal rejoicings in Italy when he recovered from
a dangerous illness at Naples in 50 B.C.*   Probably
he underrated the fighting strength of Caesar's
veteran army, and overrated his own forces in Spain.
But doubtless from the first he meant to go to the
East, where his reputation was immense, and hoped
to decide the war in his favour there.   Had he, however, made that clear at first, the Senate would have
deserted him.   People thought that Pompey had
only to stamp his foot—had he not said so himself? [71]
—and veterans would assemble and form invincible
legions: so great and, indeed, so well deserved was
his reputation.   But, as Tacitus afterwards remarked,
shortlived were the affections of the Roman People,
and Caesar's star was now in the ascendant.

Cicero landed at Brindisi on November 24th and
went slowly towards Rome.   He received 'coaxing'
letters from Caesar and Balbus, but his chief anxiety
as regards them was to repay his debt.   He owed
Caesar something between £6000 and £7000, and
had been anxious to pay the sum before he left for
Cilicia, but apparently had only given Oppius,
Caesar's agent,[72] some kind of undertaking to pay.
On December 9th he wrote to Atticus to borrow in
order to repay.   If he remains in debt to Caesar, he

---

* *Tusc. Disp.* i. 86; Juvenal, x. 283.   The rejoicing must have been
hypocritical, as Cicero says March 4th, 49 B.C., *Ad Att.* viii. 16, 1.

will lose all liberty of action. 'When I have spoken finely in the Senate on behalf of the constitution, the Tarshish man (Balbus) will waylay me as I go out and say, "Kindly pay up".' [73] There is little doubt that Cicero did discharge the debt: for had he not done so, we should certainly have heard of it later. Thus while others were receiving money from Caesar, Cicero was paying money to him.

But this, while it gave him freedom of action, did not throw any light on his path. At this moment he shows extraordinary insight into Caesar's moves, and pitiful indecision as to his own line of conduct. He still hoped for a triumph, but he was determined not to let that stand in the way of his duty, if only he could see clearly what *was* his duty. He feared a civil war would end in a tyranny whichever won. As we read his daily vacillations communicated to Atticus, it is hard to resist a feeling of contempt; but it is only just to him to reflect that, while a Caelius unblushingly says: 'Stick to your party while peace lasts; when war breaks out, join the big battalions', it was exactly the moderate men of high principle like Sulpicius the jurist (see p. 65) and Cicero who were most perplexed. Caelius joined Caesar. Cicero's only comment is: 'So far is he from influencing my attitude, that I think he ought to be sorry that he has changed his'. Sulpicius sent his son to Caesar, but stayed himself in Rome and was bold enough to take an independent line in the Senate: he is coupled with Lucius Volcatius Tullus and Manius Lepidus (consuls, 66 B.C.) as a neutral.[74] Cicero, being unable to get a lead from either Atticus or Peducaeus, on whose judgement he greatly relied, kept putting off his final decision: but on December 9th he writes to

Atticus: 'The only boat for me will be the one steered by Pompey: if asked my opinion in the Senate, I shall answer, "I am with Pompey".'[75] On December 10th he saw Pompey, who of course assumed that he had his support, but he came away despairing of any settlement. On December 23rd, Antony, the new tribune, in a harangue to the people denounced Pompey's whole life.[76] On December 25th, Pompey saw Cicero again, and then expected that Caesar would abandon the idea of being consul in 48 B.C., and would keep his provinces and army. Certainly in that way civil war could have been averted. Pompey did not foresee that some tribune would flee to Caesar with a complaint that he had been expelled, and that Caesar would then on this pretext invade Italy. This Cicero clearly foresaw as a possibility, in writing to Atticus on December 27th.[77]

Caesar was well served by the tribunes in his pay. The younger Curio, who had been almost the only vocal opponent of Caesar in 59 B.C. and was both then and afterwards regarded by Cicero as the rising hope of the Senatorial party, had been bought. He cost, it was said, £500,000—the consul Paullus went for £300,000—but was cheap at the price. So, having been elected tribune on the Senatorial ticket, Curio had changed sides. Cicero in Cilicia could treat this as a joke, but the poet Lucan was right, when he wrote long afterwards: 'Curio's change of politics turned the scale'. After playing Caesar's game most effectively until he went out of office, he went to Caesar's camp, and reappeared in Rome on New Year's Day with a proposal from Caesar of simultaneous disarmament: but the Senate refused to accept it. Then Pompey's father-in-law Scipio moved that Caesar should be ordered to disband his army, and if he refused, be declared a public enemy (*hostis*).* The new Caesarian tribunes Marcus Antonius and Quintus Cassius (not the conspirator) interposed their veto, but the motion was carried. The tribunes seem to have been threatened with violence.† Anyhow, declaring that their rights had been infringed, and accompanied by Curio and Caelius, they left Rome and reached Ariminum on January 10th. In the night between the 10th and 11th Caesar quietly crossed the Rubicon and invaded Italy. The stories told about his hesitation are mere fictions: he had long since made up his mind.

In his *Civil War* he makes much capital of the Senate's treatment of the tribunes; but in 62 B.C. he had himself advised the tribune Nepos to yield to the Senate (p. 70). When he arrived in Rome, he forcibly removed the tribune Lucius Metellus, who barred his way to the Treasury. Later when two tribunes arrested a man who hailed him as 'king', he caused a colleague of theirs to propose and carry their deposition, a course which had been so vehemently denounced when Tiberius Gracchus in 133 B.C. took it against his colleague Octavius.

If Caesar says he had no alternative but to invade Italy, he states what is not true. He might have

---

* It is held by many, *e.g.* Professor Adcock (*Cambridge Ancient History*, vol. ix. p. 636), that Caesar's legal term had already expired, and that therefore the Senate's action was strictly correct. The view taken above is less hostile to Caesar, viz. that he still had a right to remain to the end of February 49 B.C.

† Cicero denies this, writing to his family (*Ad Fam.* xvi. 11, 2) *nulla vi expulsi* (*not driven out by violence*).

remained in his province, and every one would have breathed a sigh of relief. He himself says very little about coming as a democratic leader to rescue an oppressed people from the domination of the Senate. It was to assert his right to *his* consulship, *his* province and, above all, *his* army, which was certainly a better description of it than one of the armies of the Republic. For in wellnigh ten years of warfare against very tough antagonists, he had organised a strong force of 50,000 veterans, devoted to their leader personally, as one to whom they owed everything and with whom they had shared a thousand dangers, which moreover was reinforced by the pick of conquered Gaul, the legion of the *Larks*. Then there were the two legions quartered in Italy, who were only anxious to return to their old allegiance.*

Caesar had certainly been unfairly treated. All reasonable and moderate men, not Cicero only, felt that. But when he crossed the Rubicon, it was bringing back the bad old days of Marius and Sulla. It was refusing to follow the example of Pompey in 62 B.C. Caesar felt that he was the one person capable of curing the evils of the state, and that was probably the case. But he determined to do it by the sword, and before drawing the sword he should have reflected that other Romans were as obstinate as himself. Obstinate men can only be ruled if they are convinced that the government of the ruler is

---

* There were eight legions across the Alps but rapidly approaching. One was in Cisalpine Gaul, and the Eighth and Twelfth had been summoned to come at the utmost possible speed, when the news came that on December 11th Pompey had been charged to protect Italy from invasion. The two in Italy could be counted on. There were thus eleven (*Ad Att.* vii. 7, 6). The thirteenth legion at Ariminum was at the full establishment of 5000; not all were so strong. In *B.G.* v. 49, 7, Caesar gives 7000 as the number of two legions, and a few horse.

beneficial. For the rivers of blood that were soon to flow Caesar is morally responsible. Moreover, as will be seen, the kind of rule he wished to fasten on the Roman People was thoroughly alien and hateful; and this could only end in the tragedy of the Ides of March. All the special pleading of a Froude or a Mommsen cannot disguise the fact that Caesarism was tainted at its source, and you cannot have a sweet river flowing from a bitter spring. Not without reason has 'crossing the Rubicon' become proverbial for a fatal and irrevocable step.

During the next six months Cicero first decided to go with Pompey, then to be neutral and try to bring about a reconciliation, finally to join Pompey: nothing could induce him to join Caesar.

At the moment with his embarrassing lictors he was a pitiable figure; but his support was invaluable, whether secured by Pompey or Caesar, and both assiduously courted him. Pompey gave him a command to recruit in Campania, which he obeyed, and then threw up the task. As he had actually done nothing but go to Campania, he represents later to Caesar that he had taken no part in the war, which is hardly ingenuous. He had a son-in-law and almost more friends on the Caesarian side than on the other; and they all with one accord pressed him to be neutral, at any rate not to join Pompey.

Cicero's private letters are full of gloom. He refused to be encouraged by the secession of Labienus from Caesar, great blow as that was. He falsely prophesied that Caesar would be as ruthless as Sulla, and that his programme was abolition of debt, restoration of exiles, and any and every crime. In this

of course he was wrong: for Caesar was no Catiline.
On the other hand, he was revolted by the violent
talk of the aristocrats, and equally doubtful of the
temper of Pompey. In fact, there was little, he felt,
to choose between the two: either when victorious
would be an arbitrary master (*dominus*) and overthrow the constitution. From the Caesarian side
(Balbus and Oppius) came the flattering suggestion
that he should bring about a reconciliation: and he
pathetically writes to Atticus on February 27th: 'I
remember a book being dedicated to you by Demetrius of Magnesia, *On Concord*. I should be glad if
you would let me have it. You see the part I am
studying.' His faith in the power of words is touching: but when men have taken to the sword, reason-
ing is no longer of avail.*

What surprised him most was the rapidity of
Caesar's advance and the apparent powerlessness of
Pompey to resist it. As a matter of fact, Pompey did
everything that was possible with such an unruly set
of allies. Cicero himself did nothing that he was
told. Domitius shut himself up in Corfinium in
spite of Pompey's orders, and thus simply swelled
the army of the invader. Pompey's embarkation
of his troops at Brindisi on March 17th was
quite as fine a military feat as Caesar's lightning
advance.

Writing to Atticus on March 19th from Formiae,
after reading over again a roll of letters † received
between January 21st and March 9th, Cicero gives
us the gist of his friend's advice. Both had dis-

* The moral today is that the League of Nations must be supported
by all thoughtful people.

† *Ad Att.* ix. 10, 4. One letter was gummed on to another, till they
made a roll.

approved of Pompey leaving Italy—they were not military experts—and neither thought departure advisable for themselves. Cicero significantly remarks that years ago Pompey thought of retirement from Italy, being set on reviving the part of Sulla and returning from the East to proscribe his enemies; in this he probably does Pompey injustice. No wonder Atticus had been a poor counsellor, for he had been suffering from dysuria, as well as his periodic attack of ague. He was always on principle outside politics, and had little personally to fear. Cicero always represents his friend as an optimate at heart: he was certainly a first-rate opportunist.

At some date in March, Caesar had written [78] to thank Cicero and to say that he hoped for his 'advice, influence, position and help in all ways', while Balbus and Oppius pressed him to undertake the part of peacemaker.* But the more Cicero was pressed, the more qualms of conscience did he feel at not having accompanied Pompey in his flight, though he still thought it dishonourable and pusillanimous of him to have evacuated Italy. On March 19th he replies to Caesar as follows: [79] 'On reading your letter, which I got from our friend Furnius, in which you urged me to come near Rome, stating that you wished to avail yourself of my advice and my position, I was not much surprised; but I asked myself what you meant by my influence and help. However, my hopes led me to think that *a man of your admirable statesmanship* would wish measures to be taken for the comfort, peace and harmony of the citizens, and

* According to Plutarch (*Cicero*, 37), Trebatius also wrote to say Caesar thought Cicero ought to join him, or failing that to retire to Greece and be neutral.

K

for that purpose I considered my character and inclination very suitable. If that is the case and you are touched by the desire to maintain our friend Pompey in his position and reconcile him to yourself and the state, I am sure you will find no one more suited for the purpose than I am. I have always advocated peace both with Pompey and the Senate, ever since I have been able to do so (since his return from Cilicia), nor since the outbreak of hostilities have I taken any part in the war; I have considered that the war was attacking your rights because envious and hostile persons were opposing a distinction conferred on you by the grace of the Roman people * (he means the law of the ten tribunes dispensing Caesar from a personal canvass for the consulship). But as at that time I not only upheld your rights but urged others to assist you, so now I am greatly concerned with the rights of Pompey. It is many years since I chose you two men for my special respect, and took you to be my closest friends, as you are. So I ask you, or rather I beseech and entreat you with all urgency, that in spite of all your anxieties *you would devote some time to considering how I may be enabled by your kindness* to be what decency and gratitude, nay, good feeling, require, in remembering my great debt to Pompey. If this only concerned myself, I should yet hope that you would grant my request; but to my mind it concerns your honour and the public weal, that I, a friend of peace and of you both, should be so supported by you that I may be able to work for peace between the two of you, and harmonious feeling among our fellow citizens. I thanked you

---

* *Ad Att.* vii. 7, 5: cum *id* datum est, *illud* una datum est: *id* to stand in absence, *illud* to stand while retaining his army.

formerly in the matter of Lentulus for having saved
him, as he had saved me.*

'Yet on reading the letter he has sent me full of
thankfulness for your generous kindness, I feel that
I owe to you the same safety which he has received.
If you understand my gratitude to him, pray give me
the opportunity of showing my gratitude to Pompey
too.' Caesar sent the letter to Rome for publication.
The phrases italicised above were criticised as savour-
ing of flattery, and Cicero defended himself to Atticus
for using them. 'I was not afraid of seeming to flatter
him: for I would gladly have thrown myself at his
feet to save my country.'⁸⁰

Finally on March 28th he saw Caesar himself at
Formiae, and this is the account he sends to Atticus
of the interview. 'In both matters I followed your
advice. I spoke so as to win Caesar's respect rather
than his gratitude; and I persisted in my resolve not
to go to Rome. We were mistaken in thinking he
would be easy to manage. No one could have been
less so. He insisted that my decision was tantamount
to a condemnation of himself, and if I did not come,
others would be less likely to do so. I said my case
was very different from theirs. After much talk he
said: "Well, come and discuss peace." "On my own
terms?" I asked. "Am I to dictate to you?" said he.
"Well then," said I, " I shall maintain that the Senate
does not approve of your going to Spain, or your
transporting your forces to Greece," and I added, "I
shall lament Pompey's fate." He replied, "I do not
want that sort of thing said." "So I thought," said
I, "but I don't want to be in Rome, just because

* Lentulus Spinther, consul 57 B.C., had been active in promoting
Cicero's recall from exile.

either I must say that, and much besides, which I could not suppress if I was there, or I must not come at all." The result was that, as a way of closing the interview, he asked me to think it over. I could not refuse that. So we parted. I am convinced that he doesn't like or approve of me. But I approve of myself, which I have not done for a long time.' [81]

After reading this, who will deny that Cicero possessed moral courage? Quintilian [82] also defends Cicero against the repeated charge of cowardice and lack of moral firmness (*constantia*), and quotes words of his which are not to be found in his extant writings: 'I am not timid in facing dangers, but in attempting to guard against them'. So in an extant letter of 45 B.C. he writes to one Toranius, who in Pompey's camp had been like-minded with himself, 'And so I, whom those brave and wise men, Domitius and Lentulus, accused of being timid—and so I undoubtedly was; I was afraid that that would come to pass which actually happened—am now on the contrary afraid of nothing and ready for any contingency'. The hostile critic may accuse Cicero of blindness, stupidity or irresolution as a politician, and may produce much to support the charge: but March 28th, 49 B.C., reflects more honour on Cicero as a man than November 5th, 63 B.C., and is comparable to the calmness with which he bowed his neck to the sword of the executioner on December 7th, 43 B.C.

With amazing detachment from these acute worries Cicero went off to Arpinum, the home of his family, to confer the robe of manhood on his son: Caesar, certainly much chagrined, pursued his way to Rome. He had made himself master of Italy in sixty-five days, but he wanted to justify himself; and here was a man he could neither buy nor cajole, but who, as a supporter at Rome, would have magnificently propped up the weakness of his constitutional position: and he was well aware how disreputable were some of his supporters; a *Nekyia*, or infernal troop, Atticus called them.

At Rome he did his best in the fortnight he spent there. The two Caesarian tribunes summoned the rump of a Senate on April 1st. Caesar's father-in-law, Piso, stayed away, but Sulpicius, most respected of the ex-consuls, was there and told him that he would deserve well of his country if he did not carry the war into Greece and Spain, which was exactly what he had heard from Cicero. After his departure a law was passed appointing him dictator to hold consular elections. Caesar had deliberately adopted a policy of clemency, but Curio, who visited Cicero on April 13th on his way to Sicily and Africa, said that Caesar had very nearly given way to temper and put to death the tribune Metellus who barred his way to the Treasury. The opinion of this unprincipled but shrewd young man deserves quotation and must be considered in the light of Caesar's life as a whole. Caesar had crucified the pirates, put to death the whole senate of the Veneti, exterminated the Usipetes and Tencteri,* and cut off the right hands of the

---

* Let any one read the complacent chapter (*B.G.* iv. 15) in which Caesar describes his dealings with the Usipetes and Tencteri, and wonder that Cato should propose in the Senate that he should be delivered up to the Germans. Having detained the chiefs who had come to him 'to excuse themselves for fighting and to cheat him into granting an armistice', he made a forced march of eight miles, surprised the Germans, whose women and children fled: 'Caesar sent his cavalry to pursue them'. The Germans threw away their arms, and when they reached the confluence of the Meuse and Rhine were either killed or drowned. 'Our men, without a single casualty and with very few wounded in so for-

defenders of Uxellodunum. He kept Vercingetorix in captivity for six years, and after he had appeared at his triumph in 46, had him executed; and in ten years he caused the death of a million human beings, according to Plutarch, before the civil war began. Curio said that Caesar himself was not by nature and inclination averse to cruelty, but he thought mild measures would win popularity. If however he lost popular favour, he would be cruel. He had been annoyed when he found that he had offended the lower orders by robbing the Treasury, and so though he had made up his mind to harangue the people before leaving (for Spain), he had not risked it but had gone off in a very disturbed state of mind. 'Finally Curio swore (which comes easy to him) that Caesar was very friendly to me. I said, "I have my doubts". He said he had heard so from Dolabella. I asked what he said, and he declared he said that Caesar had thanked him warmly for wanting me to go to Rome, and not only approved but showed pleasure.' We see that Caesar relied on Cicero's able and dissolute son-in-law to keep a hold on him and prevent him from leaving Italy. But in this very interview Cicero asked for and was promised Curio's protection in Sicily when *en route* for Greece. When Cicero had once made up his mind to go he was happier. Sulpicius, on the other hand, who came to see him on May 7th, shed tears, because he had offended both Pompey and Caesar.

midable a battle, the enemy numbering 430,000, returned to camp.' Now comes the crowning touch of cruel clemency. 'Caesar gave those he had detained in camp leave to go away. They, fearing execution and torture from the Gauls, said they preferred to stay with him. To them Caesar granted liberty.' That is, he left them to their own devices. What, we wonder, became of them?

After Tullia's confinement and the birth of a
seven-months child on May 19th, Cicero felt free to
start.   It was rumoured that he was going.   Caesar
wrote to say it would be a rash and unfriendly act.
Caelius, serious for once, begged him as a friend to
do nothing so foolish.*   Antony, in charge of Italy
and obviously with orders to detain him, wrote to him
as follows: 'Your resolution is perfectly sound.
One who wishes to be a mediator stays in his fatherland: one who departs is thought to have taken his
side.   But it is not for me to decide whether a man
is right to go or not.   Caesar has commissioned me
to allow no one to leave Italy.   So my approval of
your determination is of no consequence, if I cannot
in any case give you permission.   I advise you to
send to Caesar and ask him for it.   I have no doubt
you will get leave, especially as you promise to take
our friendship into account.' †   This Cicero calls a
dispatch of Spartan brevity: there is no mistaking the
military tone; Antony is under strict orders.

Finally Cicero, accompanied by his brother, son
and nephew, embarked at Formiae for Greece on
June 7th.   From the ship he wrote a letter to his
wife, which shows that he was easy in his conscience
and almost gay, when he had finally taken the step he
considered right.   'All the troubles and anxieties
with which I have made you utterly wretched (for

---

* *Ad Fam.* viii. 16 = *Ad Att.* x. 9a: 'You are mistaken, if you think
that Caesar will behave in pardoning his opponents in the same way as
in offering terms.   His thoughts and even his speech contemplate stern
and ruthless action.   He left Rome in anger against the Senate; he was
clearly roused by this tribunician opposition; I assure you there will be
no room for any appeal to mercy.'

† *Ad Att.* x. 10, 2.   It is impossible to understand what Antony meant
by 'your resolution'.   Probably that an *imperator* could go abroad, if
he chose.

which I am very sorry), and our dear Tullia who is sweeter to us than our lives, I have put away and dismissed. The reason I discovered the day after I left you: it was an attack of the liver, which I got rid of in the night. I obtained such immediate relief, that I fancy some god cured me: to that god please render due and pious thanks as you always do.* I trust we have got a very good ship: this is written after going on board. Next I shall write to our friends a number of letters to commend you and dear Tullia to their care. I should exhort you to show more courage, if I did not know that you both are braver than any *man*. Yet I trust affairs are such that I may hope you both will be very comfortable where you are, and that one day I shall have men like myself at my side to defend the Republic. For yourself in the first place take care of your health, secondly if you think fit, make use of those country places which are furthest from the military. If the price of provisions rises, you can conveniently occupy the farm at Arpinum with the town staff. Cicero, a fine lad, sends you his best love. Again and again good-bye. June 7th.'

From other sources we infer that he went to Atticus' estate at Buthrotum in Epirus, and in the autumn to Pompey's camp: there are no letters to Atticus between May 49 and January 48. Caesar, on his victorious return from Spain, as dictator nominated himself and Publius Servilius as consuls for 48 B.C. The first dictatorship lasted eleven days.

The camp of Pompey was no place for Cicero.

Cato bluntly told him he should not have come. He disgusted everybody by his querulousness, and

* Note the implication that the practice of religion is for women only, not men.

they disgusted him by their bloodthirsty talk. He particularly disliked their appropriation of the property of their opponents in the hour of their expected victory.

Into the details of the campaign in Epirus from January to August 48 B.C. it would be irrelevant to enter. The war became simply a question which of two men would be the ruler of the Roman world. Pompey's ambition was subsequently carried out by Augustus: Caesar by aiming at a tyranny more on Greek and Oriental lines, lost his life. No one can help recognising the great and generous side of Caesar's character, while condemning his ambition. The man who could burn Pompey's correspondence unread after it had fallen into his hands at Pharsalus* was no ordinary man. Yet the summing up of Dio Cassius is not unjust.[83] 'In temper they differed from one another to this extent, that Pompey desired to be second to no man, and Caesar to be first of all: the former was anxious to be honoured by a willing people, and to preside over and be loved by men who fully consent, whereas the latter cared not at all, if he ruled over even an unwilling people, issued orders to men who hated him, and with his own hand bestowed the honours upon himself.'

After the crushing defeat of the Pompeians at Pharsalus, at the imminent risk of his life, Cicero refused further connection with the die-hards: Pompey's son Gnaeus threatened to kill him at Corcyra. Quintus fell out with his brother as the source of all the family troubles: perhaps he was still a little sore about Cilicia.

* He did the same with Scipio's correspondence after his victory at Thapsus, 46 B.C.

Marcus returned to spend eleven miserable months at Brindisi. Antony gave him a grudging permission to stay in Italy: but Vatinius, governor of Brundusium, showed him kindness.[84] He had great difficulty in raising the second instalment of Tullia's dowry, and Dolabella was an outrageously unsatisfactory husband for her: but the child that had been born, though delicate, survived. He was also much irritated with Terentia over money matters. It was worse than the exile. When he hears of Pompey's death, he hardly sheds a tear. 'I never had any doubt as to Pompey's end. All kings and nations had so given up his cause as desperate, that wherever he went, I thought this would happen. I cannot help deploring his fate; for I have found him to be an upright, moral and righteous man.' [85] Not, be it observed, a general, a statesman or a leader of men. He had been weighed in the balance and found wanting. At the end of his life he lays this indictment against Pompey. 'When people disregard everything that is morally right and true, if only they may secure power thereby, are they not pursuing the same course as he (Pompey) who wished to have as a father-in-law the man by whose effrontery he might gain power for himself? He thought it advantageous to secure supreme power while the odium of it fell upon another; and he failed to see how unjust to his country this was and how wrong morally.' [86] One may remark that the odium of the first Triumvirate (59 B.C.) chiefly fell on Pompey, so that Cicero is hardly correct in that: but his moral censure, the final judgement on the man, is sound. Pompey was fifty-eight less a day [87] when he died: Caesar was murdered at the age of fifty-five.

Meanwhile Caesar spent nine months in Egypt. As he subsequently brought Cleopatra to Rome and gave her a separate establishment across the Tiber, her fascinations must have accounted for some of this delay. Cicero heard rumours that Caesar had left Alexandria in June 47 B.C. So he had, but for Pontus, not Rome.

Finally Caesar reached Italy and restored order, *inter alia* pardoning Dolabella who had been trying to bring about abolition of debt. Dolabella was more lucky in saving his skin than Caelius, whose abortive rising in 48 had brought him to a bad end. His connection with Cicero made him very valuable to Caesar. Finally there came a 'tolerably generous letter' (*litterae satis liberales*) from Caesar and then the two met on a pleasant footing. The Quinti also were pardoned, and Caesar seemed in no way prejudiced against Marcus by their unkind talk. In fact, Caesar now did everything he could to conciliate and employ those who had fought against him. Thus Marcus Brutus was entrusted with a province: Cassius was made legate, and subsequently praetor. Before the end of 47 B.C. Cicero divorced Terentia. This added to his financial embarrassments: for he had to repay her dowry. The arrangements for doing this by instalments fell upon Atticus, who never seems to have grumbled at serving his friend: Cicero urged him to concede all her demands.

After all, Cicero himself was a safe investment: for Atticus was his publisher, and now there began a period of intense literary activity, which lasted almost to Cicero's death, and no doubt enabled Atticus to recoup himself for any indebtedness.

Note.—Atticus had lived long in Greece, where the book trade was far older and better established than at Rome. So (*Ad Att.* ii. 1, 2) in 60 B.C. Cicero can ask him to circulate in Greece, of course for sale, with perhaps some presentation copies, his Greek account of his consulship, and similarly (*Ad Att.* iv. 13, 2) in November 55 he says, 'I have worked long and hard at my *De Oratore*: now you may have copies made'. It has usually been supposed that Atticus was the first to establish in Rome the publication and sale of contemporary books, which had hitherto merely been circulated by their authors. This is denied by R. Sommer (*Hermes,* 61, 389) but chiefly on the ground of a somewhat higher estimate than usual of Atticus' character. Atticus was a good friend to Cicero, but his main object in life was to make money, and his domestic staff was therefore, not exclusively of course but largely, composed of slaves who could read and write.

Cicero, who on one occasion writes that he has paid him for a book, which he did not want to be a present, and on another occasion bore with him the expense of a large-paper presentation copy, regrets (*Ad Att.* xiii. 13, 1) that he has caused his friend 'loss' by scrapping the first edition of the *Academica*—the materials and the slaves' time had been wasted —but he says the new edition will be double the size, and it will gratify Atticus' wish to have a work of Cicero dedicated to Varro. What can this mean but that Atticus got the profit or bore the loss of the edition in question? Much that Sommer says is of course correct. Everything of the sort at Rome was very inchoate before Augustus' reign. The bookshops, in one of which Clodius hid from Antony (*Phil.* ii. 9, 2 1), were poor things, and did not sell contemporary literature. Libraries were formed more by exchange and presentation copies than by purchase. Most writers circulated their own works, not being lucky enough to have an Atticus as friend. Cicero did not write for profit or expect any gain from his books. But that the parsimonious Atticus did not, before he died in 32 B.C., benefit pecuniarily by Cicero's writings it is difficult to believe.

Chapter 9

UNDER THE DICTATOR

47-IDES OF MARCH 44 B.C.

*I don't know how it was, but Caesar was most patient
with me.*   *Ad Att.* xiv. 17, 6

*Caesar could never bring himself to hate me, even in the
moment of our dissensions.*   *In Pisonem* 32, 81

THE dictatorship has already been often mentioned.
Its origin goes back to days before the history of
Rome begins. Apparently it was a Latin institution:
for the name *dictator* survived as the title of the chief
magistrate in some Latin towns. Thus Milo (pp. 88,
90, 102) was dictator of Lanuvium. When the regal
period came to an end, the Romans instituted not one
chief magistrate but two annual *consuls* or colleagues:
at first they were called praetors, those who marched
at the head of the civic levies. As they might quarrel,
it was apparently to meet that contingency that it was
decided that one of them might nominate a dictator,
who would then supersede them both. He was also
called 'master of the infantry' (*magister populi*) and
was not allowed to ride a horse himself, but by custom
nominated a 'master of the horse' (*magister equitum*),
who was his lieutenant. In token of his supreme
military authority he was accompanied by twenty-four
lictors, twice the number allotted to a consul, and

these bore, even in the City, in the bundles of rods
(*fasces*) with which they scourged offenders, axes
(*secures*) with which they could behead anyone, if
ordered to do so.   It was generally in time of war,
when the consuls seemed incompetent, that they were
appointed. The period of a dictatorship was limited
to six months.

The institution survived the anomaly of two dictators in the Second Punic War, when the reputation
of Fabius the Delayer (*Cunctator*) was temporarily
low. But as the power of summary execution without
trial had been taken away finally by a Sempronian
Law carried by Gaius Gracchus forbidding any decision affecting the status of a citizen which was not
ordered by the popular assembly, it fell into desue-
tude.   Sulla had made it very unpopular by his proscriptions. Pompey definitely rejected it when it was
suggested in 53 B.C.*: nor was the offer made to him
in 49 B.C. when it would have been really useful, for
though the Senate had committed to his charge the
defence of Italy, he could not control the senatorial
possessors of military command (*imperium*) like
Domitius and Cicero himself.   It was reserved for
Caesar to be appointed by means of a law.   Strictly
speaking, the law empowered the praetor Lepidus,
in the absence of the consuls, to name him.   His first
dictatorship lasted for eleven days. He was then
consul for 48 B.C. His second dictatorship lasted
for a year and ran out. He was consul for the third

* By Hirrus (see p. 120) and Vinicianus (*Ad Fam.* viii. 4, 3).   In
Mommsen's *History* (English Translation), iv. p. 341, 'Dictatorship of
Pompeius' (marginal abstract) is quite misleading. The text says 'the
undivided consulship'. When in 59 B.C. Gaius Cato called Pompey an
unofficial dictator, it meant only that Pompey was working the oracle
(*Q.F.* i. 2, 15).

time in 46 B.C. and Schnabel has pointed out a coin of his, on which he is described as 'Consul III' but not as dictator. His next dictatorship, conferred after his fourfold triumph, was for ten years, and he combined with it a fourth and fifth consulship. Finally when his friends offered him and he accepted a perpetual dictatorship, the title of king could be safely refused, as being unpopular and conferring no extra power. As will be seen, Cicero hoped, up to the beginning of 46 and even later, for some sort of constitution (*aliqua res publica*), but the cumulative holding of the consulship, the constitutional office, with the dictatorship, the emergency office, and the grant of a life dictatorship destroyed his hopes and those of many others. The appetite grows in eating, and increasing servility made Caesar sometimes arrogant. It may be said that, so far as laws and decrees of the Senate could make it, his position was constitutional, but as tribunician sacrosanctity and an oath of all senators to observe it had been added, it was absolutely unprecedented. The worst of it was that it was based on the power of the sword.

To-day there is a recrudescence of dictatorships. Some have been set up and fallen; some seem more durable. England tried a military despotism once under Cromwell and did not like it. Mussolini's power is more assured than that of Caesar, because it commends itself to a greater proportion of the people, and the same may possibly be the case with Hitler. But let there be no mistake about the fact that the dictatorship in Rome, though in early days constitutionally conferred and temporary, in the case of Sulla and Caesar was simply the power of the sword.

They seized the position because they were leaders of armies devoted to them.

A dictatorship is the negation of freedom. It means the death or exile of all opponents. It means the silencing of criticism in all classes of society.* It means interference with literature and the muzzling of the Press, as in Italy and Germany. It means interference with art, as in Ireland where President de Valera—really a dictator—will not allow plays of which he disapproves to be performed, even in U.S.A.† It means interference with education and religion, as in Germany where the process of dragooning the Protestant ‡ and Roman Catholic Churches simultaneously is going on before our eyes. People have the governments they deserve, and it is better when they set up a dictator for themselves, than when a Caesar appoints himself. But what happens when they cease to admire him, and is he to nominate a successor? In 1874 Dr Congreve, the chief exponent of Positivism, argued that a dictatorship in a time of transition was preservative of order and averted anarchy; but what is to happen if a dictator regards himself as in power for life?

Caesar had good reason for thinking his position permanent, and that is why he became more and more unpopular with the leading men of Rome, the

---

* 'Under the German national campaign against "carpers and critics", a woman in a village near Mainz, who had complained that the economic situation of Germany would never improve, has been ordered to report at the burgomaster's office in her village daily for three weeks and to declare "Things have already improved, and will improve further"' (*The Times*, May 15th, 1934).

† Synge, *The Playboy of the Western World*; Sean O'Casey, *The Plough and the Stars* (*The Times*, May 10th, 1934).

‡ A. Nygren, *The Church Controversy in Germany*. S.C.M. Press, 1934.

L

more he killed in battle and the more he pardoned afterwards. Not that he did not carry out changes which the time demanded, and which indeed were overdue. The enfranchisement of the Transpadanes came early in 49 B.C. by a law of the praetor Roscius, who had stayed in Rome and not gone to Epirus. Thus at last Italy was unified; and be it remembered, Pompey's father had been the first to advance the position of the Northern Italians. It is very improbable that Cicero on principle objected to this: for he had vehemently denounced the behaviour of the consul Marcellus to the citizen of Novum Comum (p. 120). Nor, we are sure, had Cicero any objection to the reform of the calendar: all he disliked was the substitution of 'July' for *Quintilis*, with its implication of royalty. He must have rejoiced at the exclusion from the juries of the needy and venal *tribuni aerarii*, about whom he once made the barely translatable joke, that they were not so much possessed of cash, as, true to their name, recipients of cash (*venal*). He certainly did not object to the limitation of the tenure of a province to one year for an ex-praetor and two years for a proconsul: he had escaped with one himself. Prejudiced as he was against agrarian laws,* he must have felt Caesar was very moderate in his grants of land, and his objection to the small remission of debt is not very strongly expressed. Finally he felt that disorder, such as Clodius had organised and tried to make permanent,

---

* But it was the second law of Caesar to evict the old tenants in Campania and redistribute the land in lots, that moved Cicero's anger, not the first. In *De Officiis*, ii. 22, 79, he thus states his objection. 'How is it fair that a man who never had any property should take possession of lands occupied for many years or even generations, and that he who had them before should lose possession of them?'

was checked with a strong hand, and that there was no scope for another Catiline. Was it then mere unreasonableness that made him a passive resister to the new régime? Why could he not support it?

The reason was that Caesar, possibly owing to his nine months in Egypt, had been so dazzled by this last surviving Hellenistic divine monarchy, that he was determined to inflict something similar on Rome. That his person should be declared sacrosanct was nothing new: any tribune had been that, at least till Cato and Metellus had found the office no protection. But that his supposed descent from Iulus, Aeneas, Anchises and Venus should be taken seriously, and that the temple of Venus Genetrix was intended to be the focus of a new cult, that a month should be named after him and his portrait be on the coinage, that his image should be carried among those of the gods next to Victory (July 45), that a statue of him with the inscription 'To the Invincible God' should be set up in the Temple of Quirinus—in fact that all the forms and ceremonies of the Hellenistic divine king should be introduced into Rome *—all this made Cicero so angry, that he hardly dared to allude to Caesar, except in writing to his most intimate and trustworthy friend, lest he should be held guilty of high treason. Personally of course he always got on excellently with Caesar, who was one of the very few men in Rome capable of appreciating his own great gifts, but he saw very little of him and did not seek his society. 'Let us give up flattery', he says to Atticus, 'and be at least half-free: and we can manage that by keeping quiet and out of sight.'

* See Ulrich Wilcken, *Alexander the Great* (translated by G. C. Richards), pp. 279-280. Dio, not Cicero, gives the inscription.

But he was not ungrateful for the positive merits of Caesar's rule. In writing to Sulpicius who was like-minded with himself, he describes Caesar as a marvel of moderation; and to Caecina he says 'I often admire the high principle, the justice and wisdom of Caesar', particularly pointing out Caesar's complimentary references to Pompey and his promotion of ex-Pompeians. Three times he pleaded before Caesar for the pardon of opponents, for Marcus Marcellus in September 46 B.C., for Quintus Ligarius in November, and some time the following year for king Deiotarus. Caesar, it is said, was much affected by hearing once again the well-known voice of the great orator: it was Cicero's forte to excite compassion. The first two were pardoned: Deiotarus' case was reserved, and the Ides of March saved him.

In the *Pro Marcello* Cicero broke a silence of six years: for since he had pleaded for Milo unsuccessfully and for Saufeius successfully in 52 B.C., his voice had not been heard in the law-courts, and hardly if at all in the Senate. Mommsen informs us that at this time 'Caesar still cherished the magnificent dream of a free commonwealth, although he was unable to transfer it either to his adversaries or to his adherents'. Doubtless in the same way Mussolini and Hitler cherish the dream of a free Italy and a free Germany: but their idea of freedom seems to exclude any difference of opinion or free discussion. Certainly at this time (September 46 B.C.) Cicero hoped that in some measure Caesar might restore the Republic. In describing the scene in the Senate when Marcellus was pardoned, to Sulpicius, then governor of Achaia, he says, 'This seemed to me so glorious a day, that I imagined I saw before me some fair vision of the Republic rising, as it were, from the dead'. Hence the exuberance of his gratitude. It was a notable case of an unlooked-for reconciliation: for Marcellus was the last of Caesar's opponents whom he could have been expected to pardon.

The following passage of the *Pro Marcello* shows his feeling that day. 'If the end of your immortal deeds, Gaius Caesar, be such that, after the overthrow of your opponents, you leave the Republic in the condition in which it now is, beware, I beseech you, lest your superhuman merit be rather admired than glorious, if indeed glory be a distinguished and widespread reputation for services to fellow citizens, to the fatherland or to mankind. This is then what remains for you to desire, this is the final act, to this you must devote your efforts *to give a constitution to the Republic (constituere rempublicam* [88]*).'* Then Caesar can say he has lived long enough, and his victories will go down to posterity. 'But unless this city is stabilised by your designs and institutions, your name will travel far and wide, but have no sure ·dwelling place or fixed abode.'

In Cicero's Letters we can follow the hopes he had of this 'constitution' and their gradual disappointment. In April 46 B.C., after the news of Caesar's victory at Thapsus had reached Rome, he writes to Varro, explaining why he is himself staying quietly at Rome, and suggesting that Varro should do the same. 'Let us', he says, 'be fixed in our determination to live together in these studies of ours, in which we previously sought only delight but now seek also our *salvation; if any one desires to employ us, not merely as master builders, but even as masons to build up the Republic, not to hang back but rather to hasten forward*

with alacrity: if no one avails himself of our services,
at any rate to write and read Political Constitutions;*
and if not in the Senate house and the Forum, at all
events in literature and books, after the manner of the
ancient philosophers, *strenuously to serve the State*, and
pursue enquiries on Morals and Laws.' Varro and
Cicero might still hope to be given appropriate
functions by Caesar; Varro was actually made lib-
rarian of the new Palatine Library. In September
46 B.C. Cicero writes to Publius Servilius Isauricus,
who had just been sent to govern Asia: 'I am not, I
think, without hope that our colleague Caesar (as
augur) will be, and indeed is anxious that we should
have a constitution (*aliqua respublica*): and it was of
great importance that you should participate in his
deliberations. But as it is more advantageous, I
mean more glorious, for you to govern Asia, I am
bound to regard it as more desirable.' Servilius was
a moderate and reasonable Caesarian, whom Caesar
had chosen, as the most respectable aristocrat available, to be consul with him in 48 B.C. In these
words the wish of course was father to the thought,
and it is only an illustration of Cicero's attempt to
teach constitutionalism to the Caesarians. Servilius
did stand by the Senate in 44 and 43, except that he
had a violent controversy with Cicero over the grant
of honours to Plancus.[89]

In May 46 B.C. the news of Cato's suicide at
Utica reached Cicero. By June 13th it had been
suggested to him that he should write an *éloge* on
Cato, and with his usual rapidity of writing, he
finished the task to his own complete satisfaction in

---

* Cicero may have been again taking up work at his treatise *On the
Laws*.

July. It is to be inferred from a letter of July 27th, 45 B.C., that the pamphlet had a second edition in 45, when he inserted the characteristic anecdote of Cato at the age of four.[90] The Italian leader, Pompaedius Silo, tried to induce the boy to influence his uncle, Livius Drusus, to support the grant of the franchise to the Italians. The boy refused, and even when Silo held him out of the window and threatened to drop him, remained 'undismayed and fearless'.

This Republican manifesto was answered by Hirtius, who in his turn was critical of Cato but very complimentary to Cicero, while Brutus who had also produced a *Cato* seemed to Cicero very niggardly of praise to himself. We do not possess Caesar's *Anti-Cato*: but on August 12th, 45, Caesar praised the style of Cicero's *Cato*, and August 26th, 45, Cicero reciprocated the compliment. Altogether the pamphlet warfare was carried on in the most gentlemanly way; while arms seemed to dominate the Roman world, the real conflict was one of ideas.

In May 45 Cicero planned and actually composed an open letter to Caesar: it was his last effort to extract a 'constitution' from the dictator. Atticus wisely showed this to Caesar's intimates, who suggested so many alterations, that it was never sent. 'If I can't make a *coup*', says Cicero, 'I won't make a fiasco.'[91] He also remarks, on hearing that Caesar would not go to fight the Parthians without leaving a settlement at Rome behind him (*nisi constitutis rebus*), that this was exactly what he had advised in the suppressed letter. But Cicero's and Caesar's ideas of a 'constitution' were poles apart, and absolutely irreconcilable.

The first note of bitterness comes in a letter of
May 17th, 45 B.C.,[92] when he has heard that a statue
of Caesar (according to Dio, inscribed 'To the
Invincible God') has been erected in the Temple of
Quirinus (the deified Romulus) near Atticus' house:
'I would rather he shared the temple of Quirinus
than that of Salus' (Safety)—a plain allusion to the
reputed end of Romulus who was said to have been
torn to pieces by the senators. A few days later
he calls Caesar 'the puppet messmate of Quirinus',
and asks how, if even Alexander, the pupil of Aristotle,
after becoming Great King, was tyrannical, cruel
and ungovernable, will Caesar bear 'his moderate
letter'.[93] And so he abandons as insoluble a
problem that might tax an Archimedes, how to give
good advice without causing offence and so doing
harm instead of good. He was ready of course to
respond to any personal courtesy, such as Caesar's
letter of condolence on the death of Tullia, dated
'Seville April 20th', which he received on July 2nd.
But on August 2nd he calls Caesar 'the king', and
says he would be alarmed by the calumnies of his
nephew, if 'the king' did not know that he, Cicero,
had no spirit left in him. On August 7th he scoffs
at Brutus' hope that Caesar will join the 'good' party.
'Where will Caesar find them, unless he hangs himself and joins them in the other world?'[94] What
Brutus' ideas were on August 7th, it is impossible
to say, as we do not know what was 'the sudden long
journey' which he planned in July. We suspect
that he was still hoping to be Caesar's principal heir.
He had recently divorced his wife, in a manner
condemned by public opinion,[95] and married Porcia,
widow of Bibulus. Cato's daughter was made of

sterner stuff than Cato's nephew and was no doubt
a convinced Republican. So now the influence of
the wife was pitted against the influence of the
mother, Servilia, who still counted for something
with Caesar. Brutus was selected to be city-praetor
for 44 B.C. What Caesar saw in him it is difficult
to say, for socially he was unendurable. Not once
only Cicero intimates to Atticus, always a backer of
Brutus, that he cannot endure Brutus' society. 'We
cannot live together', he says; 'you know what con-
stitutes social intercourse': he uses the Greek word
that corresponds to our 'conviviality'. Of this at
any rate Cicero was an impeccable judge, though his
political wisdom sometimes failed him. Brutus
could not complain of any lack of attention on
Cicero's part: for Cicero had dedicated to him in
46 B.C. the treatise called *Brutus* or *On Famous
Orators*, and also the *Paradoxes of the Stoics*. The
opposite influences on Brutus are illustrated by
Cicero's reference to the pedigree of the Junian
family, including Ahala and the old Brutus, which
Atticus had drawn up to hang in Brutus' library.[96]
This shows that the appeal to Brutus on the score of
his family traditions had already been made: probably
as yet it had not taken effect.

Later in December Cicero was honoured by a visit
from one who was now monarch in all but name. It
was at Cicero's villa at Cumae.[97] 'What a formidable guest, but he leaves no regrets behind him: for
all passed off very pleasantly. When he reached my
neighbour Philippus (the step-father of Octavian) on
the evening of the 18th, the house was so crowded
with soldiers that there was hardly a room unoccu-
pied for Caesar to dine in. There were two thousand

men. I was worried as to what would happen next day, and Cassius Barba came to the rescue and set guards over me. A camp was pitched in the grounds and the house put under guard. On the 19th he stayed at Philippus' house till 1 P.M. and saw no one: going over his accounts with Balbus, I suppose. Then he took a walk on the beach. After 2 P.M. he took a bath. He received the news about Mamurra* and exhibited no emotion. He was anointed and sat down to table. As he was undergoing a course of emetics, he ate and drank with appetite and without fear, the dinner being good and "well cooked and seasoned with pleasant discourse, and if you want to know agreeable". Besides him his suite were entertained liberally in three separate rooms: the lower freedmen and slaves had plenty and the upper sort were entertained in style. In fact, we seemed just ordinary human beings (Caesar did not "assume the god"). Still he was not the sort of guest to whom you would say "Please look me up on the way back". Once is enough. There were no serious topics, but plenty of literary talk. In a word, he was pleased and enjoyed himself. . . . That is all about my entertainment, or billeting, objectionable but not uncomfortable.' Later he gives us an anecdote of a visit he paid to Caesar in Rome to make some request for a friend. When Caesar heard that Cicero had been kept waiting, he said: 'Can I doubt that I am heartily detested, when Cicero sits waiting and cannot see me at his convenience? Yet if anyone is good-natured, he is.' Next day Cicero gives a corrected version.

---

* Mamurra was Caesar's chief engineer in Gaul and amassed such wealth that it raised the ire of the poet Catullus (Poems 29 and 57). The news is probably of Mamurra's death.

Caesar said to Matius, 'Can I be foolish enough to think that this man, good-natured though he is, is friendly to me, when he has to sit and wait for my convenience so long?' This certainly sounds more authentic.

The year 46 B.C. was really not unhappy for Cicero. He helped his friends as much as possible by his friendly relations with prominent Caesarians. 'In the old days', he says, 'when I was monarch of the courts, I had no such deference paid me by anybody, as I now receive from all of Caesar's most intimate friends.' Most of his letters of commendation preserved to us date from this period. He wrote to many political exiles giving them advice and promising his services 'to the extent of his influence': he has no access to Caesar himself but he knows his friends'. Thus besides Marcellus and Ligarius, we have letters to the exiles, Torquatus, Caecina, Nigidius Figulus and his old friend Plancius, their parts being now reversed. Never in his life had Cicero shown himself more obliging and that is a strong statement.

About this time Cicero made friendly overtures to his only rival in learning among contemporary Romans. Marcus Terentius Varro of Reate, and so, like Cicero, Italian in sympathy rather than purely Roman, was a voluminous author and a learned scholar, but had also taken a part in public life. He had always been attached to Pompey. He served under him against the pirates and Mithridates, he commanded Pompey's forces in Further Spain, was with Cicero at Dyrrachium in 49 B.C. and was subsequently pardoned by Caesar. During the year of Caesar's first consulship he is mentioned as being in Pompey's confidence, which Cicero was not, and is

described now as 'satisfactory', now as 'tortuous and
dishonest': Atticus is begged to use his influence
with Varro in Cicero's favour before and during the
exile. In 54 B.C. Cicero asked Atticus for the loan
of some of Varro's books and tried to work Varro into
his dialogue *On the Republic*, but did not actually do
so. There are several letters of Cicero to Varro in
the years 46 and 45, and Cicero dedicated to him the
recast *Academics*. From a letter written June 24th,
45, it appears that Varro had promised two years before, but not yet fulfilled the promise, to dedicate a
work to Cicero.* Ultimately he did dedicate to him
the later books of his great work on the 'Latin Language'. Varro was now seventy, a man of much
learning but little talent: in practical life he had been
a soldier. He was apt to find fault,† and Cicero describes him as an unwelcome guest at Tusculum
when he arrived unexpectedly.[98] There was very
little in common between the two men, and it is a
probable conjecture that Varro's influence with
Pompey had always been hostile to Cicero.

It remains to give a brief sketch of Cicero's domestic affairs and literary activities in the years 46 and
45. Early in 46 it would seem that for financial
reasons Cicero contemplated a second marriage. He
apparently consulted one of the Roman matrons who
acted as professional matchmakers. He tells Atticus
he will not have Pompey's daughter; and of another
lady, whom he supposes Atticus knows, he says he
never saw such a fright. The match ultimately arranged with his young ward Publilia was merely

---

* *Ad Att.* xiii. 12, 1. He is a 'slow coach'.
† *Ad Att.* xiii. 25 quotes Homer, *Iliad*, xi. 654: 'he is a fearsome man:
the blameless he would blame'.

mercenary and in every way lamentable. From the first Publilia was jealous of Tullia, and on Tullia's death (February 45) soon after the marriage the inconsolable father sent his young wife back to her family and refused to receive her parents. Even when his literary lady friend Caerellia came to intercede for Publilia he proved adamant. Cicero is not the only man who has thus made a fool of himself at the age of sixty.

It is somewhat astonishing that Cicero could bring himself to write in a friendly way to Dolabella after Tullia's death; but the aristocratic young scoundrel (he was only twenty-four, whereas when Tullia died she was thirty-four) always showed his most agreeable side to his father-in-law. Besides it was of some consequence to Cicero to get the dowry back, if he could, and there was an infant grandson whose interests had to be considered. When Dolabella wrote to say he was defending Cicero against the malevolence of young Quintus,* Cicero received the overture gladly. Though under the crushing blow of Tullia's death he politely declined an immediate visit, he received Dolabella on June 18th.

After the final defeat of the Pompeians at Munda (March 17th, 45) Cicero, seeing that politics and public life were definitely closed to him, entered on a period of astonishing literary activity. He had finished his *Consolatio* for his daughter, while disconsolately roaming on the sea-shore at Astura. Assisted by his faithful Tiro he then performed prodigies of literary composition. First he wrote a

---

* The Caesarians all resented Quintus' behaviour. Hirtius took no notice of him and Pollio actually wrote from Spain to warn Cicero about the doings of 'my blackguardly relative'.

popular work urging men to the study of Philosophy, called after his great rival *Hortensius*. Perhaps this passage of St Augustine is an extract from this treatise.

'As we meditate day and night and sharpen the edge of the intellect, which is the eye of the mind, and see that it is not dulled, our hopes rise high. Either, if our feelings and thoughts are mortal and transitory, when our human tasks are done, we shall have a pleasant setting, a painless extinction and a sort of repose from life. Or if, as was the view of the greatest and most famous philosophers of old, our souls are eternal and divine, then we must believe that if they have always been exercised in reason and research, and the less they have been entangled by human faults and failings, the easier will be their ascent and return to heaven. Wherefore whether we wish for a peaceful extinction after a life spent in these pursuits, or if we wish to pass without delay from this to a far better home, we must equally devote ourselves with all care and pains to these studies.'[99] It is much to be regretted that we have lost a work which so deeply influenced the young Augustine that he writes: 'In my unsettled time of life, when I desired to shine, out of a damnable and vainglorious ambition and a delight in human vanity, in the ordinary course of study I came upon a book of Cicero, whose speech all admire, but not so his heart.[100] This book of his contains an exhortation to philosophy and is called *Hortensius*. But this book altered my affections and turned my prayers to Thyself, O Lord, and caused me to have other purposes and desires. Every vain hope became at once worthless to me; and I longed with an incredibly burning

desire for an immortality of wisdom and began at
once to arise that I might return to Thee. For not
to sharpen my tongue (which training in that my
nineteenth year, my father having died two years
before, I was purchasing with my mother's allowance), not to sharpen my tongue did I employ that
book: it did not infuse into me its style but its
matter.' Perhaps Cicero's greatest achievement is to
have decisively influenced the youthful Augustine.
The master of words had become a master of thought.

On May 13th, 45, he writes from Astura to Atticus
that he has finished two long treatises: 'it is the only
way in which I can get away from my misery'. It is
likely that these were the two books named after
Lucullus and Catulus respectively into which the
Academics ('Treatise on the Human Understanding)
were originally divided.* By May 21st he must have
begun work on the *De Finibus*. Apparently Atticus
said to him he would have a hard job in rendering
Greek philosophical terms into Latin. He replies:
'Don't be uneasy about the Latin Language. You
will say, "What? when writing on such subjects?"
They are copies and do not give me much trouble.
I only supply words of which I have plenty.' † He
is probably too modest about his matter, but as to
his diction he is perfectly right. No one but himself
could have rendered the thought of Greek writers in
such an easy and fluent style.

In October Cicero induced himself to attend
Caesar's great games in Rome. It must have been
a bitter experience, since Caesar, who had in 46

---

* Of this he says (*Ad Att.* xiii. 25, 3): 'May I be hanged if I ever take
so much trouble to write anything again'.

† *Verba tantum adfero quibus abundo* (*Ad Att.* xii. 52, 3).

nominally only triumphed over foreign enemies, after
Munda celebrated a triumph for a victory in Civil
War, and actually accorded a share in it to two insignificant legates. Yet he writes to his brother
augur Cornificius that he has seen his *bête noir*
Plancus Bursa* without turning a hair, and listened
to the verses of Publilius Syrus and the Knight
Laberius: no doubt he enjoyed the outspokenness of
the latter. He only wants a kindred spirit with whom
to laugh at it all: will Cornificius come and be that
kindred spirit? Once more the resilience of Cicero's
disposition had asserted itself and he could be gay
again. For the rest of the year—only interrupted by
the visit of Caesar already described—he was busy
with the *De Finibus*. After completing these five
books he began the *Tusculan Disputations*, which must
have fully occupied him nearly up to the Ides of
March 44 B.C. Between December 21st, 45, and
April 7th, 44, we have no letters to Atticus to en-
lighten us: the two friends must have been near to
one another in Rome.

In the latter part of 45 the good-for-nothing young
Quintus was the chief worry of the family. He was
in debt and his father wanted him to marry a rich
wife: for just now he was pretending, only pretending, his uncle thinks, to have quarrelled with his
mother. 'Am I to renounce him altogether', says
Cicero to Atticus, 'or am I to take to crooked ways?'
Apparently Atticus advised the latter course: for we
have an amusing letter written from Tusculum in
December.[101] 'Young Quintus came to see me very

---

* Cicero had prosecuted him in 52—a rare instance of Cicero as
prosecutor—and got him exiled: but he had now returned under the
general amnesty.

down in the mouth. I asked why he was in the blues. "Can you ask," said he, "when I have a journey before me, a journey to a war, and one that is both dangerous and even disgraceful." * "What makes you go then?" said I. "Debt," said he, "and yet not even enough money for the journey." Here I borrowed from your style of eloquence: I held my tongue. He went on, "But what worries me most is my uncle" (Atticus). "Why?" said I. "Because he is angry with me." "Why do you let him be?" said I, "for I would rather put it that way than say, Why do you make him angry?" "I won't let him," said he, "for I will remove the reason." "Very right of you," said I, "but if it is not objectionable, I should like to know what is the reason." "Because my hesitation, which lady I was to marry, annoyed my mother and therefore him too. Now nothing is worth that. So I will do what they want." "Good luck to you," said I, "and I applaud your resolution. But when is it to come off?" "The time doesn't matter," said he, "as I have made up my mind to it." "Well," said I, "I advise you to do it before you start. In that way you will oblige your father too." "I will do as you advise," said he, and there the conversation ended.' But the young scapegrace did not do it. Very probably it was all a scheme for getting some money out of his paternal uncle, his maternal uncle having cut up rough: but Cicero did not rise to the bait. After all that the rascal had been saying about him in the camp of Caesar, Cicero was very lenient in seeing him at all. Next year Quintus was

---

* The commentators give no help here, but it looks as if Quintus was thinking of offering his valuable services to Sextus Pompey, who revived the Pompeian cause in Spain and then took to piracy on a large scale and troubled the Mediterranean for ten long years.

M

desperately afraid that his father would marry an heiress called Aquilia and declared he would not stand her as a stepmother. Later on he tried his luck with Antony, but fell out with him and then induced his uncle to introduce him to Brutus and Cassius. The last mention we have of him is when Cicero took him to Brutus, who dismissed him with an embrace and a kiss, but did not actually promise him employment. When this young man shared the fate of his uncle and his father, the world did not miss much.

One very curious episode of the year 45 was the intense desire of the bereaved father to immortalize Tullia, by erecting a shrine to her in some public place, where it would be seen by as many people as possible. For several months he worried Atticus to purchase a suitable site, suggesting first one and then another. Atticus knew better than to oppose the whim and pretended to humour it, but really raised objections or threw difficulties in the way of every particular suggestion, till finally Cicero dropped mentioning the subject and apparently forgot all about it. It was at any rate an amiable weakness, if it is one to which it is difficult to find any parallel.

Chapter 10

CONFUSION
AND DISILLUSIONMENT
IDES OF MARCH—DECEMBER 9TH, 44 B.C.

*Now I am not so much consoled with the Ides of March as
I was: for it was a great blunder, unless those youths
(Brutus and Cassius) by other noble deeds wipe out this blot.*
Ad Att. xiv. 22, 2. May 14th, 44

INDIRECTLY no doubt the attitude of passive resist-
ance which Cicero took up may have assisted dissatisfaction with the Dictator to come to a head: but with
the actual conspiracy which produced the tragedy of
March 13th, 44 B.C., he had nothing to do. Shakespeare, who is often remarkably true to history in
Julius Caesar, makes Brutus say in deprecating a
proposal to bring in Cicero:

> O name him not.
> For he will never follow anything
> That other men begin.

Besides, Cicero's literary activity seems to preclude
any such possibility. He cannot have finished the
Tusculan Disputations in five books much before the
Ides of March. Immediately after that he seems to
have written *On Divination*, dedicated to his brother,
and *On Destiny*, dedicated to Hirtius.

It is quite uncertain whether the little note to Basilus [102] refers to the assassination. It has been referred to September 47 B.C.* Basilus was a very minor conspirator to receive so much credit. It is not clear whether Cicero was present at the murder, though his expression 'the pleasure given to my eyes by the just death of a tyrant' [103] makes it likely: but Professors Tyrrell and Purser, in their great edition of the letters, do not think the phrase conclusive. Mr. Froude in his *Caesar* surpasses himself by quoting from Cicero,[104] 'Brutus, waving his bloody dagger, called on Cicero by name and congratulated him on the recovery of freedom', and omitting to mention that these are words attributed to Antony.† He might have mentioned that Dio Cassius puts them into the mouth of the Caesarian Calenus, who says that the murderers ran out into the Forum and called for Cicero. This goes far to show that Cicero was justified in repudiating the statement of Antony.

Had Cicero joined the conspiracy, he says he would have insisted on Antony's sharing Caesar's fate. Brutus, it appears, vetoed this; and Trebonius, who, according to Cicero and Plutarch,‡ had sounded Antony about such a plot in the beginning of 45 B.C. at Narbo, was entrusted with the duty of keeping Antony away from the scene of the murder. But at any rate Cicero would have insisted on a definite plan of operation after the murder was accomplished.

* By Professor Merrill in *Classical Philology*, viii. 48.

† Mr. Froude has also stated that the Second *Philippic* was delivered, when it was never spoken at all, and that *Pro Marcello* of a year and a half earlier was delivered a few weeks before Caesar's death.

‡ Plutarch, *Antony*, xiii.: *Philippic*, ii. 14, 34. Was this true? If true, why did Antony not betray Trebonius? on the principle *qui s'excuse, s'accuse?*

If Cicero had nothing to do with the genesis of the conspiracy, who had? It seems likely that Cassius was the leading spirit. We have heard of him as a soldier of merit, who had stemmed the tide of a Parthian invasion. He had been a Pompeian, but according to Appian after Pharsalia surrendered to Caesar the fleet he commanded. Others say this was a Lucius Cassius. But certainly Gaius Cassius became Caesar's legate * and very probably went with him to the war against Pharnaces. Whether it be true that Cassius intended to kill Caesar at the mouth of the Cydnus in Cilicia, as Cicero states,[105] or simply that he met Caesar there and was pardoned at the intercession of Brutus,[106] it is difficult to say. He did not go to Africa or Spain—neither did Antony— but remained in South Italy waiting the issue of events, and occasionally corresponding with Cicero, sometimes on points of Epicurean philosophy. In January 45 B.C. he writes to Cicero: 'I am full of anxiety as to what is going on in Spain. Hang me, if I would not rather have the old and merciful master (Caesar) rather than make trial of a new and cruel one. You know what an ass Gnaeus is' (this was Pompey's son, who had threatened to murder Cicero at Corcyra): 'you know how he thinks we (cultured people) have always laughed at him. I fear that in his boorish way he will answer our chaff with the sword.'[107] After the elimination of Gnaeus he hurried to Rome and Caesar made him praetor, but apparently did not trust him. He was a man of vehement and passionate temper and apparently worked

---

* *Ad Fam.* vi. 6, 10. Cp. *Ad Fam.* xv. 15, 3 : 'you took a line which enabled you to share Caesar's counsels and foresee what was going to happen'.

upon his brother-in-law Marcus Brutus, so as to fit
him for the family rôle of liberator. Brutus was
thirty-five; Cassius certainly over forty and, as the
senior, the driving force of the conspiracy.

An anecdote of Dio Cassius[108] may be unhistorical,
but illustrates the character of the man. On the day
after the murder, the sons of Lepidus and Antony
were sent as hostages to the Capitol, Brutus came
down to sup with Lepidus, Cassius with Antony.
During the meal Antony said to Cassius: 'Have you
perchance even now a dagger up your sleeve?' To
this Cassius replied: 'Yes, and a big one, if you too
should desire to make yourself a tyrant'.

Gaius Trebonius may have been a few years older
than Cassius, as he must have been thirty, when he
was quaestor in 60 B.C. He was an old friend of the
Cicerones. As tribune in 55 B.C. he made himself
useful to the Triumvirs, by proposing the law which
gave Syria to Crassus and the two Spains to Pompey.
He then served Caesar as legate in Gaul for five
years and was rewarded by the position of city
praetor in 48 B.C. In this capacity he foiled the mad
schemes of Caelius and was then sent in 47 to Spain,
out of which he was driven by the Pompeians in 46.
He showed his friendship with Cicero by compiling
and dedicating to him *Ciceroniana*, a collection of
Cicero's wit and wisdom.* He accepted from
Caesar the position of *consul suffectus* (consul elected

---

* In *Ad Fam.* xv. 21, 2 Cicero gratefully acknowledges the compliment. 'This book you have sent me, what a revelation it is of your
affection for me. First, because whatever I have said seems brilliant to
you (not so perhaps to anyone else), and secondly, because these mots of
mine, be they brilliant or be they not, become perfectly beautiful when
you are the teller. Why, even before my name is reached, people have
hardly a laugh left in them.'

after the usual time) near the end of 45 with the government of Asia to follow, which was very dishonourable, if he was already in the plot. On his way to Asia, he looked up young Marcus, and sent a good report of him to the not unnaturally anxious father.* A year later he was murdered by Dolabella at Smyrna.

With Decimus Brutus, whose ingratitude to Caesar was worse than that of any other conspirator, Cicero probably had little acquaintance, till he corresponded with him as governor of Cisalpine Gaul in 43 B.C.: nor are we aware of any close connection between Cicero and the rest of the conspirators. If there were sixty persons in the plot, it is surprising both that the secret was kept so well, and that they did not make up their minds what to do afterwards. Some had been Pompeians, some Caesarians: both found the idea of a new monarch intolerable. Probably most of them were under forty: it was the madness of youth.

Cicero seems to have visited the conspirators in the Capitol on the evening of the murder. Next day Dolabella assumed the *insignia* of a consul and appears to have made overtures to them. On the 17th, the day of the *Liberalia*, exactly a year after the debacle of the Pompeians at Munda, the Senate met in the Temple of Tellus. Cicero claims that he laid the foundations of the restored Republic. At least he did what he could in supporting an amnesty. The speech put in his mouth by Dio has a very plausible air in its allusions to Roman history, and to the amnesty at Athens after the defeat of the Thirty Tyrants.

---

* Young Cicero was supposed to be attending the lectures of Cratippus the Peripatetic, 'the foremost philosopher of the present age' (*De Off*. iii. 1, 5) at Athens.

It contains only a very brief reference to Caesar's acts: certainly Cicero did not oppose the confirmation of them decided on that day. Neither he nor anyone else foresaw the wide construction that Antony would put on Caesar's acts. In fact Cicero seems to have unduly underrated the cleverness and forcefulness of Antony: thus on April 9th he conjectures that Antony is concerned with feasting rather than plotting mischief. Antony as consul was in the strong position of constitutional head of the state, and he made most unscrupulous use of his position. For the reading of the will and the funeral, so vividly described by Shakespeare, the veterans flocked into Rome; and after that the liberators had to skulk about their country estates, except those who, like Decimus Brutus and Trebonius, had provinces to which to retire. It was extremely humiliating for Brutus, who though praetor dared not show his face in Rome, and Cassius, who was also praetor and equally unpopular.

When Cicero says that it was a pity Antony was not removed too, he is only speaking in the light of subsequent events: it is quite likely that had he been a conspirator he would have taken the view that the tyrant and the tyrant alone deserved to die. Soon his enthusiasm over the 'heroes' cools and he bewails the fact that liberty has been recovered, but not the Republic. He retires from Rome and renews his pleasant intercourse with prominent Caesarians. He stays with Matius, who is in despair and can see nothing but anarchy ahead. Balbus however meets him at Puteoli and bids him dismiss his fears of troubles with Gauls or Germans. On the arrival of Caesar's chief heir, the eighteen-year-old Octavius, Balbus acts as intermediary between him and Cicero. On

April 22nd Cicero says: 'Octavius is here on terms of respect and friendship with us. His people address him as Caesar, but Philippus (Octavius' stepfather) does not and so I do not either. I hold it impossible for a loyal citizen to do so.' Cicero resumes his instruction of Hirtius in rhetoric; and Pansa, the other consul-designate for 43 B.C., becomes his pupil too. He says: 'I have no love for these consuls-designate who have forced me to declaim to them so that even at the waters I can have no peace.[109] He taught them rhetoric: they taught him to enjoy good dinners. Not one of these people connected Cicero with the Ides of March.

Dolabella had successfully asserted his claim to be consul, and Antony had somewhat contemptuously acknowledged him as a colleague: after all a sole consul was a contradiction in terms. Still the relations between Cicero and Antony were quite correct. We possess three letters of Antony to Cicero. The one sent in May 49 [110] Cicero describes as nasty, because though effusively civil—he refers to Tullia as a peerless lady, and uses both Latin verbs for affection to describe his feeling for Cicero—it was meant to prevent him from leaving Italy. The second is the dispatch of Spartan brevity [111] (p. 135). The third * was sent off late in April 44 and is very politely worded. The exiles are being restored, and Antony asks Cicero as a favour to himself to consent to the recall from exile of Sextus Clodius, a retainer of his old enemy Publius.[112] He will not allow it, if Cicero withholds his consent, but recommends a closing of Cicero's

---

* *Ad Att.* xiv. 13a: *Philippic*, ii. 4, 7: the answer (*Ad Att.* xiv. 13b) was read in the Senate by Antony, and Cicero vigorously denounces this as an ungentlemanly act.

feud with the Clodii as likely to promote a quiet and honourable old age for himself. 'The young son of Publius should feel that you fell out with his father on political, not on personal grounds.' This was civil in expression, but contained an obvious threat.* In the Second *Philippic* Cicero says: 'You obtained my consent'—his actual answer was a model of polite wariness:—'For why was I to set myself against your audacity, which neither the authority of this House nor public opinion nor laws could restrain? Yet after all what reason was there to request me, if the man for whom you made the request had been already restored by a law of Caesar? I suppose he wished the credit to be mine in a matter wherein even he himself could win none, as a law had been passed.' At the moment, however, Cicero gave his consent in what the Dublin editors call 'a rather effusive letter'.[113] As late as June 21st, Cicero writes to Tiro, to whom he would certainly express his genuine feelings, that Atticus is unnecessarily alarmed: 'I certainly want to maintain my friendship of long standing with Antony without any breach, and I shall write to him, but not before I see you'. Later to Decimus Brutus he says:[114] 'I was always Antony's friend, until I found he was not only openly but gladly waging war upon the Republic'. The quarrel was certainly of Antony's making.

The dictatorship had been abolished for ever, and things looked brighter, when in May Dolabella, having the *fasces*, as the phrase was—the consuls were not simultaneously executive but took alternate

* Young Clodius might prosecute Cicero on some charge or other. Young Atratinus at the age of seventeen had prosecuted Caelius, who had attacked his father.

months—took strong measures to abolish the popular cult at Caesar's grave and restored order in Rome. Cicero writes to him on May 3rd in almost dithyrambic terms congratulating him on his action: [115] but when he winds up with 'Support the liberators', we can imagine Dolabella saying to himself 'I am not such a fool'. A straw showing which way the wind was blowing was a formal proposal for reconciliation made to him by Quintus Fufius Calenus, father-in-law to Pansa the consul-elect and a violent Caesarian. As governor of Greece after Pharsalus, Calenus had been harsh to the Pompeians who surrendered, and Cicero at Brindisi described him as a bitter enemy. In writing to Atticus, Cicero treats the overture with contempt and does not even say whether he acceded to the request or not.

In April and May Antony had been making a tour of Italy, later described in drastic terms by Cicero,[116] and when he returned to Rome, he felt master of the situation and summoned the Senate for June 1st. As the display of military force was intended to be menacing and was so understood, Cicero and those like-minded stayed away. Immediately after, on June 8th, Cicero was invited by Brutus to attend a family council held at his house at Lanuvium, which he graphically describes to Atticus.[117] All the ladies were there, Servilia, Brutus' mother, his sister Tertulla, the wife of Cassius, and his wife Porcia, the daughter of Cato. The question under debate was whether Brutus and Cassius should accept commissions to look after the corn supply in Asia and Sicily respectively—commissions which Antony had offered them, as one throws a bone to a dog. It was a dodge of Antony to get them out of Italy in a more or less honourable way, so that they had no real power. Cassius, 'with flaming eyes and fairly breathing out war', declared that he would not go to Sicily. Brutus said he would rather go to Rome. Cicero urged him not to endanger his life by anything of the kind and thought he had better go to Asia, though he would personally prefer him to stay in Italy. The feebleness of the pair is sufficiently obvious. 'They kept on bewailing the chances that had been let slip, especially Cassius'—but who had let them slip?—'and complained bitterly of Decimus.' It was all someone else's fault. 'I said "don't harp on the past," though I agreed with them.' Servilia vehemently interrupted Cicero when he criticised their behaviour, and actually undertook to get the appointment of Cassius deleted from the decree of the Senate. It is surprising that, even after Caesar's death, she had still sufficient influence to make such an undertaking. The meeting broke up without result and the account of it makes us realise the feebleness of the 'Liberators', who soon afterwards left for the East. Dolabella then nominated Cicero as his legate, or member of the staff which he would take as governor of Asia. So Cicero could travel officially to Greece and see how his son was getting on: for the reports received of him were not always favourable.

All this time Cicero had been assiduously writing. By May 11th he had finished and dedicated to Atticus, in the year of his grand climacteric, the most charming of his works, *On Old Age*, with the alternative title 'The Elder Cato': Atticus wrote to him in July that it was his daily delight to read it. In the opinion of an experienced schoolmaster this treatise still appeals irresistibly to boys who are learning Latin. Cicero is anxious to pay his debts, especially to repay Publilia's dowry. 'Pay my debts and preserve my reputation.' 'Please, my dear Atticus—see how I can cajole—do transact, regulate and govern all my affairs, while you are in Rome, without waiting to consult me. For though I have enough outstanding debts to satisfy my creditors, it often happens that my debtors do not pay up when they should. If anything of that sort happens, please consider my reputation first. Preserve it not only by borrowing but by selling out if need be.' In fact Atticus had power of attorney, and thus enabled his friend to face the situation without distraction.

More and more Cicero is disgusted with the state of things. The tyrant (*rex*) has gone, but not the tyranny (*regnum*). However he is hopeful of a breach between Antony and Caesar's young heir, of whom he says, 'He has a good disposition, if it will only last', and 'We must train him in the way he should go (or perhaps simply 'support him'), and if nothing else keep him from joining Antony'.[118]

There being nothing to detain him, he started on July 17th by sea for Athens from Pompeii,* where he had a villa. He broke his journey to stay at Velia with his old friend Trebatius, whom he had chaffed so unmercifully when he was in Caesar's camp in Gaul (Trebatius is a link between Cicero and Horace): he could take liberties with a friend so intimate that he addresses him '*Testa mi*' or '*mi uetule*', 'dear old

---

* There was as near an approach to a quarrel between Cicero and Atticus as ever in their lives over this journey. Cicero had understood that Atticus did not object, if he returned by January 1st, 43. But after his departure Atticus wrote reproaching him for deserting his country. To this Cicero replied indignantly on August 19th in *Ad Att.* xvi. 7.

chap', liberties which he never takes with anyone else. During the coasting journey from Velia to Rhegium—in the course of which he dropped in on his friend Sicca at Vibo—he adapted a work of Aristotle for Trebatius' benefit, the *Topica*, and with the help of Tiro completed it in seven days.[119] By now his rapidity of work was becoming astounding: the feverish energy of the man was stimulated to the utmost. After touching at Syracuse, he was driven back by contrary winds to Leucopetra near Rhegium. At this place he heard that the Senate had been summoned for September 1st, and that letters had been sent by Brutus and Cassius to all ex-consuls and ex-praetors begging them to be present. 'There were great hopes that Antony might yield, some agreement be arrived at, and our friends allowed to return to Rome. They added that I was missed and people were inclined to blame me for my absence.' There is no doubt that both now and later Brutus hoped to make a deal with Antony. Cicero was not the man to resist this appeal both to his patriotism and to his vanity. So he turned back. In August the situation had improved for Antony by the passing of the law 'about exchange of provinces'. This was supported by Octavian, and obtained Matius' vote. It sent Decimus Brutus to Macedonia without an army, and transferred Cisalpine Gaul to Antony with the Macedonian legions, which he hastily summoned. The inferior provinces of Crete and Cyrene were assigned to Brutus and Cassius. The difficulty for the constitutional party thenceforward, as Cicero was to find, was to justify the position of Decimus Brutus in Cisalpine Gaul, Marcus Brutus in Macedonia, and Cassius in Syria. Antony had completely out-manœuvred them and they were acting against the letter of the law.

During Cicero's return journey, on August 17th he met Brutus, whom he never saw again. Brutus told him that Piso, Caesar's father-in-law, had taken a bold and independent line on August 1st (but he had failed to carry the Senate with him in declaring Cisalpine Gaul no longer a province), and he wished Cicero had been there to back him up. Cicero reached his Tusculan villa on August 28th and entered Rome on the 31st, receiving a hearty welcome.

Next day the Senate met in the Temple of Concord, presumably for the sake of the omen, but Cicero, pleading ill-health, stayed away. His real reason was that the subject of debate, the proposed apotheosis of Caesar, was offensive to him, but he preferred to keep silence on the subject. Antony was annoyed at his absence and said he would send men to pull down his house about his ears. This neurotic outburst was of course reported to Cicero. Next day Dolabella, Cicero's son-in-law, presided: Antony had retired to Tibur. Cicero appeared, and in the First *Philippic*, without any violent language or personal invective but plainly and unmistakably, declared war on Caesarism. He thanked Piso for his speech on August 1st and regretted he had found no supporters. He agreed that Caesar's acts should be ratified but Caesar's promises and casual memoranda were not acts, and Antony had been making improper use of them and, which was worse, even failing to observe Caesar's laws. Throughout it is a denunciation of Antony's public behaviour, not of his private conduct. But he hints plainly that Antony is preparing for himself the fate of Caesar. 'How shall I influence you by what I say? For if the end of Gaius Caesar cannot induce you to prefer affection to fear, no words of my own will either profit or prevail. Those who think he was happy are themselves wretched.' 'No one is happy whose life is held on such conditions that his death will not merely go unpunished but redound to the greatest glory of his slayer.' 'Wherefore then, I pray you, look back on your ancestors, and so direct the State, that your fellow citizens may rejoice that you were born: without that it is wholly impossible for any man to be happy or illustrious or *safe*.'

This was plain speaking, and there were good hopes of a reaction. It was not merely the liberators who were disgusted with Antony: Piso had denounced him, Octavian was biding his time, Hirtius disapproved of Antony, and stating that he was in fear of his life had left Rome in May.[120] There was a chance of forming a constitutional party. But Antony being what he was, there is no wonder that on hearing of this speech he publicly renounced friendship with Cicero and devoted seventeen days to preparing a reply, and, Cicero says, to his cups.

It would of course be absurd to take to the foot of the letter every charge with which Cicero blackens Antony's character. But apropos of this charge, the Dublin editors say—and there is no higher authority —'We feel sure that the charges of drunkenness which Cicero made against Antony were not all inventions; and that the real hatred which he felt for Cicero came out when, owing to excesses, his nerves were not fully under control.'

On September 19th Box was there, but Cox was

not. The violent invective against Cicero the contents of which are examined in sections 12 to 42 of the Second *Philippic* can only have done harm to Antony's cause. Cicero's famous reply was never delivered. It was composed at leisure, and sent from Puteoli to Atticus on October 25th, approved by him, but only made public after Antony left Rome on November 28th.* In a letter of November 5th Cicero announces the completion of the *De Officiis*, a treatise in three books on morals, dedicated to his son. How could he have possibly found time to write the book? It is probable that he had for years been making notes on the subject, which only needed putting into shape. But is there any other literary man in history who, in the space of three months, could complete the most scathing invective ever penned, and a moral treatise which will always stand high in its class?

Are the two works inconsistent? The standards of antiquity and those of to-day differ widely, just as the taste of Mediterranean lands to-day differs from that of north Europe. A revolting subject cannot be treated with decency even in condemnation. While acknowledging the amazing force of the invective we cannot to-day take unalloyed pleasure in reading it. But two passages at least must be quoted.

The one describes the famous scene at the Lupercalia, February 15th, 44 B.C. (§§ 85-87). 'Your colleague [Caesar] was seated on the Rostra, clad in a purple gown, on a golden chair, with a wreath. You mount up, you approach the chair,—if you were

---

* Dr Rice Holmes says the 'lampoon' was never published by Cicero. It cannot be proved that it was, but it is unlikely that Cicero did not make it public.

Lupercus, you should have remembered you were a consul too,—you display a diadem. There is a groan all over the Forum. Whence came the diadem? You had not picked up what someone had thrown away, but had brought it from your house, a crime rehearsed and carefully planned. You persisted in putting it on his head, amid the lamentations of the people; he, amid their applause, persisted in rejecting it. You then, traitor, were discovered to be the one man who, while establishing a tyranny, and willing to have your colleague as your master, were at the same time making trial to see what the Roman People could bear and endure. Nay, you even courted compassion: you threw yourself as a suppliant at his feet. Asking for what? Slavery? You should have asked it for yourself alone, whose life from a boy showed you would submit to anything, would lightly be a slave; from us and from the Roman People at least you had not that as a mandate. Oh, how splendid was that eloquence of yours, when you harangued naked! What can be more disgraceful than that, more foul, more worthy of punishment? Are you waiting for us to goad you into speech? These words of mine, if you have any particle of feeling, tear you and cut you to the heart. I fear I may be lessening the glory of illustrious men; yet I will speak, moved by indignation. What is more shameful than that he should still live who put on the diadem, when all men admit that he was rightly slain who rejected it? But he even ordered this entry under the Lupercalia in the public records: "To Gaius Caesar, perpetual dictator, Marcus Antonius the consul by command of the people offered the crown: Caesar would not take it". By now I cease to wonder that peace discomposes you, that you hate not only the city but the light of day, that you live with the most abandoned brigands, not only on what the day brings but also only for the day. For where in peace will you plant your foot? What place can there be for you, while the laws and the courts survive, which, so far as in you lay, you abolished by the tyranny of a monarch? Was it for this Lucius Tarquinius was banished, Spurius Cassius, Spurius Maelius, Marcus Manlius were put to death, that, many generations later, by an act of desecration, there should be set up by Marcus Antonius a King at Rome?' This is oratorical passion *in excelsis*: but the peroration (§§ 115-119) is even grander: 'Recall then, Marcus Antonius, the day on which you abolished the dictatorship; set before your eyes the joy of the Senate and the Roman People; compare it with this monstrous marketing conducted by you and your friends: then you will understand how great is the difference between gain and glory. But assuredly, even as some, through a kind of disease and numbness of perception, do not perceive the flavour of food, so the lustful, the avaricious, the criminal cannot taste genuine glory. But if glory cannot allure you to right doing, cannot even fear call you away from the foulest deeds? The law-courts you do not fear. If because of your innocence, I praise you; but if because of your violence, do you not understand what he must be afraid of who in such fashion is not afraid of the law-courts? Yet if you have no fear of brave men and honest citizens, because they are kept from your body by an armed guard, your own followers, believe me, will not endure you any longer. And what life is it, day and night to dread your own followers? Unless indeed

you have men bound to you by greater favours than
Caesar had in some of those by whom he was slain,
or are yourself in any respect to be compared to him.
In him there was genius, calculation, memory,*
letters, industry, thought, diligence; he had done in
war things, however disastrous to the state, at least
great; having for many years aimed at a throne,† by
great labour, great dangers, he had achieved his object; by shows, buildings, largesses, banquets he had
conciliated the ignorant crowd; his own followers he
had bound to him by rewards, his adversaries by a
show of clemency; in brief, he had already brought
to a free community—partly by fear, partly by endurance—a habit of servitude. With him I can
compare you in lust for power, but in other respects
you are in no wise comparable.‡ But out of the very
many evils which he has inflicted on the Republic,
there has emerged this much good; the Roman
People has now learned how much to trust each man,
on whom to rely, of whom to beware. Think you
not of these things? and do you not understand that
it is enough for brave men to have learned what a
beautiful thing, what a welcome benefit, what a title

* For Caesar's exceptional memory cp. *Deiotarus*, 42: 'he appeals to
your memory, which is strong with you'; *Ligarius*, 35, 'You never forget
anything but injuries'; *Ad Fam*. xiii. 29, 6, 'I know what a memory
he has'. But Caesar did not always forget injuries: the mutinous soldiers
he pardoned in Italy he took care to get rid of in Africa in the way in
which David got rid of Uriah.

† This is Cicero's deliberate opinion. Posterity has to judge whether
he was right. Cp. *De Off*. iii. 8, 36, 'The separation of the expedient from
the morally right . . . finally leads to the desire of making oneself king
in the midst of a free people, and anything more atrocious and repulsive
than such a passion cannot be conceived'.

‡ Antony certainly possessed *Caesariana celeritas* (*Ad Att*. xvi. 10, 1):
and he was a good soldier, cp. *Antony and Cleopatra*, Act II., Sc. 1,
where Sextus Pompey, comparing him with Octavian and Lepidus, says:
'His soldiership is twice the other twain'.

to fame it is to slay a tyrant? Or will men endure you when they could not stand him? In rivalry hereafter, believe me, they will hurry to do this work, and not wait for the slow coming opportunity.

'Recover your senses, at length, I beg: consider from whom you are descended, not with whom you consort; treat *me*, as you will; be reconciled to the *state*. But you must look to your own conduct; for myself I will make my own profession. I defended the state in youth, I will not desert her in old age: I despised the swordsmen of Catiline, I will not dread yours. Aye, and even my body will I gladly offer, if the liberty of the state can be realised by my death, so that the anguish of the Roman People may some time bring to birth that with which it has so long travailed. For if nearly twenty years ago in this very temple I said that death could not come untimely to an ex-consul,* with how much greater truth shall I say it in old age! By me, indeed, Conscript Fathers, death is even to be desired, now that the honours I have won and the deeds I have performed are past.

'For these two things only do I pray; one, that in my death I may leave the Roman People free—than this no greater gift can be given me by the immortal gods—the other, that each man's fortune may be according to his deserts toward the state.'

The Second *Philippic* sealed Cicero's fate, if in the struggle to come Antony got the upper hand. Rome could not hold them both. Cicero saw in Antony the real enemy to the constitution, under which he was born and which was now tottering to its fall. Hardly any one entirely denies him the

* In *Cat.* iv. 2, 3, December 5th, 63 B.C.

motive of patriotism, but many contended then, and
still contend, that he was carried away by paltry
animosity to the man Antony? This is very doubtful. To Publius Clodius he certainly cherished
undying hate. Long after Clodius' death he would
say something happened so many days after the
'Battle of Bovillae'. But with Antony his relations
had always been very slight, and as we have seen, up
to Cicero's departure from Rome in July, had been
correct. How was it that they threw off all decencies
of society and blackguarded each other with the
foulest charges?

We must not forget that Antony began this course
on September 1st, and that Cicero did not follow
suit until the Second *Philippic* was published. In
the First *Philippic* he had given Antony a *locus
paenitentiae*. Antony's fury was raised by opposition. No doubt he was goaded on by Fulvia, the
widow of Cicero's enemy Clodius, whom he had
recently married. But she only added fuel to a fire
already burning. When it suited Antony, he threw
her over, and until he fell under the spell of Cleopatra he had not been dominated by any woman.
History, as well as the succeeding generation, has
pronounced its verdict, that even if one deducts fifty
per cent of Cicero's charges, this was a contest
between a patriot and a vicious self-seeking man.
Not even the genius of Shakespeare has made a hero
of Antony, attractive as is the picture of him in
Antony and Cleopatra. To an unbiased view he
represents the worst features of decadence in a
decadent age. Octavian had in the end to crush
him, and the poets-laureate have truly celebrated the
triumph of Octavian as the triumph of Rome. Had

Antony won, Alexandria might have taken its place as the capital of a semi-Greek, semi-Oriental Empire. Horace denounces Cleopatra without any special denunciation of Antony, but Propertius [121] has no hesitation in calling him the 'foul consort of Cleopatra'.

It was now Octavian's turn to act. His adoption had been legally carried through and he stood before Rome as the heir. It was rumoured that on October 5th he made an attempt on Antony's life. Most people thought this was a fiction put about by Antony, but Cicero credits it in writing to Cornificius in Africa and seems to allude to it in the Third *Philippic*.[122] There is at least no doubt that Octavian made repeated overtures to Cicero, who was much embarrassed to know what to do. 'I cannot trust one so young: I don't know what are his real sentiments.'

But Octavian had also acted. By November 12th he had arrived outside Rome with ten thousand veterans, who had rallied to him in Campania. Antony had been away, but, on his return from Brindisi, at Suessa he executed some centurions of the Martian Legion, which promptly deserted him for Octavian. He summoned the Senate for November 24th, and a resolution declaring Octavian a public enemy had been drafted. But the news of the defection of the Fourth Legion changed his mind. Instead, if Cicero may be believed, he hurried through, without allowing any debate, a thanksgiving in honour of Lepidus, now proconsul in Gallia Narbonensis and Hither Spain, for negotiating peace with Sextus Pompeius,* and a number of

* In the Fifth *Philippic* it suits Cicero's purpose to cause Lepidus to

decrees, which were registered in less time than they took to draft. Among other performances of the evening was the manipulation of the lot so as to alter the disposition of the provinces, in such a way that Cisalpine Gaul fell to him, instead of Decimus Brutus, and Macedonia to his brother Gaius, instead of Marcus Brutus. Then he hurried away from Rome, only to return a year later to superintend the proscriptions.

be thanked for the same reason. It was then important not to break with Lepidus.

Chapter 11

REPUBLIC OR DESPOTISM
DECEMBER 9TH 44-DECEMBER 7TH 43 B.C.

No evil can happen to a good man in life or after death.
Apology of Socrates, translated by Cicero

*Death cannot be shameful to a brave man, untimely to an
ex-consul, or a cause of unhappiness to a philosopher.*
CICERO, *In Cat.* iv. 2, 3

CICERO returned to Rome on December 9th, as we
learn from a letter which he wrote soon afterwards
to Decimus Brutus, who, unable to meet Antony in
the field, had retired into Mutina (Modena) prepared
to stand a siege. Nothing much could be done till
January came: for of the magistrates Antony had
fled, Dolabella had gone to Asia in the autumn, the
city-praetor Gaius Antonius had gone to take over
Macedonia. But Cicero went straight to Pansa, as
consul-designate for 43, no doubt to ask for protection for the Senators who were opposed to Antony:
he had to deal with a strong opposition from Antony's
friends, led by Quintus Fufius Calenus (see p. 171).

The Senate was summoned by the tribunes, among
whom Marcus Servilius took the lead, for December
20th. Hirtius was ill;[123] Pansa absented himself.
But it was necessary for Cicero to back up Decimus
Brutus in his awkward position. On the day before,

he wrote to Decimus to encourage him to resist Antony, and after the meeting of the Senate wrote again to describe how he had defended his interests. In the Third *Philippic* he carried the Senate with him in asking for protection at the meeting of January 1st, in confirming Decimus and Plancus, consuls-designate for 42, in their provinces, and in a vote of thanks to Octavian and the two legions which had deserted Antony; it was also resolved that Hirtius and Pansa should consult the Senate as soon as possible after entering on office. Passing out of the Senate House he harangued the people (Fourth *Philippic*) briefly, pointing out that if Antony had not yet been declared a public enemy, the resolutions of the Senate were tantamount to a declaration of war upon him.

Everything now depended on the incoming Consuls. They were two officers of Caesar, whom we have heard of as learning rhetoric from Cicero and teaching him gastronomy. Hirtius wrote the Eighth Book of the *Gallic War*, but as he says he was not engaged in the Alexandrine and African Wars, it seems improbable that he wrote the accounts of them which we possess. Perhaps Caesar deliberately left him in Italy in 46 B.C.: perhaps Hirtius was tired of warfare and preferred to enjoy the pleasures of the table. As a neighbour of Cicero at Tusculum, he wished to profit by the instruction of the great orator. We have heard how polite he was to Cicero, even in answering his *Cato*. But though Cicero's pupil, he was very faithful to the memory of Caesar, and could not be induced to support the liberators. The only letter of his we possess is an urgent appeal to Cicero to stop Brutus and Cassius from being so foolish as to take up arms. It is obvious, however, that he disliked Antony and left Rome, in fear of his life as he said, in May 44. On May 31st, Cicero says: 'Hirtius writes that he is much annoyed with the veterans'. He was taken seriously ill in the autumn, and never completely recovered.

Pansa was an echo of Hirtius, as Oppius was of Balbus. They were not really men of ability. When they died, Cicero says: 'We have lost two consuls, patriotic indeed but only patriotic consuls', and therefore no match for Antony. They never acted separately.[124] Sometimes Cicero distrusts them: 'They are afraid of peace'.[125] 'Hirtius could not of course say that he did not want peace, but he did say that he was as much afraid of armed action on our side as from Antony, and that after all both had reason for being on their guard, and for his part he was afraid of hostilities from both. In fact he was unreliable.'[126] 'They have no seriousness in them, and are only drowsy drunkards.'[127] Quintus wrote to Tiro with his usual strong language that both were vicious and Pansa was a drunkard, and 'the ruffian (Antony) will beguile them by companionship in his vices'. 'You would never believe what I know they did in summer quarters, when they were opposite the camp of the Gauls.'[128] Probably this means very little more than that Quintus disliked them personally. He always wrote in a truculent way and his statements are to be taken with much deduction: Hirtius had befriended both him and his son.

On January 1st and onwards, from Cicero's point of view, they behaved well: at any rate they accepted the position that the Senate was the constitutional authority, though they were very loth to fight

Antony. They called on Calenus to speak first. He proposed that before any hostile measures were taken, an embassy should be sent to order Antony not to invade Cisalpine Gaul. This moderate attitude was supported by Piso, Caesar's father-in-law, who said that Cicero was carried away by personal animosity to Antony. It is not quite clear to what meeting of the Senate Dio Cassius assigns the speech he puts into the mouth of Calenus. It is a rhetorical exercise giving a detailed reply to the charges against Antony in the Second *Philippic*. Its filthy insinuations against Cicero require no refutation: but one ingenious defence of Antony is noticeable. At the Lupercalia he was really manœuvring so as to prevent Caesar from assuming the state of king rather than offering him the crown. One who can believe that can believe anything.

The Fifth *Philippic* (January 1st) is a strong call to arms. In this speech Cicero gives the definite undertaking that Octavian will be loyal to the Republic: he seems to have regarded it as an acid test that Octavian had not protested against the election of Casca, one of Caesar's murderers, as tribune, on his entering office on December 10th.[129] Later, on July 27th, 43 B.C., he wrote to Marcus Brutus: 'it gives me great pain, when I write these lines, that though the state took me as security for the stripling, or rather the mere boy, I seem scarcely able to make good my promise'. Octavian seems to have completely hoodwinked Cicero: Plutarch says that he called Cicero 'Father', and undertook to follow his advice. At any rate Cicero procured for him on this occasion *imperium*, the rank of propraetor with a seat in the Senate, and permission to stand, notwithstanding his age, for the higher offices. Octavian took this to mean the consulship, though of course the praetorship was meant in the first instance; and to all this his stepfather Philippus added the honour of an equestrian statue, only granted previously, according to Velleius, to Sulla, Pompey and Caesar.

The debate lasted four days. Ultimately an immediate declaration of war on Antony was averted. Sulpicius, Piso and Philippus, two of whom would certainly be inclined to favour Antony, were to be the ambassadors. They were to order Antony to raise the siege of Mutina, evacuate Cisalpine Gaul, remain two hundred miles from Rome, and obey the orders of the Senate: failing obedience, war was to be declared. At a meeting held by the tribune Appuleius on the afternoon of the 4th, Cicero in the Sixth *Philippic* explained to the people that as Antony would certainly disobey, war was inevitable. The speech ends with a string of short pithy sentences, like pistol shots: 'As consul, I have held many important meetings: I have been present at many. Never have I seen one as great as yours today. You all have one mind, one object, to avert from the state the violence of Antony, to quench his madness, to crush his audacity. All ranks of society have the same desire: they are seconded by the boroughs, the colonies, the whole of Italy. Thus you have made the Senate, already firm in its own determination, firmer by your support. The time has come, citizens, later than the Roman People deserved, but so ripe that the hour cannot be postponed. There was a misfortune ordained by destiny, which we bore as best we could (the rule of Caesar): now if any comes, it will be from our own choice. That the Roman

People should be enslaved is not right: the immortal gods willed it to rule the world. The crisis is imminent: liberty is at stake. You must either win the day, citizens, as assuredly you will through your loyalty and great unanimity, or do anything rather than be slaves. Other nations can endure slavery: the peculiar possession of the Roman People is freedom.' English can hardly do justice to the terse expression and intense meaning of the passage. Cicero's hour had come, and for a few brief months he led Senate and People.

Was the cause hopeless? Everything depended on the line taken by selfish and ambitious War-Lords in the various provinces: there is no closer parallel in history than the Tuchuns of China in the last decades. No one knew, or could know, how much political wisdom was to be developed later in an inexperienced youth. It was worth while, if the struggle of Demosthenes against Philip was worth while. It is unfair to judge the fight for freedom, and Cicero its leader, solely in the light of subsequent events. An elderly civilian, just because he represented the sacred cause of freedom, became, almost in spite of himself, an immortal leader. To Dr. Johnson's great words: 'That man is little to be envied, whose patriotism would not gain force upon the plain of Marathon, or whose piety would not grow warmer among the ruins of Iona', might well be added, 'or in whom love of freedom would not be fired by the *Philippics* of Cicero'. It was not for nothing that Cicero called his speeches *Philippics*: * he knew

---

* *Brut.* ii. 3, 4: 'I now admit that your speeches may even be called *Philippics* as you jestingly wrote in a letter'. Brutus was always disagreeable even when he agreed with anybody.

and had pondered well the words of Demosthenes: 'Do not then impute it as a crime to me that Philip chanced to conquer in battle: the issue rested not with me but God. Prove that I adopted not all measures that were possible according to human calculation—that I did not honestly, diligently and with exertions beyond my strength carry them out—or that my enterprises were not honourable, worthy of the state and necessary. Show me that, and then accuse me as soon as you like.'

The extant correspondence of Cicero with the provincial governors, Cassius, Marcus and Decimus Brutus, Plancus, Lepidus, Pollio and Cornificius, shows what a high tone he adopted with them. The letters are, as the Dublin editors say, 'the high-water mark of Latin prose', and 'nowhere else do we find such a combination of noble sentiments, chastened eloquence and perfect taste'. But those to whom they were addressed were a poor and self-seeking crowd. Their replies to Cicero are mostly demands for money and honours for themselves.*

Cassius was a man of culture and a sincere, if narrow, Republican. But he was bent on making himself another Pompey in the East, and could not realise that the battle for the Republic would be decided in the West. About *Marcus Brutus* in his youth we have already heard much that indicated avarice and arrogance rather than higher qualities. To these defects he added abnormal conceit, after the Ides of March; and after all his action then cannot be acquitted of base ingratitude. One could expect nothing but obstinacy from Cato's son-in-

---

* Cornificius is the best of them, but even he complains that Cicero only commends litigants to him: what he wants is money.

law and imitator: but he was inexcusably deaf to
Cicero's repeated calls to Italy. He was jealous of
the rise of Octavian, and, if his letters are genuine
(they certainly appear to be), reproached Cicero
for servility to a new master. Meanwhile he too
was only concerned with controlling the Balkan
Peninsula.

Decimus Brutus in Cisalpine Gaul was bound to
be faithful to the Republic, for otherwise he was
doomed; so great odium had he incurred by the dis-
closure of the fact that he was named second heir in
Caesar's will. *Lepidus*, the 'barren-spirited fellow',
owed too much to Antony to be reliable, and only
pretended to be following the lead of the Senate.
Plancus in Gallia Comata was an accomplished hypo-
crite, and *Asinius Pollio* in Further Spain was fully
his equal in that respect, and also jealous of Cicero's
fame. Only *Cornificius* in Africa was to be wholly
trusted. The movements of the free lance, *Sextus
Pompey*, were quite incalculable, and only added to
the general confusion and uncertainty: Cicero appears
not to have appealed to him directly. Who was
there who could be expected to put country before
self?

In the Seventh *Philippic*, while the ambassadors
were still away, Cicero, using the senator's right to
be irrelevant, neglected the question before the house,
and urged the Senate to maintain their hostility to
Antony and admit no compromise.

During the embassy Sulpicius died, and the Ninth
Philippic, delivered the day after the Eighth, is a
warm eulogy on a learned and high-minded man,
who in extreme ill-health obeyed the order of the
Senate and gave his life for his country, as much as

if he had fallen on the field of battle. Piso and Philippus brought back 'intolerable demands' from Antony. If his veterans were rewarded, his acts confirmed, his peculations condoned, he would graciously accept in lieu of Cisalpine Gaul the government of Gallia Comata (France and Belgium, with the exception of Provence) and the command of six legions for five years, by which time he calculated that Brutus and Cassius (Octavian he left out of the reckoning) would have held consulships and provinces and be private citizens. He could then, only he did not say so, replay the part of Caesar. Only on these conditions would he relinquish Cisalpine Gaul and give up all claim to Macedonia.

This was too much for the Senate, and on February 2nd war was declared and the military garb adopted by everybody in Rome. The Eighth *Philippic* was an argument in favour of war to the knife. Hirtius had already been attacked and a state of war existed: any one going to Antony therefore should be regarded as an enemy, but any one deserting Antony before March 15th should be pardoned. In a later speech [130] Cicero admitted that Antony's impudent demands might have been conceded, but at the moment he would hear of no concession.

Even in these gloomy days a letter from an old acquaintance elicited a charming reply from Cicero showing him as attentive to his friends and amusing in his advice as ever. Paetus had warned him of plots against his life and recommended a friend. At first Cicero eschews serious subjects, and counsels Paetus for his good to dine out and give little dinner parties. 'A happy life largely depends upon sharing it with good and agreeable fellows who are fond of

o

you: our word for such gatherings is far better than the Greek "symposium". We call them "livings together" (*convivia*): for at these times most of all life is shared.* Take care of your health, and you will do this best by dining out.' Then, lest he may be thought frivolous, he adds: 'But as you love me, don't think that because I write jocularly, I have dismissed all thought of the State. Day and night my one aim and anxiety is the safety and freedom of my fellow citizens. If in this charge and public work, I have to lay down my life, I shall feel I have had a fine ending.' [131] It was not far off.

In the Tenth *Philippic*, February 13th, Cicero succeeded in maintaining Marcus Brutus' position in Macedonia. The speech contains an interesting personal touch. 'The legion, which was commanded by Lucius Piso, a legate of Gaius Antonius, has placed itself at the disposal of my son Cicero.' How the father's heart must have been full of pride in making this announcement.

But Cicero was not always able to command a majority in the Senate; for in the Eleventh *Philippic*, March 6th, he vainly pleaded for authority to Cassius in Syria to carry on war against Dolabella, who had murdered Trebonius and occupied the province of Asia.† Of course Cassius did so without the sanc-

---

* Cp. *On Old Age*, xiii. 45: 'Our fathers did well in calling the reclining of friends at feasts *convivium*, because it implies a communion of life, and is a better designation than that of the Greeks, who call it sometimes a "drinking together" and sometimes "an eating together", thereby apparently exalting what is of least value in these associations above that which gives them their greatest charm.'. . . 'I am profoundly grateful to old age, which has increased my eagerness for conversation, and taken away that for food and drink.'

† Cicero felt this deeply. He says later that by doing this dastardly deed Dolabella had made death a boon for which to pray.

tion of the Senate. No doubt those provinces were wanted for the choice of the existing consuls: for Calenus' motion that at the end of the war in North Italy they should draw lots for Asia and Syria was carried. Cicero promptly wrote to Cassius, and said that though thwarted by Pansa in the Senate, he had been given an opportunity of addressing the people by the tribune Servilius, and defended the cause of Cassius, straining his voice so that he was heard all over the Forum and eliciting unparalleled applause:[132] this speech is lost.

At the end of February, in the Twelfth *Philippic*, Cicero frustrated a scheme to send a second embassy to Antony, of which he himself had been made a member by the proposers, and the proposal of Piso and Calenus was withdrawn. A delicate compliment was paid to Cicero on March 19th, when the Senate resolved that his statue of Minerva in the Capitol (p. 107), which had been thrown down by a storm, should be re-erected. In the Thirteenth *Philippic*, March 20th, he moves a vote of thanks to Sextus Pompey for his loyal declarations, and criticises sentence by sentence a letter addressed by Antony to Hirtius and Octavian, which tried to fan into a fresh flame the old antagonism of Caesarians to Pompeians. He also thought it politic to reply civilly to Lepidus, who had written to the Senate, advocating peace with Antony and to point out to him that it was impossible. Probably that same evening he wrote a very curt letter to Lepidus, rebuking him for his rudeness in not thanking the Senate for the honour conferred on him, and warning him not to interfere.

Early in April Plancus, governor of Gallia Comata,

who had previously advocated peace, wrote to place himself under the orders of the Senate. Cicero on April 7th proposed complimentary votes to him and met with violent opposition from Publius Servilius, and a tribune who vetoed the vote. But on the 9th Cicero, in a speech which is lost, carried his proposal.

Then followed the battles for Mutina. In the first on April 15th Pansa was defeated by Antony at Forum Gallorum, but Hirtius inflicted loss on Antony, while Octavian defended his camp against Antony's brother Lucius. An interesting account of this engagement was sent to Cicero by Galba, one of Pansa's officers. On the 21st Antony suffered a decisive defeat under the walls of Mutina, Decimus Brutus making an effective sally. But unfortunately Hirtius was killed in the battle, Pansa died of his wounds a few days later, and the Republic was deprived of its constitutional heads. They were men of no mark, but the jealousies of the leading men made it impossible immediately to fill their places. Had they survived, the rise of Octavian to power would have been probably more rapid, and his alliance with Antony averted. At the moment Antony made good his escape. Decimus Brutus said he was unable to follow him: whether he spoke the truth, we have no means of judging. Soon Antony by junction with his lieutenant Ventidius was strong again, though further from Rome, but unfortunately nearer to the unreliable Lepidus.

On April the 21st Cicero delivered the Fourteenth *Philippic*, deprecating the adoption of the garb of peace, but cordially supporting the proposal of a public thanksgiving, which he said, would stamp

Antony as a public enemy: 'for no thanksgiving has ever been voted in the case of a war between citizens'. The following passage proposes the erection of a monument to those of the Martian legion who had fallen: 'Great and marvellous are the services of this legion to the State. This legion was the first to break away from Antony's robber crew; this garrisoned Alba; this joined Caesar; by following its example the Fourth legion has won an equal renown for valour. The Fourth has not lost a man: of the Martian some fell in the very hour of victory. O fortunate death, the debt to nature, but paid on behalf of fatherland! You I verily regard as born for your fatherland; your very name is from Mars, so that it seems the same god begot this city for the world, and you for this city. In flight death is disgraceful, in victory glorious; for Mars himself is wont to claim out of the battle-line the bravest as his own. Those impious wretches whom you have slain will even among the shades pay the penalty of their treason: you who have expired in victory have won the abiding resting place of the good. *Brief is the life given us by nature, but the memory of life nobly resigned is everlasting.* If that memory were no longer than this life of ours, who would be so mad as, with the greatest toil and peril, to strive for the height of honour and glory? All then is well with you, most valiant while you lived, but now also soldiers most revered; for your valour cannot be entombed, either in the forgetfulness of this generation, or the silence of posterity, when, almost with their own hands, the Senate and the Roman People have raised to you an immortal monument. There have been in the Punic, Gallic and Italian wars many armies glorious and great, yet on none of these has honour of such a kind been bestowed. And would that we could bestow greater, since from you we have received what is greatest! You turned back from the city the mad Antonius; you repelled him when he was striving to return. There shall therefore be erected a structure of splendid workmanship and an inscription cut as an everlasting witness to your superhuman valour: and in your praise, whether men behold your monument or only hear of it, never shall language of deepest gratitude be silent. Thus in exchange for life's mortal state you have gained for yourselves immortality.' Marble monuments are perishable, but Cicero, like Shakespeare, could construct a 'star-y-pointing pyramid' of splendid words.

There were certainly other *Philippics* — as on April 9th Cicero supported honours to Plancus, so on the 25th he proposed honours to Decimus Brutus —but this is the last extant speech, the orator's farewell to his countrymen, and last legacy to posterity.

To the liberal distribution of honours, and especially those to Octavian, which followed, Marcus Brutus took violent objection—there were none for him—and accused Cicero of excessive subservience to the 'boy'. Decimus Brutus found that Octavian would have nothing to do with him, and complained: 'Caesar can neither obey orders himself, nor secure the obedience of his soldiers, both of which things are equally disastrous'. It was about this time that Decimus Brutus reported to Cicero, whom he obviously thought indiscreet, that a saying of his had been maliciously reported to Octavian. The Latin word which gave offence means both 'to raise aloft' and 'to remove'. Cicero said apparently: 'the young man must be praised, honoured and raised to the skies'. Octavian resented this, and said he would not put himself in such a position that he could be raised to the skies. The story bears on its face the mark of genuineness. Cicero ought to have curbed his caustic tongue, which had, by making Clodius a relentless enemy, caused himself such misery: but he seems to have never been able to resist the temptation to utter a witticism. Anyhow, about this time came the breach between Octavian and the Senate, just when neither could really dispense with the other. If that very untrustworthy writer Dio Cassius is to be believed, the Senate was to blame for this breach by its preference of Decimus Brutus to Octavian. But as he also states that the Senate gave to Cassius Syria together with the war against Dolabella, which as we have seen they refused to do in spite of Cicero's pleadings, we cannot put much confidence in Dio's assertions. There is a story that Pansa on his death-bed warned Octavian that the Senate were only using him to get the better of Antony, and then would crush him and revive the party of Pompey. At any rate after the battle of Mutina, Octavian never again co-operated with Cicero or the Senate.

After the escape of Antony, Cicero's chief hope was in Plancus, who responded cordially to his letters: he assured Cicero that he was trying to keep Lepidus loyal, and to prevent a junction between him and Antony. Lepidus wrote to both Plancus and Cicero to assure them of his loyalty, but finally, pretending to be coerced by his soldiers, joined Antony. His loyal legate Laterensis, who had been doing everything in his power to avert this, committed suicide. Lepidus had been characterised by Cicero, as early as March 17th, 49, as 'the meanest and basest fellow in the world':[133] on April 29th this year Decimus Brutus called him 'that weathercock'.[134] There is hardly a more contemptible figure to be found in all Roman history.

Asinius Pollio wrote on March 16th to Cicero from Corduba (Cordova) as follows: 'I have learned (under the dictator) the joy of freedom, and the wretchedness of life under a despotism. Accordingly, if it is a question of everything being again under the power of one man, I declare myself his enemy, whosoever he may be.' How could Cicero doubt that a man who uttered such sentiments would oppose Antony? Yet when recalled from Spain to defend the Republic with his army, he took the longest time possible on the road, and when he had arrived, joined the big battalions. At that date, he had no alternative. But if he had really had the good intentions he professed to Cicero and started earlier, his three legions might have turned the scale.

Before describing what happened to Plancus and Decimus Brutus, let us now turn to the East and follow the fortunes of Cassius and Marcus Brutus. Cassius wrote on March 7th from Taricheae on the Lake of Galilee to announce that he had secured the province of Syria. At precisely that moment in Rome Cicero delivered the Eleventh *Philippic*, but failed to carry the Senate with him in legalising the position of Cassius; then he declared to the people[135] that Cassius would take the province on his own responsibility, and he would support him. In May

Cassius (on the eve of crushing Dolabella, which he did in July) wrote again to Cicero: 'I regard my dignity committed to your charge'.[136]   He meant, of course, that as Brutus' position in Macedonia had been legalised through the Tenth *Philippic*, February 13th, it was high time he should be treated in the same way.

What was Brutus doing?   He was behaving in a way which seemed to Cicero very unsatisfactory. First of all Cicero objected to his misplaced clemency to the Antony brothers.   As he had prevented Marcus from sharing Caesar's fate, so now he was behaving with ridiculous leniency to Gaius, whom he had deprived of the province of Macedonia by armed force: apparently Gaius repaid him by fomenting mutiny among his officers and men.   Cicero's dissatisfaction came to a head when two letters were read in the Senate on April 13th.   One was from Gaius Antonius Proconsul.   As Cicero remarks to Brutus, 'if Gaius is proconsul, you are only an interloper'. The other was a very short letter purporting to be from Brutus, couched in terms of excessive leniency to Antonius.   Labeo (one of the liberators) declared this was a forgery: Cicero obviously thought it genuine, and indignantly protested.   'How are we to deal with Dolabella, if you take this attitude?'   It is as clear as can be that Brutus had not yet abandoned the hope of doing a deal with Mark Antony, and wished to use Gaius as an intermediary.

The second cause of disagreement was the attitude of the Senate to Octavian.   Brutus was excessively annoyed by the intervention of the youth who had supplanted him as Caesar's heir, and by his close relations with Cicero personally, and through him

with the Senate. He wrote on May 15th to depre-
cate honours to Octavian.   Brutus' attitude was dictated by jealousy: but was it politic and was Cicero
imprudent?

Cicero in writing to Atticus in November 44
had summed up the difficult situation as follows: 'If
Octavian has much power, the acts of Caesar will be
more completely ratified than they were on March
17th in the Temple of Tellus, and that will be bad
for Brutus. But if Octavian is beaten, Antony will be
intolerable: so you don't know which you want.'[136a]
From the point of view of the preservation of the
Republic, Cicero had no alternative but to try and
unite the Senate and Octavian.   But he went too far;
for the veterans of Caesar, whose excessive influence
he so eloquently denounced on February 13th,[137]
who hated the liberators and were devoted to
Octavian because he was Caesar's heir, spurred him
on till his demands became intolerable.

Brutus' dissatisfaction with Cicero culminates in
the letters he wrote to Atticus in the middle of June
(i. 17), and to Cicero in the middle of July (i. 16).
It is difficult to understand how these letters have so
often been suspected as forgeries.*   The so-called

---

* Zielinski quotes Taine (*Essais* 275) as holding *Brut.* i. 16 to be
genuine and points out that the words: 'Do you think living at Rome is
equivalent to being safe and sound: it is the fact, not the place that must
guarantee that to me'. 'In Caesar's lifetime I was not safe and sound,
till after I performed that deed; nor can I be an exile anywhere, so long
as I loathe slavery and submission to insults worse than all other evils',
have a striking similarity to *Tusc. Disp.* v. 106 ff.: 'What is left to be
feared? Is it exile, which is counted the greatest of evils? If it is only
evil because of the estrangement and displeasure of the people, we have
already stated how little that counts. If to be absent from one's fatherland is wretched, the provinces must be full of wretched people. . . .
How does exile, if we look at fact and not the disrepute of the word,
differ from perpetual travelling?'

Letter to Octavian is quite obviously a rhetorical forgery: but these bear the hall-mark of Brutus, his rudeness. Thus he tells Atticus, 'Your age, your character and your being a family man (having a daughter to think of) make you sluggish and inactive'. He goes on, 'I have no longer any regard for the accomplishments with which Cicero is so liberally equipped', if his only object is to make the 'boy' propitious to him, *i.e.* condescend to grant him 'divine' favour. To Cicero he says, 'If you approve of Octavius'—he will not recognise the adoption and call him Octavian—'as a person from whom we are to beg our lives, it will appear that you did not so much run away from a master, as look out for a more friendly master'.

It was a bitter jibe, and there was some truth in it. All the romantic and educational instincts of Cicero had been stirred by the hope of training up this young man to do Caesar's work *in a better and more lasting way*. It is incumbent on us to point out that these hopes were actually in large measure realised.* The taunt would have come better from Brutus if he had done what the Senate and Cicero vainly urged on him, and returned to Italy.

This was the third cause of disagreement between the two men. At the end of May Decimus Brutus and Cicero agreed that the only possible course was to recall Marcus Brutus to Italy at once. When on June 30th Lepidus (Brutus' brother-in-law) was

---

* There is no space to pursue this subject. It may be followed out in Mason Hammond, *The Augustan Principatus in Theory and Practice during the Julio-Claudian Period*, Harvard University Press, 1933. The book maintains that Augustus meant what he says, *Monumentum Ancyranum*, c. 34: 'In 28–7 B.C. I transferred the republic from my own power into the free control of the senate and Roman people'.

declared a public enemy for joining Antony, Cicero urged Brutus to come and bring his army at once. But Brutus' only anxiety was to plead for his sister and her children, that their property should not be confiscated. On this point Cicero gave way: he says pathetically, 'I care more for your goodwill than consistency: in nothing would I rather be and be thought consistent than in loving you'. But love was wasted on the stony heart of Brutus. On June 18th, July 2nd, July (after 11th), July 14th, in varying but equally urgent language, Cicero pleaded with him to come, and bring young Cicero along with him. Finally on July 27th Cicero was summoned to a conference on the question what Brutus should do by that old intriguer, Brutus' mother Servilia. 'I replied, what I thought, viz. that it was most expedient for your position and reputation to come at the earliest possible opportunity to protect the sinking and almost falling Republic.' His last words are very touching: 'There will never be anything in which I will not say or do what I think you want, and what concerns you, even at the risk of my life.'*

But the obstinate man stayed on in Macedonia. It is reported that, before he died on the battlefield of Philippi next year, he quoted from some unknown tragedian the lines:

> Poor Virtue, thou art but a name!
> I ever served thee as the truth.
> But now I see thou'rt Fortune's slave.

Plutarch, who admired Brutus and passed on his estimate of him to Shakespeare, can only offer the

---

* And yet Cardinal Newman spoke of Cicero's 'unworthy treatment of Brutus' (*Historical Sketches*, vol. ii. p. 256). What did he mean?

remark, that disease engenders maggots in the brain!

The end of Brutus illustrates the powerlessness of Stoicism, that pagan parallel to Pelagianism, to effect a moral reformation. Brutus had attempted to model himself on his uncle, but had only succeeded in copying Cato's *gaucherie*: the avarice, jealousy and meanness which were his own besetting sins, he never even tried to curb. It is high time for the world to cease admiring such a pinchbeck hero.*

The refusal of Brutus to intervene caused events to move rapidly. The news of the combination of Antony and Lepidus reached Rome early in June. Decimus Brutus joined Plancus. Had they been reinforced, they might have effected something. Meantime Octavian maintained his independence and, spurred on by the veterans, sent four hundred of them to Rome to demand rewards for themselves and the consulship for him. To both Cicero and Plancus this demand seemed extravagant. Thereupon Octavian marched on Rome, a precocious repetition of Caesar's behaviour. When he arrived, the three legions which had been at the Senate's disposal (two from Africa, and one of recruits left by Pansa) went over to him, the city praetor committed suicide, and every one else made peace with the youthful conqueror. If Appian, a violent Caesarian, is to be believed, what he said to Cicero was: 'You are the last of my friends to come and meet me'. On August 19th Octavian was elected consul, with his co-heir Pedius.

Of the last four miserable months of Cicero's life, which apparently he chiefly spent at Tusculum, there

---

* Brutus was thirty-seven years of age at his death (Velleius, ii. 72), and was therefore born in 79.

are no complete letters and we know hardly anything. There is only a pathetic fragment to Octavian: 'I have a double pleasure in your grant of leave of absence (from attending the Senate) to me and Philippus (Octavian's stepfather): you give pardon for the past and indulgence for the future'.

It was not till November that the second Triumvirate, Antony, Octavian and Lepidus—or was it Octavian, Antony and Lepidus, a question which distracted the Roman world for many a long year? —arranged the proscriptions in which Cicero, his brother and nephew perished.* This is Plutarch's account of Cicero's death, derived largely, but not entirely, from Tiro. 'During the arrangements for the proscriptions, Cicero was in his villa at Tusculum and his brother Quintus was staying with him. On learning of the proscriptions they determined to go to Astura, where Cicero had a villa on the sea coast, and from thence to take ship for Macedonia, and join Brutus, who was reported to be in a strong position. They were carried in litters, worn out with distress, and frequently during the journey they stopped, and bringing their litters close together they bewailed their misfortunes to one another. Quintus was especially distressed, and reflected on his destitute condition: for he said he had brought nothing from home, and Marcus too had but a scanty supply of money for the journey. Accordingly he considered it best for Marcus to escape before him, and he would follow when he had obtained supplies. So after embracing they parted in tears. Not many days after Quintus was betrayed by his servants to those

* The *Lex Titia* of November 27th created them *tres viri reipublicae constituendae* for five years from January 1st, 42 B.C.

who were in search of him, and was killed along with his son.*

'Cicero, when he arrived at Astura, and found a boat, at once embarked and with a favourable wind, sailed along the coast as far as Circeii. But when the sailors wished to put out to sea immediately from that place, whether it was for fear of the discomfort of the sea-voyage,† or from not yet having given up all trust in Caesar, he proceeded by land about twelve miles towards Rome. Again becoming distracted and changing his mind he returned to Astura. There he passed the night in terrible and desperate reflections: he thought even of going into Caesar's house secretly, and slaying himself on the hearth, so as to bring a curse on it. But fear of torture diverted him from this course. Forming other wild plans, he allowed his servants to carry him by sea to Caieta (Gaeta) where he had a villa, and a pleasant retreat during the heat of summer, when the Etesian winds blow deliciously. The village had a temple of Apollo, a little above the sea. From thence came a flock of crows, which settled, screaming, on Cicero's boat, as it was rowed to land. Sitting on each side of the yardarm, some kept cawing, and others plucking at the rope-ends: all on board regarded it as an evil omen.

'Then Cicero landed, and going to his villa, lay down to take some rest. The greater part of the crows sat on the window, noisily screaming, and one perched on the bed where Cicero lay covered up, and tried little by little with its beak to draw the coverlet

---

* We note the difference. Quintus' slaves betrayed him: Marcus' servants did everything possible to save a kind master.

† This was probably the reason. Cicero was a bad sailor.

from his face. When Cicero's servants saw this, they reproached themselves for waiting to see their master slain; the lower animals they said were helping and caring for him in his undeserved troubles, and yet they themselves were doing nothing for his protection. Then partly by entreaties, and partly by force, they succeeded in taking him and conveying him in a litter towards the sea. But now the murderers were at hand—a centurion Herennius, and a tribune Popillius (Laenas), whom Cicero had defended when charged with parricide, with attendant soldiers. Finding the door locked, they broke it open. When they did not find Cicero there, and those in the house said they did not know where he was, it is said that a young man to whom Cicero had given a liberal education, and a freedman of his brother Quintus, called Philologus,[138] told the tribune that the litter was being carried by rough woodland paths to the sea. The tribune then took a few men with him and hastened to the end of the wood. When Herennius came running along the path, Cicero saw him, and ordered his servants to lay the litter down on the ground. Then as was his wont, supporting his chin on his left hand, he looked fixedly on the assassins. When they saw him, all dishevelled and unkempt, his face haggard with anxiety, most of them covered their faces, while Herennius slew him. He stretched his neck out of the litter, and was thus slain, in his sixty-fourth year.

'Herennius cut off his head, and at the order of Antony, the hands which wrote the *Philippics*. . . . When these were brought to Rome, Antony happened to be holding an election of magistrates, and when he heard and saw what was done, he cried aloud that the main object of the proscriptions had been attained. He ordered Cicero's head and hands to be fixed above the Rostra—a sight at which the Romans shuddered, for they seemed to see there, not the face of Cicero, but the image of Antony's soul.' Caesar, when Cicero praised him for his clemency at Corfinium, replied, 'There is nothing I like better than that I should be true to myself and my enemies to themselves'. Antony attempted to imitate Caesar: but he never understood or could share his greatness.

The touching narrative seems very true to life: it illustrates Cicero's usual vacillations before danger, and his courage at the decisive moment. If we may trust Quintilian's quotation from him, which we cannot verify, he knew himself, when he said: 'I am not timid in facing dangers, but in attempting to guard against them'.

Octavian's sacrifice of Cicero to Antony's animosity is almost the only blot on a great character. Did he ever feel pricks of conscience? A story related by Plutarch suggests that he did. Long afterwards he surprised one of his grandsons reading a book. The boy in alarm attempted to conceal it under his cloak. Augustus took the book from him, and stood while he read a long passage. Then giving it back to the lad, he said: 'An eloquent man, my boy, eloquent and one who loved his country'. *

Plutarch continues: 'As soon as he had defeated Antony, being consul, he associated with himself Cicero's son, under whom the Senate destroyed the

---

* The Greek word the Emperor used is not to be rendered by one English word. It implies both great thoughts and their expression. It is used of Apollos in the Acts of the Apostles xviii. 24.

P

statues of Antony, abolished his other honours and decreed that thenceforward no Antony should be called Mark. Thus Fate awarded to the family of Cicero the completion of Antony's punishment.'

Chapter 12

CICERO'S SPEECHES AND RHETORICAL TREATISES

*How often have I wished that the heavenly wisdom could
find such an interpreter in speech as was Cicero in judicial
cases or in setting forth the philosophy of the Greeks, one
in whom genuine piety might vie with powers of exposition.*
ERASMUS to Sadoleto (Allen 2315)

THE Republican poet Catullus calls Cicero 'the most
eloquent of the descendants of Romulus, that are,
that have been or that will be in years to come', and
'the best of all pleaders even as he is himself the
worst of all poets': Virgil, the poet of the Augustan
régime, does not mention Cicero, unless, as some
people have thought, the portrait of Drances, the
virulent opponent of Turnus, is a veiled attack upon
him.

> Then Drances, foe inveterate, whom the fame
> Of Turnus aye with sidelong envy stirred,
> And stung to bitterness, lavish of wealth,
> Tongue-valiant, but a frosty hand for war,
> At council-board no vain adviser held,
> In faction strong—his mother's proud descent
> Ennobling whom an obscure sire begat.
>   (JAMES RHOADES)

But as Turnus could only be Antony, it is perhaps
unlikely that Virgil had Cicero in his mind at all.   It

has been, however, contended lately that Virgil only knew the caricature of Cicero which had been spread abroad by the literary circle of Pollio in the reign of Augustus. Certainly this exaggerated his mother's high birth into royal descent, and reduced his father to the proprietor of a laundry, a statement which Dio puts into the mouth of Calenus.[139] Both statements are ludicrously false, but Virgil may have believed them to be true. One would prefer to think that the gentle poet had not ascribed Cicero's opposition to Antony to envy; but one must admit that it is possible, if he had been brought up to think so.*

When Cicero had established his health after the two years' stay in Greece and Asia Minor (p. 25), it remained good throughout his life, as even Pollio tells us: 'Nature and Fortune alike were kind to him; he had a handsome face and up to old age he always enjoyed good health'.

He must have had a magnificent voice: we have had his description of his voice resounding over the Forum with the praises of Cassius. Whatever he said, he felt. Quintus is made to say, 'Many a time have I seen in you such passion of look and gesture, that I thought some power was rendering you unconscious of what you did'.[140] In pathos he was particularly strong: when he defended Ligarius, even Caesar showed signs of emotion.[141] He also excelled in vivid characterisation of persons or classes: we seem as we read to see the Gaulish witnesses swaggering about the Forum in military cloaks and breeches, with loud and menacing voices uttering their uncouth speech, or the crafty Alexandrians

---

* Mr. Trollope's idea that the statesman who quells a mob, in the simile (*Aen.* i. 100), is meant for Cicero is most unlikely.

shrugging their shoulders and perjuring themselves
with a solemn countenance.

   He began his career as an orator with a magnificent and successful defence in a case of which more
experienced men would have fought shy (p. 22).
His next great case was an equally famous prosecution. Later he seems to have confined himself to
defences.* 'The side of the defence', he says, at the
very end of his life, 'is more honourable; still that of
the prosecution also has very often established a reputation' (among seven instances he gives his own
'defence of the Sicilians', preferring that description
to 'prosecution of Verres'). He goes on to say:
'This sort of work may be done once in a life-time,
or at all events not often, except as a service to the
country; for it is no disgrace to be often employed
in the prosecution of her enemies. And yet a limit
should be set even to that. For it requires a heart-
less man, it seems, or rather one who is well nigh inhuman, to be arraigning one person after another on
capital charges.† It is not only fraught with danger
to the prosecutor himself, but is damaging to his reputation to allow himself to be called a prosecutor,'
Was Cicero expressing his own kindly feelings here,
or the etiquette of the Roman Bar? Cicero's instance is an older Marcus Brutus 142 who made a
regular business of prosecution, and, probably in
consequence, was never a candidate for public office.
He might have instanced his young friend Caelius,
who, not content with his brilliant debut in prosecuting Cicero's colleague as consul, frequently was

   * A rare exception is the case of Bursa (p. 160 n.).
   † I.e. involving not death but loss of citizenship and therefore usually
exile.

prosecutor: 'You who accuse others', said Cicero, 'ought to be more careful of your own conduct.' [143] It is probable that those who were ambitious of office seldom prosecuted. There was the additional deterrent in Cicero's case of a naturally kind disposition. He goes on to lay down another rule. 'Never prefer a capital charge against any person who may be innocent.'

But in defence 'we need not have scruples against undertaking on occasion the defence of a guilty person, provided he be not infamously depraved and wicked. For people expect it; custom sanctions it; humanity also accepts it. *It is always the business of the juror in a trial to find out the truth; it is sometimes the business of the advocate to maintain what is plausible, even if it be not strictly true, though I should not venture to say this, especially in an ethical treatise, if it were not also the position of Panaetius, the strictest of Stoics.*' No moralist would now defend this position, and we are surprised to hear that Panaetius did. For a somewhat highly coloured parallel in the case of the English Bar, we may adduce Mr. Jaggers in Dickens' *Great Expectations*. He would never allow a client to confess to him his guilt; provided he did not know it from the defendant's own lips, he would conduct any case. This was pretty much the practice of Cicero.

Undoubtedly, however, what weighed most with him was what he goes on to say: 'briefs for the defence are most likely to bring glory and popularity to the pleader', especially if one is oppressed and persecuted as was Sextus Roscius.* In 54 B.C. when

---

* *De Off.* ii. 51. Cp. also *Ad Att.* iv. 17: 'Three candidates will probably be prosecuted. What shall you be able to say for them? you will ask. May I die if I know. Certainly I find no suggestion in those three books you praise so highly' (*De Oratore*).

Cicero was kept very busy, after saying he has to
defend a Drusus and a Scaurus, he complacently
adds, 'These will make grand titles for my speeches,
and perhaps I shall have the consuls-designate too.
If Scaurus is not one of them, it will go hard with
him.' [144] Yet Drusus was acquitted by a margin of
four votes; Scaurus, though not elected consul, by
fifty-seven out of sixty-five.

Of course Cicero's great triumph in this way was
his successful defence of Murena, when the defeated
candidate for the consulship, Sulpicius the jurist, and
Cato, the guardian of public morals, prosecuted him
for corruption, at the most dangerous stage of the
rising of Catiline.   It was very awkward for Cicero
to defend Murena.   No doubt he had been guilty
of corrupt practices as candidates usually were.
Sulpicius was a great friend of Cicero; Cato was an
invaluable political ally.   Worst of all, he had himself recently carried a new law making the penalties
of bribery much more severe, and prescribing exile
as a punishment, which had never previously been
the case.   But from the executive point of view, it
was essential that Murena should not be unseated.
His colleague's time would have then been entirely
taken up with the by-election, at which Catiline
might have been carried by a *coup-de-main*, and then
anarchy was to be feared.

The prosecution had made it easy for Cicero to
laugh the case out of court.   They had attacked
Murena on three heads, private misconduct, personal
unworthiness in comparison with Sulpicius, and
corrupt practices.   This enables Cicero to devote
extremely little of his speech to the real charge, which
he flatly denies.   'There was treating alleged': this

was done by Murena's friends. 'Seats were given away at the show of gladiators': a Vestal virgin put her seats at his disposal. 'Men were hired to meet Murena': he was simply given a great reception on his arrival from the province of Asia.

The aspersions on his character are as easily brushed aside. He did not go to Asia to enjoy himself but to fight. He is described as a dancer. That is a term of abuse which Cato ought not to apply to a consul. It usually carries with it the implication of revelling and loose living. These are not alleged: why then find the shadow of debauchery where debauchery itself is not to be found?

Cicero then set himself to the congenial task of making the jury laugh, when he compared the lawyer's qualifications with those of the soldier. 'You, Sulpicius, get up before daylight to give answers to your clients, he to reach his objective with his army in good time. Cockcrow wakes you, the bugle-blast him. You draw up a pleading: he sets a battle in array. You see that your clients are not caught: he sees that cities or camps are not captured. He knows well how to repel the forces of the enemy, you how to keep out rain water. He is practised in pushing forward the boundaries of the Empire, you in controlling those of a farm.' Your profession, Sulpicius, is useful indeed, but humdrum and ordinary: I myself would undertake to acquire a working knowledge of it in three days. It can neither bring you votes nor glory; Murena's achievements in the field have won both. And if Cato has ridiculed the Mithridatic war as waged with women, he is talking nonsense. All our most serious wars have been with Greeks: and has not Mithridates given enough trouble to Sulla, to Murena's father, to Lucullus, to Pompey himself, who would not leave the East nor regard his task as ended till he heard of Mithridates' death?

The most amusing part of the speech is where he rallies Cato on his unbending and austere Stoic principles. 'Marcus Cato's splendid and super-human qualities, you must know, gentlemen, are his own: his hardness is due not to nature but his teacher, one Zeno, whose disciples are called Stoics.' These are his sentiments and precepts. 'The philosopher is never influenced by favour, never pardons an offence. No one shows pity but worthless fools. No true man ever yields to entreaties or is placated. Philosophers alone are, though misshapen, beautiful, though mendicants, rich, though enslaved, kings; we who are not philosophers, are runaways, exiles, enemies, madmen. All sins are equal; any offence is a shocking crime: to wring the neck of a cock unnecessarily is as bad as strangling a father. The philosopher has no opinion, he always knows; he regrets nothing, is never deceived, never changes his mind.' Cato has not only learned these maxims, he lives by them. 'Have the tax farmers any petition? See that influence has no weight. Do suppliants come in misery and wretchedness? You will be a base scoundrel if you do anything under the influence of compassion. Does a man admit that he has sinned, and ask pardon for the offence? It is shocking to pardon a sin. But the offence is said to be trivial: no matter, all sins are equal.'

To this Cicero briefly opposes the milder teaching of the New Academy. It is said that Cato used an ambiguous phrase, which might mean either 'How

witty our consul is!' or 'What a ridiculous exhibi-
tion he is making of himself'.

Then later he eloquently appeals to Cato to think
of the public danger. 'In this critical state of affairs,
it is for you, Marcus Cato, who are born not for me
or for yourself but for your fatherland, to see what is
going on, and to retain as helper, defender and ally
in the state, a consul who, as the time most requires,
is marked out by fortune for cherishing peace, by
training for waging war, by courage and experience
for any emergency whatsoever.' Opportunism can
seldom have been more appropriate, or wit more
timely, than in Cicero's defence of Murena.

Cicero took the same line in defending Flaccus
in 59 B.C. Flaccus was the praetor in 63 who
arrested Volturcius and the Allobrogian envoys. He
was the immediate predecessor of Quintus Cicero as
governor of Asia in 62, and some time afterwards
was prosecuted for extortion, but Cicero and Hortensius between them succeeded in securing for him
an acquittal. Cicero takes the line that the condemnation of Gaius Antonius, whom earlier in the
year he had not been able to save, was vengeance for
the death of Catiline, and that now Flaccus is
attacked to be a victim for the death of Lentulus.

He alludes to his successful defence of Murena,
'because, while Catiline was still waging war on the
Republic, the judges agreed with me that it was
necessary to have two consuls on the first of January'.
'Wise and grave judges when deciding in criminal
trials have always considered what the interests of
the state, the general safety and the general neces-
sities required.' But by this time the argument had
lost all its force, and the case was obviously a bad

one. Cicero does his best by ingeniously attacking the credit of Greek witnesses, sometimes in a very amusing way. One Phrygian witness who came from the treeless Axylon district had died, and Flaccus was accused of having made away with him. The fact was, said Cicero, that the man who had already done his worst and like a bee discharged his sting, having never seen a fig tree in his life before, ate so greedily of figs that he died in consequence! In this trial Hortensius made a handsome eulogy of Cicero as consul.[145]

About the *Verrines*, the *Catilinarians* and the *Philippics* enough has already been said in previous chapters. As little as possible should be said about the two vulgar invectives against Vatinius as witness, and against Piso. It is only pleasant to note, that while Cicero's feuds with Clodius and Antony were irreparable, and he probably was never on good terms again with Piso,* he was commanded to defend, and did successfully defend Vatinius. He, good-natured vulgarian that he was, showed his gratitude by befriending Cicero after Pharsalus, and corresponded with him when governor of Illyricum, promised to do his best to find a runaway slave for him, and even chaffed him about his having recommended—no doubt at second-hand—some disreputable rascal.[146]

Cicero's speech for Cluentius in 66 B.C. has always been considered a *tour de force*. It is certainly a powerful masterpiece of denunciation; and as Cicero, according to Quintilian, boasted that he had by his speech thrown dust in the eyes of the jury, it is

---

* He exclaimed 'I love even Piso', when, at the beginning of the Civil War, Piso refused to join Caesar.

impossible for us to unravel the actual truth. Cicero
was embarrassed by two facts. He had himself
previously defended an accomplice of Oppianicus
senior, and had to ridicule his own previous performance. Moreover, the man he was defending
against a charge of poisoning brought by Oppianicus
junior,* had, eight years previously, prosecuted
Oppianicus senior for poisoning, and had won his
case. But it was notorious that in that trial there
had been wholesale bribery. The president of the
court and several members of it, as well as a disreputable go-between, had been tried. Cicero has to
dispel what he calls an 'inveterate prejudice' which
he had once himself shared.

His method is simple. The bribery had been by
the defendant, but he had fallen out with his own
agents: the man Staienus who had been convicted
was employed by Oppianicus, not Cluentius. This
is probably the point in which Cicero took the jury
in. He is successful in everything but in making
us believe that his client was the *innocent* victim of a
vicious mother and an evil stepfather. The light
thrown on the inner life of an Italian country town,
and the medical profession in particular, is lurid.
The series of murders stated to have been committed
by Oppianicus with impunity is less incredible when
we are told that he was a Sullan partisan. The narrative is characterised by the most dramatic vividness.
It culminates in the description of the wicked

---

* It was a filial duty at Rome for a son to attack the prosecutor of a
father. Thus the Luculli prosecuted Servilius (*Acad.* ii. 1, 1), and M.
Calidius having accused Q. Gallius of corrupt practices in 66, Gallius'
two sons accused Calidius on the same charge in 51 (*Ad Fam.* viii. 1, 1;
9, 5). Antony obviously warns Cicero that he might be prosecuted by
young Clodius (*Ad Att.* xix. 13a, 2).

mother Sassia, who according to Cicero had supplanted her daughter in the affections of her son-in
law, had married the murderer of her first husband
on condition that he did away with the three children,* and had cut out the tongue of a slave and
crucified him. 'What manner of journey think you
did this woman make to Rome? I heard and learnt
it from many, living as I do near Aquinum and
Fabrateria. How they flocked together in those
towns! What groans went up from men and women
alike to think that a woman of Larinum was starting
thence to go all the way from the Adriatic coast to
Rome with a great retinue and large funds, the better
to contrive the ruin on a capital charge of her own
son! I will go so far as to say that there was not
one of them but thought that every place by which
she passed needed to be purified; not one but felt
that the earth itself, the common mother of us all,
was suffering pollution from the feet of that accursed
mother. And so in no town was she allowed to halt;
of all those many inns she found not one whose host
did not flee before her hateful glance: she was fain to
entrust herself to night and to solitude, rather than
to any city or hostelry.

'And of her present intentions, designs, and daily
plottings which of us does she imagine to be ignorant?
We are well aware whom she has approached, to
whom she has promised money, whose loyalty she
has tried to undermine with a bribe: nay more, we
have found out about her midnight sacrifices which
she thinks so secret, her infamous prayers, and her
unholy vows by which she calls even Almighty God
to witness her crime: not realising that the favour

* Sallust makes a similar statement about Orestilla and Catiline.

of Heaven may be gained by duty done to God and man, and by righteous prayers, not by base superstition and victims offered for the success of crime. But well I know that Almighty God has spurned from His altars and His temples this woman's rage and cruelty.' It is a wonderful and telling indictment. But to blacken Sassia, though it inevitably tended to whitewash Cluentius in the minds of the jury at the moment when they heard the orator, hardly clears his reputation with the leisurely reader of the speech.

After Sassia comes Clodia in Cicero's gallery of infamous women. He was called on in 56 to help his young friend and former pupil Caelius out of the scrape into which he had got himself. He had quarrelled with Clodia, given her a coarse nickname which stuck, and dubbed her Clytaemnestra as being as fatal to her husband Metellus Celer as the Argive queen was to Agamemnon. Moreover, he had twice over, against the advice of Cicero,[147] prosecuted one Atratinus. 'In order to put an end to the gossip about his vicious and slothful life (what he did he did against my will and in spite of my strong remonstrances) he prosecuted a friend of mine for corrupt practices. Even when acquitted he pursues him still, drags him back into court, will not be guided by any of us, and is far more violent than I could wish.' Clodia with the fury of a woman scorned induced the younger Atratinus, who was only seventeen and probably her latest victim, to bring Caelius into court on charges of assault and poisoning. Caelius defended himself but also obtained the assistance of Crassus and Cicero.

Cicero cannot altogether whitewash the character

of his young friend and is obliged to put forward the
plea that young men must be allowed to sow their
wild oats.   At the same time he presents Clodia
with this dilemma.   If she is as bad as rumour says,
Caelius cannot be severely censured for his connection with her: 'If you are not such a woman—and I
would much rather believe that you are not—then
what is it that they impute to Caelius?'   'Either
your modesty will supply us with the defence that
nothing has been done by Caelius with undue wantonness; or else your impudence will give both him and
everyone else great facilities for defending themselves.'   Cicero's nickname for her, the Medea of
the Palatine, must have annoyed her as much as those
of Caelius: for as Jason threw over Medea, so Caelius
had broken his liaison with her.   The most thrilling
passage of the speech is where Cicero describes the
death-bed of Metellus Celer, and goes on: 'Shall yon
woman proceed from this house and dare to talk of
the rapid operation of poison?   Will she not fear the
house itself that it may utter some accusation or the
walls that are privy to guilt?   Will she not shudder
at the recollection of that fatal and melancholy night?
I return to the actual charge against my friend, but
the mention of the end of this great and gallant man
has hampered my speech with tears and overcome my
mind with grief.'   Caelius was acquitted, and we
hear no more of Clodia: probably she died before her
equally notorious brother met his end in 52.   This
leads us on to the speech for Milo.

This speech on behalf of Milo, when arraigned
before a special court, guarded by the troops of
Pompey, is not that actually delivered by Cicero,
who was himself intimidated and did not show at his

best, but it is the elaboration of it afterwards published. It is said that when a copy of the published
speech was sent to Milo in exile, he said it was a
good thing it was never delivered, for then he would
not be enjoying the flavour of the mullets of Marseilles. This was a high compliment to Cicero's
influence over any ordinary Roman jury, which we
have seen illustrated in the case of Cluentius: but
doubtless on this occasion the trial was intended to
be a mere form, and the conclusion was foregone.
Cicero refused to take the line of justifiable homicide,
and endeavoured to prove that Milo caused Clodius
to be killed in self-defence. The wonder is, by the
way, that no murder had taken place before, as for
the last five years the pair had been looking for one
another: it is extremely probable that Clodius had,
as Cicero states, prophesied the death of Milo in
three or four days. As obviously no one could be
condemned for a death which was caused in self-
defence, Cicero maintains that the only question the
jury has to decide is, which plotted the death of the
other. Clodius had everything to gain by Milo's
death: for he would then be praetor under favourable consuls. Milo had nothing particular to gain,
because he was sure to be elected consul and would
then be the official superior of his enemy. Cicero
omits the possibility, which no doubt represents the
fact, that it was an accidental meeting, and in the
brawl, Milo's forces being superior in numbers,
Clodius lost his life.

There are many ingenious points in the speech.
It was said that the death of Clodius was made more
shocking because it took place amid the monuments
of his ancestors: 'They ask me to believe that Appius

the Blind constructed the road not for the use of the people, but as a place wherein his descendants might with impunity play the highwayman'.* He then goes on to relate how Clodius murdered a knight with impunity on that same Appian Way, just as he had previously plotted the death of Pompey and himself. Then he adds in a fine passage of sustained irony: 'But how absurd of me to dare to compare Drusus, Africanus (whose murders were never avenged), Pompey and myself with Publius Clodius! These acts were tolerable: none can with equanimity endure the death of Publius Clodius! The Senate mourns, the equestrian order is inconsolable; the whole community is bowed down with affliction; the municipalities wear the garb of woe; the colonies are heart-broken: why, the very fields are pining for a citizen so kindly, so beneficent, so gentle!' (The irony that consists in stating as true that which is obviously the opposite of the truth is not nearly as common in ancient as in modern speeches.) To the question 'Why did Milo emancipate the slaves who had defended his life?' Cicero replies by scouting the idea that it was to prevent them from being examined. That could not be to ascertain the facts, for the fact that Milo killed Clodius is not disputed: rather it was to reward them for their loyal service.

The peroration is in Cicero's grandest manner, but the eulogy of Milo is overdone, and the pathos is forced. There was no getting out of the fact that one hooligan had killed another, and Rome would be better without the survivor. But as a desperate

* *Pro Caelio* 14. 'Was it for this that I made the Appian Way, that you should travel along it escorted by other men than your husband?' Cicero is using again the same *cliché*, in the *Pro Milone*.

Q

effort to save a friend, whose political help had been invaluable to Cicero, as a fine specimen of invective, the *Miloniana* can still be read: but it pales beside the real force of the *Catilinarians* and *Philippics*. As to the force of Cicero's invective, he mentions,[148] that he once made Hortensius unable to reply, that similarly Curio the elder was silenced and that he struck Catiline dumb.

This brief survey of some of Cicero's orations may fitly end with a little speech in which, at the height of his prestige after the suppression of the conspiracy of Catiline, he defended the Roman citizenship of the Greek poet Archias of Antioch, whom he had known in boyhood. Archias had been made a citizen of Heraclea in southern Italy, which had treaty relations with Rome, and had long been domiciled in Italy, when a law was passed granting Roman citizenship to all persons who had such qualifications and gave in their names to the praetor within sixty days. According to Cicero this was done, but as the records of Heraclea had been destroyed, his status could only be attested by the Luculli, his patrons and friends. Cicero asks leave to treat the matter in a style unusual to the law courts.* He sketches his client's brilliant career and calls the attention of the court to the importance of literary studies generally and especially of poetry. Ennius, a native of Rudiae, was made a Roman citizen: shall this citizen of Heraclea be expelled from Rome? It is very wrong to suppose that his Greek poetry has

---

* The 'novel and unforensic style' which Cicero asks leave to adopt has nothing to do with language or schools of oratory. It consists in the strictly irrelevant introduction of the *Encomium on Literature*, and the ingenious suggestion that the poetry of Archias has celebrated and will continue to celebrate the greatness of Rome.

less distinction than Latin: for Greek is almost universally read, while Latin is confined within narrow limits. It may be asked why he himself feels such interest in Archias. 'It is because he provides refreshment for my spirit after the clamour of the courts and repose for senses jaded by their vulgar wrangling. Do you think that I could find material for my daily speeches on so manifold a variety of topics, did I not cultivate my mind with study, or that my mind could endure so great a strain, did I not study to provide it with relaxation? I am a votary of literature and make the confession unashamed: shame belongs rather to the bookish recluse who knows not how to apply his reading to the good of his fellows, or to manifest its fruits to the eyes of all. But what shame should be mine, gentlemen, who have made it a rule of my life for all these years never to allow the sweets of a cloistered ease, or the seductions of pleasure, or the enticements of repose to prevent me from aiding any man in the hour of his need? How then can I be justly blamed or censured, if it shall be found that I have devoted to literature a portion of my leisure hours, no longer than others without blame have devoted to the pursuit of material gain, to the celebration of festival or games, to pleasure and the repose of mind and body, to protracted banqueting, or perhaps to the gaming-board or to ball-playing? I have the better right to this concession, because my devotion to letters strengthens my oratorical powers, and these, such as they are, have never failed my friends in their hour of peril. Yet insignificant though these powers may seem to be, I fully realise from what source I draw what is highest in them. Had

I not persuaded myself from my youth up, thanks
to the moral lessons derived from wise reading, that
nothing is to be greatly sought after in this life save
glory and honour, and that in their quest all bodily
pains and all dangers of death or exile should be
lightly accounted, I should never have borne for the
safety of you all, the brunt of many a bitter encounter,
or bared my breast to the daily onsets of abandoned
persons. All literature, all philosophy, all history
abound with incentives to noble action, incentives
which would be buried in darkness were the light
of the written word not flashed upon them. How
many pictures of high endeavour the great authors
of Greece and Rome have drawn for our use, and
bequeathed to us, not only for our contemplation,
but for our emulation? These I have held ever
before my vision throughout my public career, and
have guided the workings of my brain and my soul
by meditating on patterns of excellence.'

It may be said that the great men of the past,
whose merits have been celebrated in literature, were
themselves unlearned. It is true that learning
without natural ability is not so good as natural
ability without learning: but an Africanus or Laelius
in whom both were combined outshone all others.
'But even if there were no such benefit but pleasure
only to be derived from study, nevertheless this
mental relaxation would be counted most humane
and liberal. Other relaxations do not suit all times,
ages or places: these studies are the food * of youth,
the delight of old age, the ornament of prosperity,
the refuge and consolation of adversity; they give
joy at home, they are no hindrance abroad; they are

* Perhaps the right reading is 'stimulus' or 'employment'.

our nightly companions, they go abroad with us, they are our companions in rustic retirement. Even if we could not touch or taste them ourselves, we should be bound to admire them, when we saw them in others.' * Fifteen years later Cicero was to exemplify the truth of his words.

Cicero was not only an orator, he wrote on the theory and history of oratory. Passing over his early treatise *On Invention*, we may regard as his chief works the *De Oratore* in three books of 55 B.C. dedicated to his brother, and the treatises of 46 B.C., *Brutus* or *On Famous Orators* and the *Orator* dedicated to Marcus Brutus, and this notwithstanding that there was great difference between the styles favoured by Brutus and Cicero respectively. For there were three contemporary schools of oratory.

First there was the florid Asiatic style, the acknowledged master of which was Hortensius. Cicero in his early speeches (*e.g.* for Roscius of Ameria) had been in danger of falling into this: he criticises his own effort later as declamatory and redundant.[149] That speech does sometimes use two essentially synonymous words, when one would have sufficed: but how grand and sonorous this may be, is illustrated to us by the Book of Common Prayer.

In fact the best English parallel to the sonorous Latin of Cicero is the equally sonorous language of the Prayer Book. The reason is that the rhythmical structure of the Prayer Book is derived, with certain adaptations to our language, from the rhythmical prose, first brought to perfection in Latin by

* *Tusc.* v. 36, 105: 'What is more delightful than leisure devoted to literature? That literature I mean which gives us the knowledge of the infinite greatness of nature, and, in this actual world of ours, of the sky, the lands, the seas?'

Cicero.[150] The Litany will make this instantly plain. In the three phrases 'Lords of the Council', 'all the Nobility', 'wisdom and understanding' we have the three commonest cadences of Ciceronian prose, afterwards stereotyped by the Papal chancery, and commonly called the 'Cursus'. These are identical with three-quarters of the cadences (*clausulae*) in Cicero's extant speeches (17,902 according to Zielinski). It was in the effective variation of these cadences that Cicero excelled. The Roman public was extremely appreciative of rhythmical construction, as Cicero shows by a quotation from a speech by the tribune Carbo,[151] but he condemns the excessive use of the third instance above (*dichoreus*) by the Asiatic school.

The triplets of which Cicero is so fond, *e.g.* 'Sicily with hides, clothes, corn, dressed, fed, armed our forces', frequently occur in the Prayer Book, *e.g.* 'full, perfect and sufficient, sacrifice, oblation and satisfaction'. A House of Commons speech also illustrates this: 'The honourable gentleman combines the language, the style and the gestures of the Bar, the stage and the pulpit'. The only difference is that rhythm in English requires 'and', while Cicero always has *asyndeton*, that is, he omits the conjunction. The triplet 'to strengthen such as do stand, to comfort and help the weak-hearted, and to raise up them that fall' is thoroughly Ciceronian.

Cicero hammers an idea into his hearers by repetition in varied language, but there is seldom anything in him of what he himself calls 'empty and ludicrous volubility',[152] and you cannot, as a rule, shorten his sentences without spoiling their rhythmical construction. As an orator he must have been more

forcible when heard, than he seems when read.
'You cannot add anything to Cicero,' said Quintilian:
but one can as little take anything away.   One does
not agree with Dr. Johnson, who proposed to improve Gray's 'Elegy' by shortening the lines.

That the defect of the Asiatic style was exuberance and diffuseness is agreed, and Cicero had been
cured by Molon of this tendency.   His style remains
much the same from Verrines to Philippics.   But
there was also the so-called Attic style, which Brutus,
Caesar and, above all, Calvus adopted.   Brutus disliked Cicero's style: Cicero regarded Brutus' as
lacking in force.   Shakespeare again probably does
Brutus more than justice: for of his speech at the
meeting on the Capitol, Cicero says: [153] 'If I had
pleaded that cause, I should have written with more
fire'.   Brutus had the elegance of the Attic style,
but the force and passion of Demosthenes were
impossible to him; he could not fulminate.   The
letters of Brutus give us some idea of his style, and
this sentence may help to illustrate it: 'Living at
Rome, do you regard that as being safe: the thing,
not the place, must guarantee that to me'.[154]   The
order of the last words would infallibly with Cicero
have been different.   Brutus' order is much nearer
to that of English: Cicero no doubt thought it tame.

We have no extant specimen of Caesar's oratorical
style: none of his speeches have been preserved.
But in the pleading for Ligarius, Cicero adopted a
style much nearer to the Attic than usual, in the
hope of thus being more persuasive.   The peroration
may be quoted in illustration: 'In nothing do men
more nearly approach the gods than in saving men:
your position has nothing prouder in it than the

power, your character nothing nobler than the wish,
to preserve all you can. The case might perhaps
call for a longer speech, your character a briefer.
Deeming it therefore more expedient that you yourself should speak rather than I or anyone else, I will
now close: merely will I remind you that if you grant
life to the absent Ligarius, you will grant it to all
those present.' It is difficult in English to convey
these delicate differences: but surely it must be felt
that for Cicero this was an unusual peroration. He
spoke in a manner which was likely to appeal to
Caesar, paying him the subtle compliment of imitat-
ing his style.

Calvus was a young poet and orator of distinction,
who like Catullus was a strong anti-Caesarian. When
only twenty-seven years of age he was opposed to
Cicero in the trial of Vatinius, 54 B.C. Calvus had
no high opinion of the leader of the Roman Bar: he
thought him 'sloppy and flabby';[155] but Cicero
would have replied, 'You may be more terse, but
nevertheless you do not succeed in showing force'.
This is the substance of Cicero's very kindly criticism of him. He was very sorry that, after the death
of Calvus, a letter criticising him had got out.[156]
He acknowledged his talent, his wide and abstruse
reading, he deplored his choice of the Attic style,
but admitted that he was a perfect exponent of it.
But he lacked 'blood' and 'force'. Thus though
the connoisseurs appreciated him, he did not go
down with the vulgar, as Cicero certainly did.

It would be impossible to give any adequate idea
of Cicero's rhetorical writings. Cicero did not over-
rate the part which theory plays in the making of an
orator. 'Speech is not developed out of theory, but

theory out of speech.' [157] 'Theory once learned puts
itself into practice, and produces its effect.' 'But no
theory can give the sense of what is appropriate.' [158]
As has already been stated he always held strongly
that philosophy, by which he meant culture, was an
essential element in the forming of an orator. 'My
own talent for speaking', he says in the *Orator*, 'or
whatever value may be ascribed to it, has been fed
not in the workshop of rhetoric but in the alleys of
the Academy'. These works show a wide acquaintance with the orators of Greece and Rome, they are
characterised by great sanity and kindliness of judgement, and the references of Cicero to himself, as an
acknowledged exponent of the art, are in good taste
and even modest. The same is the case when he
deals with his literary performances. His boastfulness begins when he touches on politics and his own
political performances; because they are so bitterly
criticised by his enemies, he feels it necessary to
magnify and even exaggerate them. That is the
real ground of his somewhat impudent request to
Lucceius, to disregard the canons of history, and
'bestow on our love a little more than may be allowed
by truth'.*

But the Attic style prevailed after Cicero was
dead. Caesar had praised his copiousness: but the
next generation thought him redundant. Sometimes we think him so, too: but then comes a noble
outburst of passion, and he takes his place by
Demosthenes. Between Livy † and Quintilian ‡ no

* *Ad Fam.* v. 12, 3. Cicero says he is downright shameless: 'for a
letter does not blush'.
† Livy said it would require a Cicero to praise him as he deserved.
‡ *Instit. Orat* xi. 106: 'No word can be taken from Demosthenes:
no word added to Cicero'.

Roman did justice to Cicero. But the anonymous yet illustrious Greek, whoever he was, who somewhere in the neighbourhood of A.D. 40, wrote the treatise *On the Sublime*, at any rate found in Cicero something to illustrate that theme. Finally, when Vespasian appointed Quintilian professor of rhetoric, owing to the public lectures he delivered, Cicero came to his own again. It would have been ungrateful if Rome had not paid the tribute due to her most patriotic son. In the *Brutus* there is not a single speaker for a whole century of whom he does not say the best that he can: 'I didn't think', says Atticus, 'I should have heard you praising an Autronius or a Staienus'.

It is not often that a first-rate exponent of art can satisfactorily describe the secrets of the art, though Sir Joshua Reynolds did something of the sort for painting. Cicero by his oratorical trilogy atones for the conceit, of which he was sometimes guilty, by his judicious estimates of many Greek and Roman orators.

A pleader at the Bar has the one object before him, to persuade. If we think Cicero's methods sometimes very unfair and his arguments fallacious, we must put that down largely to the character of the Roman juries.* Pliny the Elder points out how he seemed to be able to do anything with the Roman People in his consulship. Under the spell of his voice, they rejected the Agrarian Law, that is their daily bread: they forgave Roscius for reserving seats in the theatres to knights; and the sons of the proscribed forbore to seek office: 'before your genius Catiline ran away'.[159]

* 'The taste of the Romans was always the controller of the eloquence of orators' (*Orator*, 24).

Then Pliny indulges in a lyrical outburst, rare in
so sober and dull a writer. 'Hail thou that first of
all wast named father of thy fatherland, thou first
didst in the garb of peace earn a triumph and the
laurel of the tongue, being equally the father of
Roman eloquence and Latin literature (as the dictator
Caesar, once thy enemy, said of thee), and didst win
a laurel greater than that of any triumph, in proportion as it means far more to have extended the
boundaries of Roman intellect than those of the
Empire.'

Chapter 13

CICERO'S PHILOSOPHIC WORKS

I have written more in this short time since the downfall of the Republic than I did in the course of many years while the Republic stood. De Officiis, iii. 1, 4

CICERO wrote two works in imitation of Plato, *On the Republic* and *On the Laws*. The completion of the first and the beginning of the second belong to the period between 54 and the middle of 51, when he went to Cilicia. This is proved by a letter written to Atticus partly from Delos and partly on board ship,[160] in which he says, 'I shall expect a letter from you of a more statesmanlike character, as you are just now running through my treatise (*De Republica*) with our friend Thallumetus', obviously a slave or freedman in Atticus' publishing establishment. Atticus had apparently expedited the publication: for Caelius writes to Cicero after the latter's departure: 'Your political treatise is universally popular'.[161] The public seems to have hailed the work as an attempt to secure an adjustment of political and economic conflicts by conciliation and compromise.

We have unfortunately only fragments of the six books *De Republica*.* It is a dialogue supposed to

* The Loeb edition (tr. Keyes) presents these in a readable form, cp. *Ad Att.* vi. 1, 8 (Feb. 20th, 50), 'six books'.

have taken place in the garden of the younger Africanus in 129 B.C. between a number of leading Romans.   It presents the Roman State as the ideal balance of the three simple and good forms of government, kingship, aristocracy and democracy. The third book dealt with justice as the necessary basis of a commonwealth.   Scipio is made to say, 'As in music harmony is produced by the proportionate blending of unlike tones, so is a state made harmonious by agreement between dissimilar elements, brought about by a fair and reasonable blending of the upper, middle and lower classes just as if they were musical tones'.   (St Augustine [162] enables us to read on.)   'What the musicians call song is concord in a state, the strongest and best bond of permanent union in any commonwealth; and such concord can never be brought about without the aid of justice.'   In a lost passage the thesis that a state cannot be carried on without occasional injustice is refuted; and then Scipio lays down, 'A Republic (*respublica*) means an affair of the People (*res Populi*). The People is not any fortuitous aggregate, but an aggregate allied by an agreement as to justice and by common participation in advantage.'   It is unfortunate that we have not more of the practical suggestions of the treatise as to the means whereby this harmony might be recovered and 'the colours restored to the ancient painting'.   Ennius wrote:

The commonwealth of Rome is founded firm
On ancient customs and on men of might.

But now 'the loss of our customs is due to the lack of men, and we retain only the form of the commonwealth, but have long since lost its substance.

Leadership properly belongs to those who are really, not conventionally, the best.'

The famous 'Dream of Scipio', with which the treatise closed, is a powerful argument for high aims and standards, by exhibiting the best men of the past living a life of pure spirit in the Milky Way, and listening to the music of the Spheres. The moral which the elder Africanus enforces on the younger is: 'Therefore if thou wilt look on high, and contemplate this resting place and everlasting home, thou wilt no longer attend to the gossip of the vulgar herd nor put thy trust in human rewards for thy exploits. Virtue herself, by her own charms, must lead thee on to true glory.'

The treatise *On the Laws* was probably begun in 52 B.C., for it contains a reference to the death of Clodius.[163] Cicero may have been working at it in 46 B.C.,[164] but as it is not in his list of philosophical works in the beginning of the second book *On Divination*, it seems almost certain that it was only published after his death. It is much more of a real dialogue than is usual with Cicero. Quintus, Atticus and himself hold conversations on his estate at Arpinum, first in a wood containing the oak of Marius, then on the bank of the river Liris, and then on an island in its tributary the Fibrenus. We have three books practically complete, but the treatise must have been in five books.[165] As one would expect, the laws, drafted in archaic language, are for an ideal Rome. They first regulate the ancestral worship: no dissenters are allowed. Secondly they prescribe the duties of the magistrates. Two are to have royal powers. As they lead, judge and confer, they may be called praetors, judges or consuls.

'When serious wars or civil dissensions arise, there may be a dictator for not longer than six months.' The faults of the tribunate are admitted, but the institution is defended, in spite of the outrages of Clodius,[166] and even Pompey's action at the time is excused. This is an instance of Cicero's magnanimity at the end of his life which had not been sufficiently noticed.

The really important period of Cicero's literary production in philosophy is however 46–44 B.C. Until he provided the educated Roman with a complete introduction to philosophy, the word itself had hardly been established in the Roman language, and the thing was in the main a foreign and expensive luxury exclusively enjoyed by the wealthy, who liked to keep each his tame Greek philosopher and pick up fragments from conversation with him, carried on of course in the Greek language. In the twinkling of an eye Cicero changed all that. In the space of about two years he did what no one else was capable of doing, not even Varro; he created a philosophical vocabulary for Latin and he supplied readable discussions of the whole field over which philosophy then ranged, with the exception of what we now call Natural Science, though even to that he made frequent reference. In considering this amazing feat, we ought not so much to consider what is the value of Cicero to us—any actual mistakes he made should of course be pointed out—but what was the value of Cicero to his own age and to the whole history of thought in the West. From that point of view it will be found that the great scholar Zielinski was guilty of no exaggeration, when he said: 'The history of civilisation knows few moments equal in importance to the sojourn of Cicero in his country-seats during the brief period of Caesar's sole rule'.

Cicero had laboriously pursued the study of philosophy throughout his life in every interval allowed by his arduous labours in politics and at the Bar. An accident greatly assisted his studies. Servius Claudius, a man of letters, who could detect by ear a spurious verse of Plautus, died in 60 B.C., and left his library to Paetus, Cicero's witty Epicurean friend. He, thinking that it would be of greater use to Cicero than to himself, made a present of the whole to Cicero, who received it with the greatest joy. No doubt it was of material assistance to him: but when it failed him, he could always borrow from Atticus in Rome, consult the magnificent library of Lucullus at Tusculum, or the equally comprehensive collection of Faustus Sulla at Cumae, on which he 'feasted' in 55.

We have seen how as a youth he had been introduced to the three most fashionable schools of philosophy by listening to Phaedrus the Epicurean, Diodotus the Stoic and Philo the Academic (p. 15). He chose the latter as his chief guide, and returned to him at the end of his life, though more influenced than perhaps he realised by Stoic doctrine. In his later two years in Greece he strengthened his aversion to Epicureanism, and listened with pleasure at Athens to the eclectic Academic Antiochus of Ascalon, and the eclectic Stoic Posidonius at Rhodes. Whether he ever read Plato and Aristotle as intensively as we do to-day is more doubtful: yet there is abundant proof of his familiarity with their writings. Though priding himself on belonging to a 'school', he was not in the least illiberal, and gladly entrusted his son to the care of the Peripatetic Cratippus, because he found that he was then the leading philosopher at Athens.   He certainly had read all that had been written on philosophic subjects by Greeks for the last hundred years: thus he says of a particular subject that it had not been dealt with satisfactorily by anyone since Panaetius.   He means, 'you must not criticise me for not quoting *e.g.* Hecato: it is simply because I don't think him worth quoting'.   It is most significant that he says to Cato that they have both been devoted from boyhood to philosophy, 'than which there is nothing I hold dearer in life, nor has a greater boon than it been granted by the gods to mankind: and this genuine philosophy of ancient times (which some people look on as a sign of an idle and indolent life) we are almost the only people who have brought into the Bar, political life and almost into the battlefield'.   Finally near the end of his life, after saying that he was 'driven to the bosom of philosophy by his own enthusiastic choice, and that in his present heavy misfortunes he has sought refuge in the same harbour from which he first set sail', he thus eloquently apostrophises her: 'O philosophy, thou guide of life, O thou explorer of virtue and expeller of vice!   Without thee what would have become not only of me but of the life of man altogether?   Thou hast given birth to cities, thou hast called scattered human beings into the bond of social life, thou hast united them first of all in joint habitations, next in wedlock, then in the ties of common literature and speech, thou hast discovered Law, thou hast been the teacher of morality and order: to thee I fly for refuge, from thee I look for aid, to thee I entrust myself, as once in large measure, so now wholly and entirely.

R

Moreover, one day well spent and in accordance
with thy lessons is to be preferred to an eternity of
error.' [167]

When we read this, first we have little doubt that
the feeling which prompted these words was *mutatis
mutandis* the same as the Psalmist's, 'One day in thy
courts is better than a thousand'. Secondly we see
that to Cicero philosophy meant Culture or Civilisation in the widest sense. It is doubtful if Cicero can
be described as a metaphysician at all: it would be
harsh to deny him the name of philosopher because
like a practical Roman he thinks first of the uses to
which philosophy can be put. His first aim was to
open to his fellow countrymen the wealth of Greek
thought. The preface and dedication of the Tusculans may here be quoted: 'On at last securing a complete or at any rate a considerable release from the
toils of advocacy, and from my senatorial duties, I
have once more—chiefly, Brutus, owing to your
encouragement — returned to those studies which
though stored in memory had been put aside through
circumstances, and are now revived after a long interval of neglect. My view was that, inasmuch as the
system and method of instruction in all the arts which
bear on the right conduct of life is bound up with the
study of wisdom which goes by the name of philosophy, it was incumbent on me to throw light upon
that study by a work in the Latin tongue; not that
philosophy could not be learned from Greek writers
and teachers, but it has always been my conviction
that our countrymen have shown more wisdom everywhere than the Greeks, either in making discoveries
for themselves, or else in improving on what they had
received from Greece—in such subjects at least as

they had judged worthy of the devotion of their efforts.* For morality, rules of life, family and household economy, are surely maintained by us in a better and more dignified way; and beyond question our ancestors have adopted better regulations and laws than others in directing the policy of government. What shall I say of the art of war? In this sphere our countrymen have proved their superiority by valour as well as in even a greater degree by discipline. When we come to natural gifts apart from book learning they are above comparison with the Greeks or any other people. Where has such earnestness, where such firmness, greatness of soul, honesty, loyalty, where has such surpassing merit in every field been found in any of mankind to justify comparison with our ancestors? In learning Greece surpassed us and in all branches of literature; and victory was easy where there was no contest.' In the same sort of spirit, though the analogy is far from complete, a patriotic Englishman might have written in introducing the philosophy of Kant to English readers.

Others besides Cicero had felt that he could perform this task of interpreting to Romans the best thought of Greece. Thus Matius, most interesting and most chivalrous of the Caesarians, not only befriended Cicero when he came back to Italy as a discredited Pompeian, but urged him to write philosophical treatises.[168]

When he set out to do this, he found little more than the words philosophy, physics, dialectic already naturalised in Latin: he had the delicate task of de-

---

* Hitherto they had not—broadly speaking—thought abstract studies worth borrowing.

ciding on the right Latin equivalent for a Greek technical term, and some of his terms are very difficult to render into English. Thus while the Greek word for moral obligation has a natural equivalent in the Latin *Officium*, and he could coin the word 'quality' for the corresponding Greek, it is hard to understand that his treatise *On the Ends of Goods and Evils* means really 'on the opposing views as to the chief Good and the chief Evil.' Yet he was completely intelligible to his readers, and is comparatively easy to read even for us today.

But what a public he had to address, proud and suspicious, intolerant and, in a word, *Philistine*! When his speeches are criticised for their unfair, *ad captandum* irrelevant arguments, men forget that his chief object was to persuade, and that to persuade a Roman jury then was a different thing from persuading an English jury today. His defence of literature in the *Pro Archia*, fine as it is, is largely camouflaged by a suggestion that the poetry of Archias, especially because of the wide circulation it would obtain in Greek-speaking countries, would extend the fame of the Roman People. Nor was this prejudice against culture confined to the middle and lower classes. When three philosophers, Diogenes the Stoic, Carneades the Academic and Critolaus the Peripatetic, came as Athenian ambassadors to Rome in 155 B.C., the Elder Cato procured their expulsion for fear they should corrupt the youth. This is illustrated in Cicero's early treatise *On Invention*. 'The proposition "If one ought to be wise, therefore it is proper to pay attention to philosophy", requires proof, because many think philosophy is no good, and most people think it harmful.' Even after the labours of Cicero, when it had been established as the practice that higher education could be pursued in either rhetoric or philosophy, Tacitus says that his father-in-law Agricola went in for philosophy more deeply than was 'permitted to a Roman and a senator',* and his mother induced him to desist from its study. To be sure, the Stoic Republicans under the Empire had made philosophy seem to be suspect of treason, and, in spite of Quintilian, Cicero had gone out of fashion again when Tacitus wrote. But if Cicero's aim was entirely dictated by patriotism, to show that 'the poverty of the Latin language' of which Lucretius complained was more imaginary than real, to prove that Latin oratory was capable of as lofty flights as Greek, and to introduce to his countrymen the best thought of the Greeks, he could never have dreamed of the vast influence his writings would have in the centuries to come.

At first a Tertullian could say, 'Beware, you who have by subtlety framed a Stoic, a Platonic, a dialectic Christianity. We need look no further when we have the Gospel. If only we believe, nothing more is needful.' But Clement of Alexandria compares the ignorant bawlers who fight against Greek philosophy to the companions of Odysseus stopping their ears with wax against the Sirens' song; Jerome is so steeped in Cicero that, even after he vowed to read him no more, Cicero's writings persisted in his memory; and the use which Minucius Felix, Lactantius and even St Ambrose make of Cicero is obvious. Naturally the Saint corrects Cicero at times. Twice

* Tac. *Agric.* iv. 4. Cp. *Tusc. Disp.* ii. 1, 1: 'Neoptolemus in Ennius says that he must play the philosopher, but only in a few things: for of doing so entirely he did not approve'. Cicero rejects this attitude.

over in the *De Officiis* [169] Cicero says: 'No one should harm another unless provoked by wrong'; St Ambrose says—he could do no less—'This exception is however removed by the authority of the Gospel'.

As we have seen (p. 158), St Augustine traced the beginning of his conversion to the reading of Cicero's *Hortensius*. A passage in his letters unmistakeably refers to Cicero.[170] He is thinking of Christ preaching to the spirits in prison (1 Peter iii. 19). 'If we saw that all who were found there were set entirely free, who would not count it joy if we could prove this? Especially we should rejoice on account of certain men, who by their literary labours have become our familiar friends, whose eloquence and genius we admire, not only poets and orators who in many passages of their works have held up to contempt and ridicule the false gods of the Gentiles, and sometimes even confessed the one True God, though they shared with others in their superstitious worship, but also those whose writings we do not possess, but whose lives we have learned to be after a fashion praiseworthy, so that save for the worship of God in which they went astray, observing the vain public worship which was obligatory and serving the creature rather than the Creator, in all other respects of character they are rightly held as models for imitation, not merely to citizens but to strangers too, for frugality, continence, chastity, sobriety, contempt of death for the salvation of their country and keeping faith.' The marvel is that Christian writers found so little in Cicero to correct. Petrarch said: 'you would fancy sometimes that it is not a pagan philosopher but a Christian Apostle speaking', and Erasmus said of the Tusculans: 'When I was fond of those juvenile studies, Cicero never pleased me so much as he does now when I am grown old; not only for the divine felicity of his style but also for the sanctity of his heart and morals. In short, he inspired my soul, and made me feel myself a better man.' [171]

In a famous letter to Atticus, Cicero says: 'Make yourself perfectly easy about the language I employ, I have plenty at my command; but my matter is not original'.[172] There he does himself injustice; for while he is always following some Greek authority, first one and then another, he is all the time adapting, curtailing, illustrating by Roman history and contemporary events. Elsewhere he does himself less injustice: 'Panaetius whom I am following, not slavishly translating, in these books does not approve of lavish expenditure on public works'.[173] Incidentally it may be remarked that, if we possessed complete references to Cicero's sources, it would throw a flood of light on the development of later Greek philosophy.

Materials had, no doubt, accumulated with Cicero for years, but his great period of writing began after Tullia's death. First he composed a conventional *Consolatio*, a passage from which is quoted in the Tusculans: [174] 'No beginning of souls can be discovered on earth; for there is no trace of blending or combination in souls or any particle that would seem born or fashioned from earth, nothing even that partakes of moist, or airy or fiery.* For in these elements there is nothing to possess the power of memory, thought and reflection, nothing capable

* Therefore we cannot go back to the early speculations of the Ionian thinkers.

of retaining the past or foreseeing the future and grasping the present,—and these capacities alone are divine,—*and never will there be found any source from which they can come to men except from God.** There is then a peculiar essential character belonging to the soul, distinct from the common and well-known elements. *Accordingly whatever it is that is conscious, that is wise, that lives, that is active, must be heavenly and divine and for that reason eternal.* And indeed God Himself, who is comprehended by us, can be comprehended in no other way save as a mind unfettered and free, severed from all perishable matter, conscious of all things, and moving all things, and self-endowed with perpetual motion.' At the moment Cicero wrote these words he was evidently convinced that his dear daughter's soul still existed.

There is one other reference to the *Consolatio* in the Tusculans: [175] the Master has spoken of the release of the soul from the shackles of the body, and the Hearer says: 'you have sorrowed over life sufficiently in your *Consolatio*, and when I read it I wish for nothing better than to quit this world; having heard what you have just said, I wish it much more'.

Next he adapted the *Protrepticus* of Aristotle in the lost *Hortensius*, named after his great rival at the Bar. Of this we have one fragment which is illuminating: 'If when we have passed from this life we were permitted, as the myths say, to live for ever in the islands of the blessed, what need would there be of oratory? for there would be no judicial proceedings. We should not need the virtues of

---

* Cicero of course writes 'god', which might be translated 'a god'.

courage, justice, temperance, or even moral prudence; for there would be no scope for their exercise. We should only be blessed with knowledge and pure contemplation.' It follows that we love knowledge for its own sake. One can see that out of compliment to Hortensius the orator Cicero has added oratory to Aristotle's four cardinal virtues.*

After thus exhorting his Roman public to the study of philosophy, which took him perhaps not more than a week or two, Cicero plunged into his subject and on May 13th, 45 B.C., announced that he had finished two big treatises. It seems likely that he means the first draft of the *Academics*: for Cicero was always an Academic. He had for a time been attracted by the more eclectic teaching of Antiochus, but in later life had returned to the earlier position of Philo, the teacher of his youth. This might be described as the Old Academy, because it went back to the Socratic beginnings. Socrates was always an inquirer who did not dogmatise, but said that he was only wiser than other men because he realised his own ignorance. Plato, his gifted disciple, had erected on this basis an epistemological system, but his successors had developed a merely negative scepticism. The Academy of Philo limited itself to teaching mental suspense; there was no possibility of reaching *absolute* truth, but while one could not pretend to *knowledge*, there was a *clearness* of sense impressions which carried conviction as to their truth. Antiochus went further and professed to recover the true doctrine of Plato.

* This ingenious observation comes from Professor Werner Jaeger's brilliant book on Aristotle, admirably translated by R. Robinson (Oxford, 1934).

Cicero in his works gives the exposition of contradictory views by different interlocutors: his dialogue form was more that of Plato's *Laws* than Plato's *Republic*. The first draft of the *Academics* was in two books. In the first of these Catulus expounded the extreme scepticism of Carneades; this is lost. In the second, which we have, Lucullus attacks scepticism, which is then defended by Cicero. Cicero after pointing out the uncertainty of sense-perception, argues that probability is enough ground for action, just as certainty is not necessary for memory or the arts; and that as the dogmatists disagree with one another in logic, in physics and in ethics, suspense is the most truly philosophical attitude.

But presently Cicero was dissatisfied with his work. As he had long thought of introducing Varro into one of his dialogues and dedicating it to him, he recast the treatise into four books, of which we possess only part of the first. In it Varro expounds the dogmatism of Antiochus in ethics, physics and logic, and that of the Stoics, while Cicero holds that Philo's probability is true Platonism, but we have very little of his exposition.

By May 29th Cicero had finished part of his *De Finibus*, which is in five books as we have it, dedicated to Brutus. In the first two Torquatus expounds Epicureanism, and Cicero refutes it, adopting the Stoic standpoint. In the second two books Cato expounds Stoic ethics and Cicero criticises him. In the fifth book the ethics of Antiochus are expounded and criticised. The next two works, the *Tusculan Disputations* in five books and *On the Nature of the Gods* in three books, must have employed Cicero's time very fully down to the Ides of March 44 B.C.

In the latter work the Epicurean and Stoic theologies are expounded and the Academic position is stated in contradistinction to them.   The Academic spokesman, Cotta the pontiff, is careful to say that he upholds the traditional religion of Rome, and his philosophical position is entirely independent of that. Then in the work *On Divination* Cicero combated superstition, which he had already called the 'name of a fault' as distinguished from the praiseworthy name of religion.[176]   This is his conclusion : [177] 'Speaking frankly, superstition which is widespread among the nations has taken advantage of human weakness to cast its spell over the mind of almost every man.   This same view was stated in my treatise *On the Nature of the Gods*; and to prove the correctness of that view has been the chief aim of the present discussion.   For I thought that I should be rendering a great service both to myself and to my countrymen, if I could tear up this superstition by the roots.   But I want it distinctly understood that the destruction of superstition does not mean the destruction of religion.   For I consider it the part of wisdom to preserve the institutions of our forefathers by retaining their sacred rites and ceremonies. *Furthermore the celestial order and the beauty of the universe compel me to confess that there is a surpassing and eternal Nature which deserves the respect and homage of men.*

In his book *On Destiny* he is a determinist but not a fatalist.   It is not true to say 'if you are fated to get well, you will get well, whether you consult a physician or not', but you should say 'you will consult a doctor and get well; both are decreed by fate'. 'Natural causes may produce vices in us, but the extirpation of these vices is not the result of natural causes but the will.'

Cicero's two books *On Glory* are lost, but we are sure that in them he said there was a true and a false glory and that virtue like a shadow followed true glory, and that he also said that the desire for posthumous fame is a token assuring us of a life after death.

The *Tusculan Disputations* must have arisen out of the discussions at Tusculum in 46 B.C. with Pansa, Hirtius and Dolabella, which would follow and be a relaxation after the rhetorical exercises with which the day began. Book I sets out to destroy the fear of death: he prefers with Plato to believe in the immortality of the soul. The soul is conscious that it is in motion and also that it is self-moved, by its own and not an outside power, and that it can never be abandoned by itself: this is the assurance of its eternity. But the nature and place of the soul are left undetermined.

In Book II he deals with the endurance of pain. The Stoics said pain was not an evil. Apropos of this Cicero tells how Pompey, after his return from the East, visited Posidonius, desiring to hear him lecture. As Posidonius was laid up with an attack of gout, he paid him a complimentary call. On receiving him, Posidonius said he could not allow so distinguished a visitor to go away without hearing him, and from his couch discussed the proposition 'Nothing is good except what is honourable': when attacked by a paroxysm of pain, he said, 'It is no use, pain: for all the distress you cause, I shall never admit you are an evil'. From this we infer that some Stoics were pre-Christian Christian Scientists.

In Books III and IV he deals with varying attitudes to distress and its alleviation and to the passions and their remedies. In Book V he aims at showing that virtue is sufficient for happiness. Here he even goes with the Stoics so far as to hold that the wise man can be happy under torture. The crucial case of Regulus, the Roman hero whom he so often celebrates, seems to have led him to this conclusion. The passage in which he compares Dionysius the tyrant of Syracuse with Archimedes the Syracusan mathematician is perhaps the most famous.[178] The work is the most characteristic of all Cicero's writings and is full of a sane optimism.*

If the Tusculans are the most characteristic, the *De Officiis*, a manual of ethics dedicated to his son and carefully written down to the level of his comprehension, is the most popular of Cicero's works. 'Herewith,' he says, 'my son Marcus, you have a present from your father, a generous one in my humble opinion; but its value will depend on the spirit in which you receive it. And yet you must welcome these three books as fellow guests, so to speak, with your notes on Cratippus' lectures. As you would sometimes give ear to me also, if I had come to Athens (and I should be there now, if my country had not called me back with unmistakeable accents when I was well on my way), so please give as much time as you can to these volumes; for in them my voice will travel to you.' 'We Academics', he says, 'do maintain that nothing is known for certain. But probability supplies us with a sufficient guide of life.' After this vindication of his school against the charge of uncertainty in

---

* It was probably the first classical book to be printed (A.D. 1465).

morals, he freely adapts Stoic ethics; for in the first two books, *On Moral Goodness* and *Expediency* respectively, he is following, expanding and illustrating the work of Panaetius, which, though nearly a century old, he thinks has not been superseded. In the third, *The Conflict between the Right and the Expedient*, he tells us his model deserted him, and his casuistry is extremely interesting. The work only professes to be popular, as this passage proves: 'I am afraid some one may wonder why I am now separating the virtues, as if it were possible for any one to be just who is not at the same time wise; for it is agreed among all philosophers, and I myself have often argued, that he who has one virtue has them all. The explanation of my apparent inconsistency is that the precision of speech we employ, when abstract truth is critically investigated in philosophical discussion, is one thing; and that employed, when we are adapting our language entirely to popular thinking, is another. And therefore I am speaking here in the popular sense, when I call some men brave, others good, and still others wise; for in dealing with popular conceptions we must employ familiar words in their common acceptation; and this was the practice of Panaetius.' Again he says: 'I ask you, my dear Cicero, to assume with me, if you can, that nothing is worth the seeking for its own sake except what is morally right. But if Cratippus * does not permit this assumption, you will grant me this at least, that what is morally right is *most* worth the seeking for its own sake. Either

---

* Peripatetics would hold that there were natural goods, *e.g.* health and honour, worth seeking for their own sake, though not so much so as *moral* good. These things (Aristotle's 'external goods') the Stoics called 'indifferent'.

alternative is sufficient for my purposes: and besides these there is no other alternative that seems probable at all.* Of the cardinal virtues, justice is derived from the social instinct, wisdom from the impulse to inquiry, bravery from the will to power: but temperance is not a merely negative quality. It is a desire for propriety (*decorum*), which makes the individual do and choose what suits his individual endowments: it is in fact the perfection of the individuality, the sustaining of one's particular rôle in life, and the careful choice of a career. It will manifest itself in outward appearance and in inward self-control, in speech (oratory and conversation), even in the building of a house.' In fact one would not be doing Cicero an injustice if one made it equivalent to gentlemanliness. In this the father was thinking, above all, what he would like his son to be.

The passage which illustrates the antagonism of Caesar and Cicero deserves quotation (iii. 21, 82). Caesar was said often to have on his lips the lines from the *Phoenissae* of Euripides: 'If wrong may e'er be right, for a throne's sake, Were wrong most right: be God in all else feared'. 'Our tyrant deserved his death for having made an exception of the one thing that was the blackest crime of all. Why do we gather instances of petty crime—legacies criminally obtained and fraudulent buying and selling? Behold, here you have a man who was ambitious to be king of the Roman People and master of the whole world; and he achieved it! The man who maintains that such an ambition is morally right is a madman; for he justifies the destruction of law and liberty and

* Note his refusal even to consider the Epicurean view.

thinks their hideous and detestable suppression glorious. . . . Expediency, therefore, must be measured by the standard of moral rectitude, and in such a way, too, that these two words shall seem in sound only to be different but in real meaning to be one and the same.'

One would like to quote whole pages of the *De Officiis*. There is only room for a few of his aphorisms. 'They give us no bad rule who bid us treat our slaves as we should our (free) employees: they must be required to work; but they must be given what is justly theirs.' [179] 'There are no rules for conversation, but I am inclined to think there might be.' 'Conversation should be easy and not dogmatic: it should have the spice of wit. One who engages in conversation should not debar others from participating in it, as if it were a private monopoly: but, as in other things so in a general conversation, he should think it not unfair for each to have his turn. He should observe first and foremost what the subject of conversation is: if it is grave, he should treat it with seriousness; if humorous, with wit. Above all, he should take care that his conversation does not betray some defect in his character. This is likely to occur when people, in jest or in earnest, take delight in making malicious and slanderous statements about the absent. Subjects of conversation are usually affairs of the home or politics or the practice of the professions and learning. Accordingly, if the talk begins to drift off to other channels, pains must be taken to bring it back again to the matter in hand—but with due consideration to the company present; for we are not all interested in the same things at all times or in the same degree.

We must observe too how far the conversation is agreeable, and as it had a reason for its beginning there should be a point at which to close it tactfully.'[180]   No wonder Cicero's society was eagerly sought.

'The only excuse for going to war is that we may live in peace unharmed.'[181]   'Peace has her victories no less than war.' *   'Freedom suppressed and again regained bites with keener fangs than freedom never endangered.'[182]   'It is an excellent rule not to do a thing, when there is a doubt whether it is right or wrong; for righteousness shines with a brilliance of its own, but doubt is a sign that we are thinking of doing wrong.'[183]   Most noticeable of all is the sternness with which Cicero denounces that form of political expediency which does evil with patriotic motives: that is not true patriotism.†

Cicero rounds off his series with *Cato Major* or *On Old Age*, and *Laelius* or *On Friendship*, both dedicated to his best and lifelong friend.   They are now getting old, but old age does not unfit for deeds, and counsel is the typical deed of the old man. The body is still, if not physically strong, fit for all ordinary uses.   The best and real pleasures are still open to the old, and the approach of death has no terrors.   'The fruit which is hard to pluck when

---

* I. 22, 74.   He is of course alluding to 63 B.C.

† In an arbitration case, i. 10, 33: the destruction of Corinth, iii. 11, 46. Cicero does not hesitate to stigmatise what he regards as wrong in this respect.   Just as he laments the destruction of Corinth by the Romans, he objects to a model of Marseilles being carried in Caesar's triumph of 46 B.C.   'I might mention many other outrages against our allies, if the sun had ever beheld a more infamous outrage than this.   Justly therefore are we being punished.'   'It is while we have preferred to be the subject of fear, rather than of love and affection, that all these misfortunes have fallen upon us.'   *De Officiis*, ii. 8, 28, 29.

it is unripe, when it is ripe falls to the ground of itself.'

The treatment of friendship is based on virtue and intellectual agreement. It is only possible among good men. Away then with the base utilitarianism which sees the source of friendship in the need of help! In that case the weak would be more capable of friendship than the strong, whereas the reverse is the case. If a friendship ceases, it never existed; for true friendships are eternal.

One notices two things. To Cicero Eros is repugnant, and romance is dangerous. Elsewhere [184] he writes: 'The whole passion ordinarily termed love is of such exceeding triviality that I see nothing that I think comparable with it.' After quoting the comedian Caecilius on Love as the supreme god, he ironically exclaims: 'How glorious the reformation of life that poetry inspires! it thinks Love, the promoter of shame and inconstancy, fit for a place in the company of gods'. Certainly Eros did not show to advantage in contemporary society (p. 77). Friendship on the other hand has a reasonable basis.

The other point is the problem how Atticus, a lifelong Epicurean, and Cicero, a cordial hater of Epicureanism, got on so well together. The only possible answer is that they sympathised and touched in so many other directions. Moreover, in philosophic differences of opinion there was a certain mutual toleration in the first century B.C.

It would entail a discussion of four centuries of Greek thought to treat adequately the philosophical writings of Cicero. Their value to us is chiefly that they give us some idea of the lost works of Greek philosophers. Their value to the Romans was that they popularised the best fruits of Greek thought in an agreeable and easily intelligible form: that is why some of his writings are still the best introduction to serious study for the young. Their value in the history of civilisation is incalculable:* for they preserved to the West what would otherwise have perished. That is why Petrarch and the scholars of the Renaissance so deeply reverenced the name of Cicero. Others have pointed this out in detail;† it is sufficient here to say that in these writings Cicero of all the ancients comes most near to modern man.

Finally it may be said that while Cicero never abandoned the position that it is impossible to *prove* the truth of religion, he was to all intents and purposes a Theist. He habitually speaks of Nature as a personal agent, where we should substitute God. Thus he says in words quoted above: 'The beauty of the universe and the order of the heavens compel us to confess that there exists a surpassing and eternal Nature which deserves the respect and homage of man'. Then in the *Philippics* he says: 'Brief is the life given us by Nature, but the memory of life nobly given back is everlasting'.[185] This seems to invite the question to whom life is given back. He must have answered 'To the Giver'. A whole string of passages in the *De Officiis* shows Nature as leader (*dux*), as that which man obeys, as that which brings us to birth and clothes us with characters; and he

* Copernicus was led to his discoveries by *Acad.* ii. 37, 123, where Antipodes and revolution of the earth on its axis round the sun are mentioned as theories held.

† Notably Zielinski, *Cicero im Wandel der Jahrhunderte* (1912).

speaks of the reason in Nature which is both divine and human law.[186]

It wanted very little to make Cicero's writings Christian: that little was actually done by one Hadoardus in the Carolingian age.*

* Zielinski, *op. cit.* p. 117, note.

Chapter 14

CICERO'S LETTERS

Some people say there is nothing like viva-voce *communication, but I learned far more from your letter than from my talk with Curio.* CICERO, *Ad Att.* ii. 12, 2

CICERO's rules for conversation have already been given (p. 256); they are well illustrated by his ordinary letters to intimate friends. 'In letters', says he, 'I use the language of every day.' 'I have one style', he says to Trebonius, 'for what I think will be read only by those to whom I address my letters, and another for what I think will be read by many.'[187] To Paetus, a very intimate friend, he says: 'I don't always adopt the same style. What similarity is there between a letter and a speech in court or at a public meeting? Why, even in law cases, I do not deal with all in the same way. Private cases, if petty ones, I conduct in a plainer fashion: those involving a man's civic status or his reputation in a more elaborate style.'[188] So to his intimates his self-revelation was complete. Once Quintus says, 'I saw a complete picture of you in your letter'.[189] To Atticus he says, 'I talk to you as I do to myself'.[190]

The letters are invaluable to us, both as a revelation of the man Cicero and for the light they throw on the last years of the Republic. 'The quality in Cicero's (private) letters', says Professor Tyrrell,

261

'which makes them most valuable is that they were not (like the letters of Pliny and Seneca and Madame de Sévigné) written to be published. The letters are absolutely trustworthy; they set forth the failures and foibles of their writer, as well as his virtues and his triumphs. The portraits with which they abound were never to be shown to his involuntary sitters, so that there was no reason why they should not be faithful.' There was no thought of their publication till near the end of his life. It must have been suggested when on July 9th, 44, he says, 'There is no collection of my letters, but Tiro has about seventy, and some can be got from you. These I ought to see and correct. Then they shall be published.' [191] Apparently he never found time to do it. After his death Tiro, his invaluable secretary, who devoted the rest of a long life to his master's writings, arranged and published the sixteen books 'To His Friends' which we possess. Many of these are written in the formal style of his speeches, if he was addressing a mere acquaintance, or if while addressing a friend he wished the letter to be shown to others. A good instance of the latter is his account of his triumphal return from exile.*

The letters to Atticus, with which went those to Quintus and Brutus, were not given to the world till long afterwards. Nepos saw those addressed to Atticus, but distinguished them from the published volumes. He says that any one reading them will almost have a connected history of the age: unfortunately, however, there are large gaps. Only eleven are prior to 65, and then they fail up to January 61. They are then fairly continuous up to December 45,

---

* *Ad Att.* iv. 1, 1. No doubt Atticus circulated this letter.

but between then and April 44 there are none, nor
for the last year of Cicero's life. Asconius, who
wrote in A.D. 54, does not know them, and they are
first quoted by Seneca in A.D. 66. It seems likely,
therefore, that they were first published about A.D. 60.
The Dublin edition contains 832 letters by him and
99 written by others to him.

It is surprising that we are unable to judge the
style of Cicero's most frequent correspondent, Titus
Pomponius Atticus; it was for the reason that he
suppressed all his own letters. His watchful eye,
however, was deceived into allowing extracts from a
roll of a dozen letters written by him in February and
March 49 to appear in *Ad Att.* ix. 10. From them
we can see that he wrote in an easy style and used
Greek expressions more freely even than Cicero. He
was of course a student and scholar, with the special
subjects of Roman history, antiquities and genealogy,
as well as a wary and successful man of business. His
business relations, however, he took trouble to conceal.
It is a probable suggestion of the Dublin editors that
the usurer Caecilius who would not lend even to a relative under twelve per cent, and who left his nephew
Atticus £80,000, was the Jorkins to his Spenlow.

Among Cicero's other correspondents Sulpicius
and Matius both wrote him notable letters. Sulpicius wrote from Athens a letter of condolence on
the death of Tullia.[192] This passage is famous:
'This is an incident which brought me no slight comfort, and I should like to tell you of it in case it may
be able to alleviate your sorrow. On return from
Asia, as I was sailing from Aegina towards Megara,
I began to survey the landscape. Behind me was
Aegina, before me Megara, on my right Piraeus, on

my left Corinth, towns at one time most flourishing, now lying prostrate and demolished before my very eyes. I began to think for myself: "So! we puny mortals resent it, do we, if one of us whose lives are naturally shorter, has died in his bed or been slain in battle, when in this land alone there lie flung before us the corpses of so many towns. Pray control yourself, Servius, and remember that you were born a human being." Take my word for it, I was not a little fortified by that reflection.' Sulpicius does not regard immortality as certain. 'If there be any consciousness among the dead', he says, but Plato and Cicero too, *quâ* philosophers, always leave it an open question. It is likely that both Sulpicius and Cicero, *quâ* religious men, had no doubts.

Matius' letter does him great credit.[193] Cicero had remonstrated with him on voting for the law which transferred Cisalpine Gaul to Antony, and for managing games vowed, but not actually exhibited, by Caesar and now held by his great-nephew and heir. Matius makes a spirited protest against the obloquy heaped on him for mourning Caesar's death. 'I did not like the Civil War, but Caesar was my friend, and I will not be intimidated by your *champions of liberty* into losing my own freedom of saying what I think. I arranged the games as a matter of private obligation to young Caesar. I have called on Antony as consul to pay my respects: and so do the people who denounce me, but unlike me they go for what they can get. What arrogance is this to restrict my private intercourse! Caesar never prevented me from associating with anyone I pleased. (He means "that is why I was able to keep on friendly terms with you, Cicero".) However I am not afraid either that the sober self-restraint of my life will fail as time goes on to triumph over the mendacity of gossip, or that even those who do not love me on account of my constancy to Caesar, will not prefer to have friends like me rather than like themselves.'

Matius had a right to use this language; for when Cicero was under a cloud, he had been kind to him. But one may admire both men, without granting that Matius did well to support Antony. Cicero's good opinion of Matius was of long standing: for he wrote to Trebatius in Gaul, 'I am so glad that you have become intimate with that charming and learned man Gaius Matius; be sure you win his sincere regard'.

Among Cicero's other correspondents Cassius has an easy literary style, Brutus writes stiffly.* Caelius is gossipy and slangy. Cato's one letter is a mirror of the man. Aristocrats like the Metellus brothers do not show well in their letters. We may infer that there was only one person in Rome who could rival Cicero as a letter writer, and that was Caesar himself. Unfortunately we only possess four short letters from him, of which this is a specimen.[194] After hearing of Caesar's clemency at Corfinium, Cicero wrote to express his warm approval and Caesar replied: 'Caesar Imperator to Cicero Imperator greeting. You are right in inferring of me—for you know me well—that there is nothing further from my nature than cruelty. While I take great pleasure in that fact, I am proud to think that my action wins your approval. I am not disturbed because it is said that those whom I have set free have departed to wage war on me again; for there is nothing I like better

* The genuineness of the letters of Brutus has been contested, but without good grounds.

than that I should be true to myself and they to themselves. I hope I may meet you at Rome that I may avail myself of your advice and resources as usual in everything. You must know that nothing pleases me more than your Dolabella. I shall be grateful to him for this also; for he cannot do otherwise than arrange it. Such is his kindness and goodwill towards me.' From the letter which Cicero wrote to Caesar about Trebatius [195] we see that Caesar could be jocose. He says jestingly, 'Either I will make Trebatius king of Gaul, or (if an ingenious emendation is adopted) my pal in plundering the Segontiaci'. But we also see how uneasy Cicero was in writing to him: he thinks a compliment advisable, and so adds to the common phrase 'from hand to hand' the words 'that hand as distinguished for military triumphs as for loyalty in friendship'. (Unconsciously he has lapsed into his grand style.) He then reflects that this may be too much for Caesar, so he adds: 'I am (or perhaps "let me be") a little too fulsome, though you can barely stand that sort of thing: but to-day I think you will'. One feels instinctively that in quick wit, knowledge of the world and social gifts, the two men were on the same footing, and miles ahead of any other living Roman.

All his correspondents are outshone by Cicero in brilliance and felicity of expression. His quotations from Latin and Greek authors are apt and to the point. When they are hackneyed, he can assume Atticus' knowledge of them, and only give a couple of words. He uses a Greek expression to supply a lack in Latin * or to hit a nail on the head more

* Thus there is no convenient Latin word for the Greek one which gives us 'scope'; and 'impossible' had not yet been coined.

exactly. Occasionally he does it to baffle anybody who might intercept and try to read a letter not meant for him. Thus there is a long passage in Greek accusing Philotimus, Terentia's steward, of fraud.[196] Atticus was safe enough, but if his wife Pilia got hold of the letter, its contents would go straight to Terentia. There is a long passage in Greek on the political situation,[197] and it was decidedly safer to use Greek expressions when he said 'As I have long known Pompey to be the most incompetent of statesmen, so I know him now to be the most incompetent of generals',[198] particularly as this was very unjust. Technical terms of finance, medicine and navigation were also mostly Greek. As the knowledge of Greek disappeared, these expressions suffered at the hands of the copyists of MSS., and the problems thus presented have not all been unravelled.*

Cicero's reputation as a wit was shown by the *Ciceroniana* of Trebonius already mentioned (p. 166) and by Caesar's order that Cicero's witticisms should be transmitted to him in Gaul: it is said that Caesar could detect a joke that was not genuine. Cicero was an inveterate punster, and puns are out of fashion today. But his readiness of repartee was exceptional among the Romans, who were on the whole a dour people. This is a specimen of playing on proper names. A disreputable Roman knight was travelling in Asia Minor and left his baggage at the house of a man who died, which led to its examination and the highly compromising discovery of five small busts of Roman married ladies. 'Among them', says Cicero, 'was one of the sister of your friend

---

* The ingenuity of Professor Tucker in solving these problems has not received sufficient recognition.

Brutus—a brute indeed to associate with such a fellow—and one of the wife of Lepidus—a nice sort of man to take this so lightly.'

These are specimens of his fancy. 'Your villa, unadorned as it is, seems to me like a moralist reproving the frivolity of other villas.' 'You have a first-rate landscape gardener: he has enveloped everything with ivy, even the spaces between the columns, so that the Greek statues seem to be in business as landscape gardeners advertising their ivy.' Quintus quoted the portent of mice gnawing the shields at Lanuvium as foretelling the Marsian War. Cicero says, 'As if it mattered a whit whether mice which are day and night gnawing something, gnawed shields or sieves! Hence by the same token the fact that at my house mice recently gnawed my copy of Plato's *Republic* should fill me with alarm for the Roman Republic; or if they had gnawed my Epicurus *On Pleasure*, I should have expected a rise in the price of food!' A very interesting letter to his elderly invalid friend Marius was written after Pompey's great games in 55 B.C. He congratulates him on missing them and enjoying the delightful scenery of his Pompeian villa instead. 'You treated the gladiators with contempt: Pompey himself admits that he wasted on them both time and oil.'

In the Tusculans,[199] much in the manner in which Dr. Johnson defended prize fighting, Cicero defends the gladiatorial combats of old times between condemned criminals, as schooling the eye against pain and death. For the bloody contests of his own time he had an abhorrence,[200] and speaks of eagerly getting away from the gladiators of Marcus Metellus.

It is interesting to find that Cicero had quite a

modern appreciation of the beauties of Nature. Here is a string of quotations to prove it, in which he uses the word *amenity* to express natural beauty. 'After the great heat [of Rome] I have refreshed myself at Arpinum by the great beauty of the river.' 'Astura is a beautiful spot within view of Antium and Circeii.' 'I was looking for streams and solitude to make life more endurable; but continued rain has kept me indoors' (Arpinum). 'Nothing can be more charming, the villa, the beach, the sea view, the low hills, everything' (Astura). 'You ask whether I take more pleasure in hills and a view or a walk by the sea. Both have such amenity, that I don't know which I prefer.' [201] It looks as if Atticus shared his tastes. A similar feeling is expressed in his speech of thanks to the people after return from exile. 'As for my country (*patria*), O ye immortal gods, it is scarcely possible to express how dear, how delightful it is to me. How great is the beauty of Italy! how renowned are its country towns! how varied its scenery! what lands, what crops are there! How beautiful is the City!' [202]

The letters to less intimate friends are often quite in the style of the speeches, especially if they were intended to be shown to others. Thus the long letter to Lentulus Spinther in Cilicia [203] is intended as a defence of his political *volte-face*, as it seemed to one who had been far from Rome for nearly three years. Most of its arguments hold water, but there is one false statement: 'If I had had a completely free hand, I should be behaving in politics as I now am'. He does not like to admit that the protection of Pompey and Caesar, while rewarded by a post to Quintus and favours to himself, has been dearly bought at the cost of complete subservience. But the cleverness of it is amusing. 'The jealous optimates flirted with Publius Clodius: so I thought I would pay them out by flirtations with Publius Vatinius.' This is illustrated by a most apposite quotation from the *Eunuchus* of Terence. The Captain is jealous of his mistress' favours to a rival. 'Give her tit for tat', says the parasite Gnatho, 'and rouse her jealousy by pretending to be in love with another lady.' The cleverness of this is that it suggests that as the optimates do not really love Clodius, neither does Cicero Vatinius.

Cicero is more honest when he makes no secret of the fact that Pompey and Caesar had insisted on his outward reconciliation to Crassus, as a result of which he had to have Crassus to dinner and promise to defend him. He had obeyed but vented his feelings to Atticus by saying 'What a rascal'. If he disliked Crassus, there was at any rate this tie between the two men. Cicero had introduced to public life Publius, Crassus' second son, who he says treats him as a second father. When Publius fell with his father at Carrhae, we may be sure that no one more sincerely mourned for him than Cicero. As a specimen of Cicero's style when writing to a mere acquaintance, we may take a letter to Torquatus in exile at Athens, of January 45 B.C.[204]

'The general opinion, and it grows stronger every day, is this, that although the causes of the combatants differ very materially, *there will after all not be much difference in the results of victory on one side or the other.* Of the Pompeian party, we have already, I think I may say, had some experience; as regards Caesar, there is not a man but reflects how much to be dreaded is the anger of a conqueror with his sword unsheathed.

'At this point, if you think I am aggravating your grief, when I ought to be assuaging it by trying to console you, I confess that I can discover no other consolation for our calamities than the consciousness of a right purpose, and that there is no serious evil other than wrong conduct. And since we are so free from that charge, that our sentiments have ever been of the soundest, and it is the result of our policy rather than the policy itself that is the subject of censure, and since we have done our duty, let us bear what has come to pass with self restraint. . . . You remember the bitterness of my grief, in which my sole consolation is, that I saw further than anybody else, when *what I desired, however unfavourable the terms, was peace.* And though this was due to chance and no prophetic inspiration of mine, I still find a pleasure in the hollow credit of having been farseeing.

'In the second place, and this is a source of consolation common to both of us, if I were now called upon to quit the stage of life, the Republic from which I should be torn, is not one which it would pain me to forego, especially when the change would deprive me of all perception. My age too makes it easier for me, and the fact that my life is now at its close: not only is it gladdened by the thought of a course well run, but it forbids my fearing any violence in that change to which nature herself has nearly brought me. And lastly the man, I might even say, the men who have fallen in this war were of such a character, that it seems an act of shamelessness not to accept the same doom should circumstances compel it. For my own part, there is no contingency I

do not contemplate, and there is no calamity so crushing but that I believe it to be hanging over my head.
But since there is more evil in our anticipation of it
than in the very thing we dread, I am ceasing to fear,
especially as what hangs over me not only involves
no pain, but will itself be the end of pain.' When
Cicero wrote these words, he certainly did not expect
to live nearly three more years.

Lucceius wrote to Cicero in May 45 regretting his
long absence from Rome. If he is living a solitary
life in order to write books, he can understand it, but
if he is simply abandoning himself to sorrow, daily
lamentations are doing him no good. So he begs
him as a personal favour to come back to society and
his normal habits of life. But Cicero, while promising an early meeting, was not to be coaxed into good
spirits. As a matter of fact his literary work did
more and more absorb him and divert his mind from
painful thoughts.

There are very many letters 'To His Friends'
that it would be interesting to quote; but a word
must be said about him to whom we owe their publication, Tiro his freedman, who modestly added at
the end of the collection the letters from the Cicero
family he had preserved. Cicero manumitted him
in 54 B.C. Quintus at once wrote to express the
greatest pleasure and approval, giving his brother
a sly dig by reminding him of his past disapproval of
the manumission of Statius in this delicate form: 'If
Statius' faithful service is so constant a pleasure to
me, how inestimable should these same good qualities
be in Tiro, when we think of his literary and con-
versational powers and his refinement'. The regard
of Quintus for Tiro is shown by several letters, one

of which ends with the most extravagant language
of affection.

On the way back from Cilicia, Tiro had to be left
behind ill at Patras. As before when Tiro was ill,
so now Cicero is full of the most tender solicitude
about his lodging and medical attendance. After
leaving him, he writes from every stopping-place,
seven letters in the course of a fortnight, sending
affectionate messages from his brother and the boys.
That Cicero had no secrets from him is shown by his
long letter in January 49 on the political situation:
and finally he became so indispensable that he even
arranged his master's dinner parties.*

The gem of the book is a letter from young Marcus,
who had been wasting his time at Athens, in which
it is amusing to note that the boy uses superlatives †
more profusely even than his father, who was prone
to them. 'Though my most kindly and beloved
father's epistle gave me the greatest pleasure, still it
was your most delightful letter that crowned my joy.'
'You may with confidence be the trumpeter of my
reputation, as you promised to be. For the errors
of my youth have caused me such grief and agony
that not only do my thoughts shrink from what I
have done, but my very ears shrink from hearing it
talked about.' 'Since at that time I caused you grief,
I shall now guarantee that the joy is double as much.'
He is most intimate with his professor, Cratippus,
who comes to dine with him and bandies jokes with
him; and he has given up association with the dis-

---

* *Ad Fam.* xvi. 22, 1. Tertia, wife of Cassius, must not be asked with
Dolabella.

† By the time of the Vulgate, the superlative has almost lost its superlative meaning, and often takes the place of the positive. This process
may have begun colloquially much earlier.

T

reputable Gorgias in deference to his father. The young gentleman, one feels, protests too much. Then he begins to chaff Tiro. 'I congratulate you on buying a farm. You are become a Roman country gentleman. I seem to see you buying rural implements, hobnobbing with your steward, or keeping the pips from dessert in the corner of your cloak. I am sure the farm was bought as a joint investment of us both, and I am sorry to have failed you, but I *shall* assist you if only fortune assists *me*. Please send me a secretary, if possible a Greek: that will save a lot of trouble in writing out lecture-notes!' Tiro obviously was wont to intercede for the young scapegrace with his father.

Tiro devoted most of the rest of his life—he lived to be a hundred years old—to the task of editing his master's remains. Quintilian says [205] he abbreviated Cicero's speeches: there may have been good authority for this; but on the basis of what has come down to us, no one would have suspected it. Antiquity knew many more letters, which we have lost, to Pompey, Caesar, Octavian, Cato, Hirtius, Pansa, to Calvus, Caerellia and his son, and some less notable persons. Thus there were in antiquity nine books to Brutus.

Caerellia was a rich lady well on in years, who surreptitiously got hold of Cicero's *De Finibus* and copied it out. Letters from Cicero to her—no doubt on literary subjects—have not come down to us. The filthy insinuations of Dio Cassius as to her relations with Cicero, if not sufficiently refuted by her age, are at any rate put out of the question by her intercession for Publilia. Ausonius says that there was a lurking wantonness in the correspondence of Cicero and Caerellia, but Ausonius had a dirty mind, and was quite capable of seeing nastiness where none existed. To his intimates Cicero is always at his best. Tiro seems to have included in Book VII. letters conspicuous for their wit and sparkle. But the letters to Paetus, his witty Epicurean friend (ix. 15-26), are fully equal to those to his elderly and gouty friend Marius, and his legal protégé Trebatius Testa, or to one Marcus Fadius Gallus.

To the latter he bewails a severe gastric attack, which arose thus. Caesar's sumptuary law had forbidden extravagant dinners: so a recent augural banquet had largely consisted of vegetarian fare, but the vegetables were flavoured with such seasonings that they thoroughly upset Cicero.

It relieved Cicero's feelings under the dictator to make facetious and highly dangerous witticisms to safe persons. 'Don't write about Cato: Caesar is back from Spain', is put in the form: 'The schoolmaster is here sooner than we thought. I fear he will send whoever sticks to Cato to the Styx.' [206] To Paetus is addressed the long letter on decency in language. The Stoics hold that the wise man should call a spade a spade. Cicero gives reasons for objecting to the public use of certain words: 'I preserve and shall preserve the modest reserve of Plato'. There is only one obscene jest which Cicero reports of himself and he immediately apologises for it. Needless to say it was provoked by Clodius: Cicero could not at times restrain his tongue. The letters in the later part of Cicero's life most fully illustrate his vivacity, his resilience and his delicate sympathy. The last quality is best shown in the letter to Paetus (p. 193).

In 1345 Petrarch discovered a MS. of Cicero's

letters to Atticus, Quintus and Marcus Brutus (*i.e.* all
we now have) in the Cathedral Library of Verona.
He could not have read more than a few of them,
when he dashed off a letter in Latin to Cicero, dated
'Verona, 15th July in the 1345th year after the birth
of the God, whom you did not know'. The discovery seemed to him damning to Cicero's reputation
as a politician. He took as genuine the spurious
Epistle to Octavian, and regarded as just Brutus'
taunt, 'You do not flee a master so much as seek a
more friendly master'. He thinks that a moralist
should have behaved better, and laments that he had
taken any part in politics, even that he suppressed the
Catilinarian conspiracy. He seems to have taken
too much account of Cicero's varying estimates of
Dionysius, his family tutor, of Quintus and young
Quintus and of Dolabella. He asks, 'What madness
hurled you against Antony?' It is a typical rhetorical
outburst, based on the hastiest perusal of the Letters
and probably a very insufficient knowledge of Roman
history. It is plain that Petrarch was strongly influenced by the Brutus legend, which it has been one
of the objects of the foregoing pages to discredit.
How many similar rhetorical exercises must have
been composed in the first century A.D. That they
made their way into the pages of a—professedly
sober—history, is shown by the speech which Dio
Cassius puts in the mouth of Fufius Calenus (p. 171).

Erasmus is the only letter-writer in all history who
can rival Cicero in output.* A Spaniard writing to

---

* He is like Cicero too in badness of handwriting. Cicero admitted
he could not decipher what he wrote himself, but Tiro could. *Ad Fam.*
xvi. 22, 1. To his brother who complained that he could hardly read
his last letter, he says it was because he uses the first pen he can find.
This time he will use 'a good pen, well mixed ink and cream-laid paper'

Erasmus in 1530 apparently had compared Erasmus to Cicero and himself to Deiotarus: for Erasmus says he is not comparable to Cicero, but he values his friend more than 'any Asiatic prince' (Allen 2299). The two men were, however, comparable in more ways than one.

Both were men of great wit and superficial flippancy covering a real seriousness. Both must often in their lifetimes have been thought insincere, and have been criticised on this head much more in later years. Both accomplished marvels in the revival of an interest in all that is of deepest concern to mankind. Cicero excites our admiration more by his end. Erasmus, though a reformer at heart, had submitted to the Church, and died in his bed: Cicero upheld the banner of a free Republic to the end, and gave his life for her.

(Q.F. ii. 15b, 1). For Erasmus, cp. Allen 2290: 'I have employed a secretary not to torture you with my bad writing'.

EPILOGUE

Neither Livy, nor Tacitus, nor Terence, nor Seneca, nor Pliny, nor Quintilian is an adequate spokesman for the Imperial City. They write Latin; Cicero writes Roman.

CARDINAL NEWMAN, *Idea of a University*, p. 282

THE life of Cicero suggests the hackneyed question, 'Which is mightier, the pen or the sword?' That really means in this case: Which do you admire, Cicero or Caesar? Is it not possible to do justice to both?

They were in many ways extremely similar. Both were adepts at winning influence and untiring in doing personal favours, and both were lucky in having devoted friends. It is true that Caesar won his enemies by bribery, and did not always secure their good opinion when he had bought them (p. 134); but his personal qualities won for him the loyalty of a Matius. Both were generous and, as a rule, forgiving. There were exceptions in both cases. Both cared little for money in itself except as an instrument of power. Caesar's attitude to money was exactly that of Cecil Rhodes. Both may be acquitted of the sordid avarice which disgraced so many of their contemporaries. Finally, both were devoted to the culture of the mind.

But the differences between them were more numerous. Cicero was essentially a man's man and

278

had no romantic side: to Caesar, even if one rejects the vulgar scandals about him, the society of women was an essential part of life.

Cicero became a great figure in politics rather by accident than because he sought anything beyond the ordinary career of a Republican statesman. Caesar was ambitious of something that soared above that: he was a 'born dictator'. Thus there was this moral barrier between them. Cicero held with Plato that to do violence to one's fatherland was as bad as doing it to one's father: Caesar had no such scruples. Cicero hated bloodshed: Caesar did not seek it; but if he thought it necessary, had no pricks of conscience. Cicero's triumphs were won in peace: Caesar, at the age of over forty, suddenly became one of the few great generals of the world. He made no changes in the art of war, but he was a born leader. Cicero was saluted father of his country,* for foiling an anarchic plot in 63 B.C.: Caesar for annihilating his fellow citizens in the battle of Munda, 45 B.C. Cicero permanently influenced the thought and expression of the Roman world, and through it the nations of modern Europe: Caesar inaugurated an imperial period which only ended in 1918. The world is anxiously asking itself at this moment, 'What is to follow?' and hoping that it will not be the ruthlessness and *Schrecklichkeit* shown by our modern imitators of Caesar but the kindlier spirit of reconciliation which Cicero seems to have advocated in his works *On the Republic* and *On the Laws.*

Cicero wondered what history would say of him in six hundred years' time. He has now passed his

* By Catulus, *In Pis.* 3, 6.

second millennium (January 3rd, 1895). It was about that time that the opinion of scholars about him began to change from denunciation to appreciation,[207] and it would be difficult to find any one today who would echo the language of Drumann, Mommsen or J. A. Froude; but probably this fairer estimate of him has not reached that outside public which knows little of Roman history and is unable to read Cicero in his own tongue.

The foregoing has been an attempt, without concealing Cicero's vanity, passionate disposition and occasional insincerities, to point out that all the charges against him are based on material supplied by himself, so that this is one of the rare cases in which the duty of posterity is to vindicate the man against himself. Cicero has exhibited with his own pen his frequent vacillations, but he has also, though readers often fail to notice it, shown extraordinary insight into the actions of others, and even foretold in a remarkable way what would happen. Cornelius Nepos, who knew him and lived on into the reign of Augustus, says: 'Cicero not only foretold what happened in his lifetime, but even predicted what is taking place to-day'.[208] We should view his failings with leniency, if convinced that he was consistently patriotic: the perusal of the foregoing pages may, it is hoped, have inclined the reader to that conviction.

To one charge against Cicero one must give a definite No. He often during the course of his life had the vision of an ideal statesman, an Africanus or a Pericles, 'a ruler and steerer of the ship of state'. It has been said that he cast himself for that rôle, but that is surely a mistake. Down to Pharsalus he had envisaged Pompey in that position, and Pompey, too, has been unduly depreciated. Pompey, when given constitutional powers—and the Sullan horrors which he witnessed probably restrained him from taking the reins by force—was efficient enough. But his habitual reserve had made Cicero and others estimate his ability more highly than he deserved.

How gladly Cicero would have accepted Caesar as a 'constitutional ruler' it is to be hoped the foregoing pages have proved: but as Caesar was unwilling to give the Republic a constitution and was fascinated by the glamour of a Hellenistic throne, Cicero would have none of him.   Just in the same spirit he lost his life in opposing Caesar's pinchbeck imitator Antony.

Another point, seldom discussed, may be raised here. To us who look back on the death-throes of the Republic it is obvious that the two secret combinations of three powerful men to impose their will on the Republic led directly to its fall.   Cicero fell a victim to the second Triumvirate. Why did he not point out in some of his writings the evil of secret combinations?

It may have weighed a little with him that he refused an invitation to join the first, in which case it would have been a Quattuorvirate. But the real answer is that the first Triumvirate contained Pompey, his political idol, and Pompey was at first supposed to be the mainspring of the combination: at any rate Caesar ingeniously contrived to unload on to him the brunt of the unpopularity of the year 59 B.C.* After that it was Cicero's policy to detach

* Velleius (*R.H.* ii. 44) says: 'Caesar saw that, by shifting on to Pompey the odium of the power which they shared, he would strengthen his own position'.

Pompey from Caesar and ally him with the Senate. He nearly succeeded in so doing, and would have, had not Caesar acted with true Caesarian celerity in 56 B.C. After that Caesar had to be reckoned with as a power, until the Senate was driven into an alliance with Pompey, and things drifted into civil war. Cicero was clever enough to avoid being manœuvred into an approval of Caesar's position, and finally, to escape that entirely and to satisfy his conscience, went to Pompey's camp. It was honourable of him to go rather than confess his whole life to have been a mistake. If he sometimes afterwards regretted going, it was only because he felt he had done no good.

Cicero's position in Rome was one of great influence, because in the total absence of the Press, the Pulpit and the University, he in his single person supplied something of all three. That is why in the life of Cicero, as a man of principle and a consistent statesman, March 27th, 49 B.C., does him more honour than December 5th, 63 B.C., and is comparable to the calmness with which he met the executioner's sword on December 7th, 43 B.C. The Latin language has an untranslatable word *humanitas*: a Professor of Latin in Scotland has always born the title 'Professor of Humanity'. Whether the word means unfailing sympathy with brother man, be he slave or noble, foreigner or fellow citizen, or kindliness and obligingness of disposition, or social *bonhomie* and acceptableness, or culture in its widest sense of the word, in each and all of its senses, it would be hard to find a better exponent than Cicero.

APPENDIX

1 *Ad Att.* xiii. 42, 2.
2 *Pro Murena,* 8, 17.
3 Pliny, *Nat. Hist.* xviii. 3.
4 *De Oratore,* ii. 265.
5 *Ad Fam.* xvi. 26, 2.
6 *De Off.* iii. 80.
7 *Brutus,* 223.
8 Quintus, *Comm. Pet.* 10.
9 *Ad Att.* xii. 49, 2.
10 *De Officiis,* i. 8, 25.
11 *Ad Att.* i. 16, 15.
12 *De Legibus,* i. 1.
13 *Ad Att.* ii. 1, 11.
14 *De Prov. Cons.* 17, 40.
15 *Pro Murena,* 10, 22.
16 *Ad Fam.* xiii. 54, 1.
17 *De Leg. Agr.* iii. 5: *De Legibus,* i. 15, 42.
18 *Cui bono?* the favourite question of the judge Cassius, does not mean 'What is the good of a thing?' but 'To whom was it profitable?'
19 *Div. in Q. Caec.* 41; *Pro Clu.* 51; *Pro Deiot.* 1, 1. Plutarch (*Cic.* 35) says he sat up all night before he defended Murena.
20 Fragment of the *Hortensius,* 18.
21 *Ad Att.* iv. 17, 3.
22 *Ad Att.* ii. 4, 5, a *saltus*: *Ad Fam.* xiv. 1, 5, a *vicus.*
23 *Ad Att.* xi. 24, 3.
24 *Ad Fam.* ix. 26, 2.
25 *Ad Att.* ix. 11, 3.
26 *Ad Att.* xiii. 1, 3.
27 *Ad Att.* ii. 17, 2.
28 *Div.* xiii. 41: *Actio,* ii. 2, 73. 181.
29 *Actio,* ii. 1. 44, 112.
30 *Ad Fam.* x. 32, 3.
31 *Ad Att.* i. 4, 2.
32 Virgil, *Georgics,* iv. 127.
33 This was a chaplet of oak leaves, awarded for saving a citizen's life, the ancient equivalent of the V.C.
34 Suetonius, *Divus. Julius,* 9.
34a Asconius quotes Cicero as having said in his candidate's speech: 'With Cn Piso's connivance you desired to massacre the optimates'.
35 *Ad Att.* i. 14, 3. Crassus *may* only have wished to draw Cicero, and thus to annoy Pompey.
36 Plutarch, *Crassus,* 13.
37 *Ad Att.* ii. 6, 2.
38 *Ad Att.* xiv. 17, 6.
39 *Orator,* 37.
40 *De Officiis,* ii. 24, 84.
41 *Ad Att.* i. 14, 2.
42 *Ad Att.* ii. 9, 1; *De Harusp. Resp.* 38; *Pro Cael.* 49.
43 *Ad Att.* ii. 3, 3.
44 *Pro Sestio,* 28, 60.

[45] *De Domo*, 41.

[46] *Ad Att.* ii. 24, 3.

[47] *Pro Sestio*, 35, 77.

[48] *Ad Att.* iv. 1, 5.

[49] Cp. *Ad Quint. Fratr.* iii. 1, 1-6.

[50] *Ad Att.* iv. 2, 7.

[51] *Q.F.* ii. 2, 1.

[52] *Ad Att.* iv. 3, 5.

[53] *Ad Quint. Fratr.* ii. 3, 2.

[54] *Ad Fam.* i. 1, 3; 7, 4. *Dio. C.* 39, 12, 3.

[55] This is proved by C. Saunders in *Classical Philology*, xii. 304.

[56] *Conformity Asserted*, by L. Womack, D.D. London, 1664.

[57] *Ad Att.* iv. 10, 2; iv. 9, 2.

[58] *Ad Att.* ii. 5, 2.

[59] *Ad Att.* x. 8a.

[60] *Phil.* xiii. 12.

[60a] As this is a special case, we must not exaggerate the extent to which the published speeches differed from those delivered. Cornelius Nepos testifies that the speech for Cornelius was published *verbatim* as delivered.

[61] *Ad Att.* v. 1.

[62] *Ad Fam.* i. 9, 4.

[63] *Ad Fam.* iii. 1, 1.

[64] *Ad Fam.* iii. 4, 1: *liber auguralis*.

[65] *Ad Att.* xiv. 1, 2.

[66] *Ad Fam.* v. 20, 9.

[67] *Ad Att.* xi. 1, 2.

[68] *Ad Att.* xi. 13, 4.

[69] *Ad Att.* xi. 7, 1.

[70] E. G. Hardy, *Some Problems in Roman History*, p. 126 ff.

[71] Plutarch, *Pompey*, 57.

[72] *Ad Att.* v. 4, 3.

[73] *Ad Att.* vii. 3, 11.

[74] *Ib.* 3.

[75] *Ib.* 5.

[76] *Ad Att.* vii. 8, 5.

[77] *Ad Att.* vii. 9, 2: 'If some tribune flees to him with a tale of expulsion'.

[78] *Ad Att.* ix. 9, 3.

[79] *Ad Att.* ix. 11a.

[80] *Ad Att.* viii. 9, 1.

[81] *Ad Att.* ix. 18.

[82] *Inst. Orat.* xii. 1, 16.

[83] *Roman History*, xli. 55, 1.

[84] *Ad Att.* xi. 5, 4.

[85] *Ad Att.* xi. 6, 5.

[86] *De Off.* iii. 21, 82.

[87] Velleius, *R.H.* ii. 53.

[88] *Pro Marc.* 27-29. Cp. *Ad Fam.* xiii. 11, 3.

[89] *Ad Brut.* ii. 2, 3; *Ad Fam.* x. 12, 3, 4.

[90] *Ad Fam.* xvi. 22, 1.

[91] *Ad Att.* xiii. 27, 1, May 25th, 45 B.C.

[92] *Ad Att.* xii. 45, 2.

[93] *Ad Att.* xiii. 28, 3.

[94] *Ad Att.* xiii. 40, 1.

[95] *Ad Att.* xiii. 9, 2: *diuortium non probari*.

[96] Nepos, *Atticus*, 18; *Ad Att.* xiii. 40, 1.

[97] *Ad Att.* xiii. 52. Cumae, not Puteoli, as *Ad Att.* xiv. 11 shows.

[98] *Ad Att.* xiii. 33a, 1.

[99] *Confessions*, iii. 4, 7.

[100] *Cuius linguam fere omnes mirantur, pectus non ita.*

[101] *Ad Att.* xiii. 42.

[102] *Ad Fam.* vi. 15.

103 *Ad Att.* xiv. 14, 4.
104 *Philippic* ii. 12, 28.
105 *Philippic* ii. 26.
106 Plutarch, *Brutus*, 6.
107 *Ad Fam.* xv. 19, 4.
108 *Roman History*, xliv. 33, 7.
109 *Ad Att.* xiv. 12, 2.
110 *Ad Att.* x. 8.
111 *Ad Att.* x. 10, 2.
112 *Philippic* ii. 4, 9: Clodius is not named.
113 *Ad Att.* xiv. 13b.
114 *Ad Fam.* xi. 5, 2.
115 *Ad Att.* xiv. 17a.
116 *Philippic* ii. 39, 100.
117 *Ad Att.* xv. 11.
118 *Ad Att.* xv. 12, 2.
119 *Ad Fam.* vii. 19.
120 There is an allusion to this in *Philippic* i. 37.
121 *Elegies*, iii. 12, 31.
122 *Ad Fam.* xiii. 23, 2: *Philippic* iii. 19.
123 *Ad Fam.* xii. 22, 2; *Philippic* viii. 5.
124 *Ad Att.* xv. 22, 1.
125 *Ad Att.* xiv. 22, 1.
126 *Ad Att.* xv. 1, 3.
127 *Ad Att.* xvi. 1, 4.
128 *Ad Fam.* xvi. 27, 2.
129 *Ad Att.* xvi. 15, 3.
130 *Philippic* xii. 11.
131 *Ad Fam.* ix. 24.
132 *Ad Fam.* xii. 7, 2.
133 *Ad Att.* ix. 9, 3.
134 *Ad Fam.* xi. 9, 1.
135 *Ad Fam.* xii. 7, 2.
136 *Ad Fam.* xii. 12, 2.
136a *Ad Att.* xvi. 14, 1.
137 *Philippic* x. 18: 'If the minds of this House are to be directed by the nod of the veterans, and all our deeds and words are to be regulated by their will and pleasure, we should pray for death, which Roman citizens have always preferred to slavery'.
138 Plutarch, *Cicero*, 49.
139 *Roman History*, xlvi. 4, 2.
140 *De Divin.* i. 37, 80.
141 Plut., *Cicero*, 39.
142 *Brutus*, 34, 130.
143 *Ad Att.* vi. 1, 21.
144 *Ad Att.* iv. 15, 9.
145 *Ad Att.* ii. 25, 1.
146 *Ad Fam.* v. 9 and 10a.
147 *Pro Caelio*, 76.
148 *Orator*, 37.
149 *Orator*, 30, 107.
150 Cicero's observations about oratorical rhythm are in *Orator*, 180-203.
151 *Orator*, 213-14.
152 *De Orat.* i. 5.
153 *Ad Att.* xv. 1a, 1.
154 *Brut.* i. 16, 6.
155 Tacitus, *Dialogue*, 18.
156 *Ad Fam.* xv. 21, 4. See also *Brutus*, 283.
157 *De Oratore*, i. 146.
158 *Ib.* i. 132.
159 *Natural History*, vii. 117.
160 *Ad Att.* v. 12, 2.
161 *Ad Fam.* viii. 1, 4.
162 *De Civitate Dei*, ii. 21.
163 *De Leg.* ii. 17, 42.
164 *Ad Fam.* ix. 2, 5, where he suggests to Varro that they should both 'pursue inquiries on morals and *Laws*'.
165 Macrobius, *Sat.* vi. 4, 8.
166 *De Leg.* iii. 11, 25, 26.
167 *Tusc. Disp.* v. 2, 5.

168 *Ad Fam.* xi. 27, 5.

169 *De Officiis,* i. 7, 20: iii. 19, 76.

170 *Epp.* 164, 4.

171 I owe this quotation to Dr. J. E. King.

172 *Ad Att.* xii. 52, 3.

173 *De Officiis,* ii. 17, 60.

174 *Tusc. Disp.* i. 27, 66.

175 *Tusc. Disp.* i. 31, 76.

176 *De Nat. Deo,* ii. 28, 72.

177 *De Div.* ii. 72, 148.

178 *Tusc. Disp.* v. 20, 57; 23, 64

179 *De Officiis,* i. 13, 41.

180 i. 37, 132, 134.

181 i. 11, 35.

182 ii. 7, 24.

183 i. 9, 30.

184 *Tusc. Disp.* iv. 32, 68.

185 *Philippics* xiv. 12, 32.

186 *De Off.* i. 3, 11; 21, 72; 28, 100; 29, 103; ii. 21, 73.

187 *Ad Fam.* xv. 21, 4.

188 *Ad Fam.* ix. 21, 1.

189 *Ad Fam.* xvi. 16, 2.

190 *Ad Att.* viii. 14, 2.

191 *Ad Att.* xvi. 5, 5. These were certainly not the letters of commendation, but letters of special interest.

192 *Ad Fam.* iv. 5. This is imitated by St. Ambrose, *Epp.* i. 39, 3.

193 *Ad Fam.* xi. 28.

194 *Ad Att.* ix. 16. The others are ix. 6a, ix. 13a, x. 8b.

195 *Ad Fam.* vii. 5.

196 *Ad Att.* vi. 5, 2.

197 *Ad Att.* ix. 4.

198 *Ad Att.* viii. 16, 1.

199 *Tusc. Disp.* ii. 17, 4.

200 *Ad Fam.* vii. 1, 3.

201 *Q.F.* iii. 1, 1; *Ad Att.* xii. 9; 19, 1; xiii. 16, 1; xiv. 13, 1.

202 Post reditum ad Quirites, 4.

203 *Ad Fam.* i. 9.

204 *Ad Fam.* vi. 4, 1.

205 *Inst. Orat.* x. 7, 31.

206 This brilliant rendering is due to Mr. Glynn Williams, the translator in the Loeb Library.

207 Lord Rosebery named his Derby winner, in 1905, Cicero!

208 Nepos, *Atticus,* 16, 4.

ADDITIONAL NOTES

P. 44. *Cicero's country-houses.*—The French Abbé, Capmartin de Chaupy, who explored classic sites in Italy in the eighteenth century, gave the number of Cicero's villas as nineteen, but as a matter of fact they seem to have been twelve in number by the end of his life. First came the ancestral house at Arpinum, in connection with which he constructed a rustic shrine of Amalthea (*Ad Att.* i. 11). But of all he loved his Tusculanum best. After being at Astura for a while in 44 B.C. he writes: 'The country here is lovely, quiet and free from interruptions; but somehow or other "Home, sweet home", and I am jogging back to Tusculanum'. In speaking about his Tusculan villa he always used endearing diminutives, and probably the villa was of no great size, as land thereabouts was very valuable. The hall is an 'atriolum' (*Ad Att.* i. 10, 3), the colonnade is a 'porticula' (*Ad Fam.* vii. 23, 3), and the covered walk which he wants to copy elsewhere, is an 'ambulatiuncula'. Yet the grounds contained a gymnasium full of works of art, the gem of which was his Hermathena, a bust of the goddess on a square pillar (*Ad Att.* i. 1, 5); there were also a Lyceum and Academy connected by shady paths. Here the bulk of his literary work was done; here the Tusculan Disputations were held; here he rested from his labours in Rome; and here he awaited the sentence of death. The site of the villa is placed by Lanciani at the Colle delle Ginestre where the path descends to Grottaferrata; a roof-tile, stamped with his name, found hereabouts in 1741–6, is now in the Museo Kircheriano. Later the house was occupied by the poet Silius (Martial, xi. 49, 2), who starved himself to death probably there in the year A.D. 100. Of Cicero's villas at Antium, Astura, Formiae (really between Formiae and Caieta, see p. 207), Cumae, Puteoli (probably bequeathed to him by the banker Cluvius), Pompeii, and his *deversoriola* (little lodging-houses) at Sinuessa (where Cornificius would not stay, *Ad Fam.* xii. 20), Tarracina, Aquinum, Cales, and Anagnia, we naturally know less: those at

287

Tusculum and Formiae were singled out by his enemies for destruction, and those at Tusculum and Pompeii (*Ad Att.* i. 11), he says, 'loaded him with debt'.

P. 137.   That Cicero did not enjoy his sojourn in Pompey's camp is shown by his exclamation on May 11th, 44 B.C. (*Ad Att.* xiv. 21, 4): 'Anything rather than camp-life!'

P. 145.   'Signor Mussolini by retaining the monarchy, has possibly provided for the great danger of all dictatorships—the vacuum following the disappearance of the dictator.   When his day is done, a smooth transition to a constitutional monarchy, in which the achievements of Fascism would be preserved, should be a possibility.   None can say what will happen to Germany after Herr Hitler.'—*The Times*, November 10th, 1934.

INDEX

THE END